LIVING WELL AND DYING FAITHFULLY

Living Well and Dying Faithfully

Christian Practices for End-of-Life Care

Edited By

John Swinton & Richard Payne

William B. Eerdmans Publishing Company
Grand Rapids, Michigan / Cambridge, U.K.

Published 2009 by
Wm. B. Eerdmans Publishing Co.
2140 Oak Industrial Drive N.E., Grand Rapids, Michigan 49505 /
P.O. Box 163, Cambridge CB3 9PU U.K.

Printed in the United States of America

14 13 12 11 10 09   7 6 5 4 3 2 1

Library of Congress Cataloging-in-Publication Data

Living well and dying faithfully: Christian practices for end-of-life care /
edited by John Swinton & Richard Payne.
p. cm.
Proceedings of a symposium held in 2006 at Duke University.
ISBN 978-0-8028-6339-3 (pbk.: alk. paper)
1. Terminal care — Religious aspects — Christianity — Congresses.
2. Death — Religious aspects — Christianity — Congresses.
I. Swinton, John, 1957- II. Payne, Richard, 1951-

R726.L556 2009
616′.029 — dc22

2009026553

www.eerdmans.com

We gift this book to Alison and Terri.

Without your love, patience, gentleness, kindness, and joyfulness, none of this would be possible. Thank you for the blessing.

Contents

ACKNOWLEDGMENTS x

Foreword xii
Stanley Hauerwas

Introduction: Christian Practices and the Art of Dying Faithfully xv
John Swinton and Richard Payne

Practices of Living to Die Well

1. Practicing the Presence of God: Earthly Practices in Heavenly Perspective 3
John Swinton

2. Dying Well 17
Amy Plantinga Pauw

3. "Make Love Your Aim": Ecclesial Practices of Care at the End of Life 30
Karen D. Scheib

Practices of Faithful Suffering

4. Suffering in Communion with Christ: Sacraments, Dying Faithfully, and End-of-Life Care 59
M. Therese Lysaught

5. The Practice of Prayer and Care for the Dying 86
Allen Verhey

6. "Why Me, Lord?": Practicing Lament at the Foot of the Cross 107
John Swinton

7. Practicing Compassion for Dying Children 139
Tonya D. Armstrong

Practices of Healing and Hope

8. Healing in the Midst of Dying: A Collaborative Approach to End-of-Life Care 165
Abigail Rian Evans

9. Compassion: A Critical Component of Caring and Healing 188
Christina M. Puchalski

10. Hope in the Face of Terminal Illness 205
Richard Payne

11. More than Sparrows, Less than the Angels: The Christian Meaning of Death with Dignity 226
Daniel P. Sulmasy

12. Embracing and Resisting Death: A Theology of Justice and Hope for Care at the End of Life 246
Esther E. Acolatse

Conclusion: Attending to God in Suffering: Re-Imagining End-of-Life Care 272
John Swinton and Richard Payne

CONTRIBUTORS 277

INDEX 282

Acknowledgments

This book emerged from a unique collaboration between Professor John Swinton, who directs the Centre for Spirituality, Health, and Disability (CSHAD) at the University of Aberdeen, Scotland, UK (www.abdn.ac.uk/cshad), and Professor Richard Payne, who directs the Duke Institute on Care at the End of Life (ICEOL), which is centered in Duke University. In 2006 Professors Payne and Swinton brought together an interdisciplinary group of expert scholars to explore the role of Christian practices in end-of-life care. For three days they met together at Duke University, North Carolina, where they shared papers, argued, discussed, and worked through some issues crucial to understanding the significance of Christian presence in this area of health care. The results of this meeting are recorded in the various chapters of this book. In bringing together such a group, the book offers some unique and insightful perspectives that help us to see the importance of practices that are intentionally Christian for the ways in which we understand both life and death.

As with all such ventures, there are many people that we should thank. We would like to thank Jonathan Wilson-Hartgrove for his help and insightful editorial suggestions. We are grateful to Hans Reinders for being with us throughout the symposium and for his excellent and helpful critical reflections on the papers. We are grateful to the administrative staff at ICEOL and CSHAD. In particular, we are grateful to Renee Caron for her administrative skills and friendly manner even in times of strife! In addition, we are thankful for the input of Keith Meador and Amy Laura Hall. Keith and Amy Laura decided not to go forward with their chapters, but we very much appreciated their input during the symposium. Thanks also to Amy Plantinga Pauw, who unfortunately could not be with us at the symposium but kindly gave us permission to reprint her essay on dying well. There are, of course, many others whom we should thank, and we hope no one is offended by the brevity of our acknowledgments. All that is left is to thank Jesus for his faithful presence to us throughout this project and to offer the book as a sacrifice to God's glory. We hope it will be a blessing to many.

JOHN SWINTON
RICHARD PAYNE

Foreword

"How do you want to die?" I often ask that question of lay audiences. By "lay audiences" I mean people who are not associated with medicine. They are the only "lay audiences" that I take to exist in our day. At one time, of course, to be a layperson meant that you were not clergy, but now "laity" refers primarily to our role as patients. That transformation in how we understand what it means to be laity suggests the role that medicine plays *in* our lives and the power it has *over* our lives.

That medicine now seems to have the power that the church once had invites many to assume that doctors should be blamed for how our death and dying have now been "medicalized." However, this is not another book critical of the medical establishment. That is partly because the writers of these essays see clearly that the problems go deeper than the medicalization of our deaths. It is also because they recognize that the critical issue is to be found in how patient and physician alike answer the question, "How do you want to die?"

I have found that most people answer the question this way: "I want to die quickly, painlessly, in my sleep, and without being a burden." Most of us do not want to be a burden because we don't trust our children and/or other primary caretakers to make decisions about how we will die. We want to die quickly, painlessly, and in our sleep because when we die we do not want to know we are dying. Accordingly, we ask physicians to keep us alive up to the point that we will not know we are dying – and then we blame them for keeping people alive to no point. It is a wonderful double-bind game we play out on ourselves as well as on those committed to caring for us through the office of medicine.

That we, patient and physician alike, are caught in this mutual game of deception is why this is such an important and helpful book. Drawing on the theological wisdom of centuries, the writers of these essays remind us that dying is an art. We often assume that we must learn to live well, but we have forgotten that we also must learn to die well. Of course, there is a connection between learning to live well so that we might die well, but we seem to have lost that vital connection in our time. The result is that we are not able to trust one another enough to share the fears and hopes that so often surround our dying.

In particular, the writers of these essays help us see how language is crucial for our ability to maintain the connection between dying and living well. They suggest that such a language is available to us in the everyday practices of the church. The resources that we need to recover our ability to speak to one another about death are to be found in the worship of God, the sacraments, prayer, the psalms of lament, and the significance of everyday acts of compassion. Could it be that simple? It is that simple. Like everything crucial for living, simple wisdom is required.

Wisdom, moreover, is why this is such an extraordinary book. These essays are filled with wisdom because they have been written by those who have learned how to die either by being with the dying or by listening to those who have learned to listen to the dying. It is appropriate that this book be classified as "practical theology," since these essays exemplify the way that theology should be properly done. For if theology is not about the recovery of the hard-won wisdom of the Christian people across time, then it hardly deserves the name "theology."

God, after all, is what theology is "about." God, moreover, is at the heart of the practices that make possible our ability to die well. At one time, Christians feared the kind of death we say we want in answer to the question "How to you want to die?" They feared a sudden death because that meant they had lost the opportunity to prepare to face God. They wanted time to be reconciled with those whom they had wronged, the church, and, most of all, with God. Like us, they loved life and did not want to die, but death did not determine their dying. Their dying was determined by their confidence in the love of God.

The recovery of our ability to live confidently in the face of death animates the essays in this book. So a book about death turns out to be a book about life. A book about how we should care for one another at the end of life turns out to be a book about how we should care for one another before we come to the end of our lives. That such is the case I take to be an indication that this book has been written by those who have been shaped by the language of the faith. Thank God.

STANLEY HAUERWAS
Duke Divinity School

INTRODUCTION

Christian Practices and the Art of Dying Faithfully

John Swinton and Richard Payne

Dying is a spiritual event with medical implications.

Gwen London,
former director of the Institute on
Care at the End of Life, Duke University

What does it mean to die well? This may seem like a strange question. Because death is often perceived as the end of our aspirations and the denial of death is the implicit norm, the idea that dying might be an experience wherein we encounter well-being and fresh modes of transformative hope sounds, to say the least, odd. Isn't death something to be avoided? Shouldn't we battle against suffering by every means possible?

Most of us do not seek out death or suffering, and all of us are blessed by the gifts of medicine that enable us to avoid or at least to minimize our fear of such things. But dying well is often defined by our expectations and hopes that medicine will provide us with a pain-free death. The more we depend on techno-medicine[1] to define our understandings of illness, dying, and death, the stranger it seems to

1. By the term "techno-medicine" we mean a mode of medical thinking that prioritizes technology and technological intervention above issues of value, purpose, hope, love, and meaning. Not all medicine is practiced in this way, but the promises of modern science and technology can engender an expectation that it should be. It is that false and dangerous expectation as it is held by physicians and patients alike that we would call "techno-medicine."

ask how we might die well – or, even more strangely, to die faithfully. One of the primary questions that this book seeks to answer is this: Is dying well simply a matter of developing and utilizing technical excellence to alleviate suffering, or is there another way in which we might understand it?

In this book we suggest that there is in fact a different way to approach death and dying, a way that is rooted in the Christian tradition and that offers transformed understandings and practices that can work alongside current knowledge to bring healing and hope even in the midst of dying. In order to achieve such a task, we must begin to think differently.

Rethinking Death and Dying

There is little question that medicine as a healing art has made huge advances within the field of end-of-life care. In terms of such vital areas as pain control, surgical and pharmacological interventions, advanced and sophisticated medical technology, and the various curative and palliative practices that have emerged in recent years, there have been clear advances that have brought much relief to many people. This book does not offer an alternative to the positive advances of medicine. Quite the opposite, it recognizes and celebrates medicine's vital contribution to the field of end-of-life care.

Nevertheless, this book also recognizes and strives to capture the deep unease experienced by many people with the way end-of-life care is assumed to be primarily a medical issue. Why is our first port of call medicine and not theology? Why do we find it almost impossible to think of end-of-life care without thinking first of medicine?

At first glance these may seem like foolish questions. Surely medicine has "obvious" priority because of its ability to deal effectively with suffering and pain and its potential for allowing us to live long and fruitful lives. Theology is helpful in underpinning some of the moral dimensions of medicine, but we usually assume that when the rubber hits the road, medicine "must" take priority within end-of-life care.

This book challenges such a perception and asks whether this perception of the relationship between medicine and theology in the context of end-of-life care is in fact accurate. Does this way of imagining the relationship between medicine and theology really offer the most healing approach available to us? Suffering, death, and dying have meaning, and the shape of these meanings has a profound impact on how a person approaches these experiences. Issues of meaning and the transformation of meaning are not epiphenomenal to the central task of end-of-life care. They are central to it. The danger for us today is that within a techno-medical worldview which is often implicitly or explicitly death-denying, end-of-life issues can easily find themselves stripped of this vital meaning-making dimension. When this happens, it is easy for us to forget that suffering, terminal illness, and death have personal and corporate meanings that reach beyond the boundaries of imaginations and narratives that are shaped by medicine alone. Within such a context the suggestion that "Death has been swallowed up in victory" (1 Cor. 15:54) can only be seen as denial and foolishness.

And yet such an assertion presents us with the heart of the gospel. Christians confess that not even death can separate us from our Creator. As the apostle Paul puts it,

> I am convinced that neither death nor life, neither angels nor demons, neither the present nor the future, nor any powers, neither height nor depth, nor anything else in all creation, will be able to separate us from the love of God that is in Christ Jesus our Lord. (Rom. 8:38-39)

If this is so, then two important things become clear. First, to "die well" requires more than can be told within the narrative of scientific medicine alone. Dying well requires a wider narrative that transforms the stories told by medicine by placing them in a different context and engaging them in forms of conversation that draw out fresh perspectives and new promises. The key point is not simply what medicine does but *where* it does what it does. Medicine is always practiced within *creation* – that is, it is carried out within a world which is not our own. The boundaries and goals of medicine, as with all things, are therefore defined and shaped by God's story of creation and redemption. Science and scientific medicine remain important, of course. But, viewed in this way, they are not seen to be an autonomous source of knowledge and practice. Rather, we discover that they are contingent, dependent on and answerable to the redemptive heart of a Creator God. Viewed in this way, the relationship between theology and medicine is significantly reframed. *We do medicine in a theological context rather than doing theology in a medical context.* As we will see, this is an important reframing.

Second, for Christians the meaning of suffering is discerned within a specific narrative of creation and redemption, death and resurrection — a narrative that inevitably transforms our assumptions about the meaning of death and what it might mean to die well. In order to die well, we need to learn to see beyond our culturally constructed assumptions about what it means to be healthy and what is important in life. Death and dying are not just inevitable; they are also valuable aspects of human experience. We need to rediscover the fact that the process of dying is a deeply meaningful and spiritual human experience within which the search for God, meaning, hope, purpose, forgiveness, and even salvation should be seen as central to the tasks of end-of-life care. In order to open ourselves up to a fresh consideration of what can be learned in dying and death, we need a theological framework that includes but is not defined by the gifts of medicine, the alleviation of suffering, and the prolongation of life.

Loving God in All Things and at All Times

If the apostle Paul is correct in his assertion that nothing can separate us from the love of God, then the central theological question that should guide Christian approaches to end-of-life care and that will sit at the heart of this book is this: *How can the faithful who are dying (and those who care for them) be enabled to love God and to hold on to the reality that God is love even in the midst of their suffering?* This question does not in any sense diminish the significance or importance of the gifts of medicine. The alleviation of suffering remains very important. However, in the new understanding discussed here, the role and function of medicine are shifted. Medicine is placed within a theological framework that profoundly impacts its intentions and goals.

The key task that should underpin Christian practices of end-of-life care might therefore be summed up in the words of Matthew 22:37-40. Here Jesus says,

> "Love the Lord your God with all your heart and with all your soul and with all your mind." This is the first and greatest commandment. And the second is like it: "Love your neighbor as yourself." All the Law and the Prophets hang on these two commandments.

This text helps us reframe the primary focus and intention of end-of-life care. If enabling such a way of love is central to the lives of those who seek to embody God's good news in all of their practices, then it should clearly be central to the practices of end-of-life care. This being so, suffering cannot simply be defined by the presence of the constituent parts that make up the usual meaning of the term: pain, anguish, alienation, brokenness, death, and so forth. From the theological standpoint of the authors of this book, suffering has deeper meaning. Pain, anguish, alienation, and brokenness remain profoundly important, and we continue to do all we can to alleviate them. However, we strive to alleviate them not only because people do not want to experience such things, but because suffering can serve a deeper negativity as it functions to separate us from the love of God, self, and others. Elaine Scarry puts it this way in her reflections on the effects of pain: "Pain comes unsharably into our midst as at once that which cannot be denied and that which cannot be confirmed . . . whatever pain achieves it achieves in part through unsharability, and it ensures this unsharability through resistance to language."[2]

Suffering distances us from ourselves and pushes us away from one another and from God. Left unattended, it can destroy the threefold pattern of love that Jesus highlights as the heart of the gospel. The pain, the sense of injustice, the isolation, the depression, and the anguish of suffering easily destroy faith both for those who experience suffering and for those who are forced to be spectators of another's suffering. As we experience pain, illness, suffering, and dying within our own bodies, it can be very difficult to continue to love God with heart, mind, and soul. As we watch a loved one eaten away by cancer or dying slowly in the latter stages of dementia, it can be almost impossible to hold on to the love of God and to worship God as creator, healer, sustainer, and redeemer.

2. Elaine Scarry, *The Body in Pain: The Making and Unmaking of the World* (New York: Oxford University Press, 1985), p. 4.

When we view suffering and the process of dying in a reframed way, the practices of end-of-life care take on a different texture and intention from our normal expectations. We assume that medicine, alongside all of the disciplines involved in end-of-life care, is practiced within a theological framework that has as its primary goal the sustenance of love for God, self, and others. Technologies that are utilized by medical practice have a similar goal and are intended to move an individual in a similar direction. We alleviate pain not just because it is a good thing to do (which of course it is), but primarily because pain can be a profound obstacle to the human ability to love God, self, and others. We engage in end-of-life counseling not to provide an unfocused sense of hope in the midst of hopelessness. Rather, we counsel people in order to enable them to develop the resources to find hope in the reality that they are loved by God above all things, and that the truth of the resurrection has the power to transform situations where there appears to be nothing but hopelessness.

As we reframe end-of-life practices in the light of the profound theological insight that we are loved beyond all things and that our primary task is to learn to love God in all things and at all times, that nothing can separate us from the love of God, medicine is released to serve a vital role within the coming Kingdom of God and to participate faithfully in the movement toward that time when there will be no more tears, suffering, or death.[3] As, in this way, we encounter end-of-life care in its contemplative mode (Chapter 1), we begin to discover what it means to do medicine in a theological context rather than simply doing theology in a medical context (Chapter 5).

Christian Practices: A Practical Theology

This book is an exercise in practical theology. Put simply, *practical theology is theological reflection on the practices of the church as they interact with the practices of the world with a view to enabling faithful discipleship.* We use the term "Christian practices" here in a quite specific way to refer to forms of divinely inspired individual and communal actions that are rooted in and comprised of theological meaning and that have radical practi-

3. Revelation 21:4.

cal import in relation to the purposes of God-in-the-world.[4] In Christian practices, theoretical and practical knowledge come together to enable faithfulness. The meaning and implications of these moments of embodied theology are not always apparent. A primary task of practical theology is therefore to reflect critically on the practices of the church and the institutions of the world, such as medicine, so that the deeper meanings of our practices can be understood and worked with intentionally in the service of God.

Practices are skills that are learned in particular communities (Chapter 1), which are formed and shaped by specific traditions and which contain implicit and explicit social and theological histories. They are forms of embodied theology that communicate and reveal meaningful theological truth. Such practices are intended to ensure the sustenance of faith and faithfulness in all circumstances. Christian practices are particular forms of Christian action designed to meet human needs, but in a way that requires and enhances faithful participation in the continuing practices of God in, to, and for the world. They bring about relief of human suffering, strive to enhance human well-being, and reveal and embody something of the nature of the God who inspires and indeed inhabits such practices.

Importantly, the concreteness of Christian practices offers the possibility of constructive engagement and interaction with other forms of healing practices. Take, for example, the Christian practice of lament (Chapters 2, 5, and 6). At one level, this form of Christian practice provides a person with an opportunity for catharsis, which enables the expression of deep hurts and brokenness. But the context of that catharsis is vital for understanding its theological function. Lament is first and foremost a form of *prayer* that enables individuals honestly and sometimes starkly to verbalize their hurt, brokenness, and anger toward God. This release is expressed within the context of prayer and, ultimately, praise. As we practice lament, so we learn to worship God in all things at all times and in all places.

Again, the practice of healing (Chapters 4 and 8) has a level at which its primary focus is the alleviation of suffering and the possible

4. For a more complete development of this point, see John Swinton, *Raging with Compassion: Pastoral Responses to the Problem of Evil* (Grand Rapids: William B. Eerdmans, 2007).

movement toward cure. However, any theology of healing must be deeply embedded in the biblical concept of shalom, which primarily has to do with holiness and right relationship with God. Other aspects of healing such as peace, comfort, community, and justice emerge from the central meaning, but they are not dependent on cure. Thus the meaning of healing in end-of-life care might be quite different from that which is normally assumed, and it may require different means to attain this particular kind of healing.

Likewise, forgiveness (Chapters 2 and 4) at one level is simply an attempt to mend a relationship which has, for whatever reason, been broken. However, reflected on within the theological framework we have offered thus far, forgiveness points toward the cross and the overarching forgiveness offered by God to the world. In this context, forgiveness is not an act of the will but a response that we practice in light of the recognition that we are forgiven and deeply loved by God.

A similar multilayered perspective on various forms of Christian practices as they relate to end-of-life care is offered throughout this book in relation to such things as the sacraments (Chapter 4), love (Chapter 1), compassion (Chapters 7 and 9), hope (Chapter 10), dignity (Chapter 11), justice (Chapter 12), spiritual formation (Chapter 1), healing (Chapter 10), and even the more challenging suggestion that dying is itself a Christian practice (Chapter 2). Each author articulates these practices differently, but there is an underlying unity in their shared belief that Christian end-of-life care has the dynamic of reconciling love as its primary goal. Properly understood in their theological and practical dimensions, practices such as these offer real and fresh opportunities for the development of forms of healing that are not otherwise available, but that are often deeply desired by those who are dying.

Christian Practices and Spiritual Formation

Perhaps most importantly, continual engagement in Christian practices forms people in particular ways. Practices do not provide us with the rules that will enable us to live well. Instead, they form us into the kinds of people who can do nothing other than live well and die well. As we practice compassion in community, we become compassionate people – not people who simply act compassionately because it is a nice thing to do, but people who know no other way than the way of compassion. When we pray regularly, we do so not out of duty but rather because we long to communicate with the God who loves us even when that communication is fraught with anger, hurt, and lament. In this way we become a praying people whose lives are shaped by this precious act.

Such formation does not enable us to avoid pain and suffering. Indeed, as M. Therese Lysaught makes clear in Chapter 4, these practices that become our habit may turn out to be very difficult to continue in the face of pain and suffering. But such formation does enable us to become the kinds of people who at least have the resources to see things differently even in the midst of dying.

Living Well to Die Well

The connection between practices and formation is important. One of the obvious but nonetheless challenging observations about many of our current end-of-life care practices is that they tend to focus on suffering and dying only at the end of life. The World Health Organization defines palliative care this way:

> Palliative care is an approach that improves the quality of life of patients and their families facing the problems associated with life-threatening illness, through the prevention and relief of suffering by means of early identification and impeccable assessment and treatment of pain and other problems – physical, psychosocial, and spiritual.[5]

This definition is not, of course, inaccurate, but it is inadequate for our current purposes. Underpinning the chapters of this book and implicit within the approach to Christian practices outlined above is the fact that *dying well requires that we live well,* not just at the end of our lives but throughout the whole of our lives. In other words, as John Swinton makes clear in Chapter 1, the time to begin to develop the types of practices that this book will argue are vital for faithful end-of-life care is not

5. World Health Organization, *Cancer Pain Relief and Palliative Care* (Geneva: World Health Organization, 1990).

when we are struck by illness, but rather during our everyday lives, as we experience seasons of illness and health. As we learn to practice the presence of God in all things and at all times, we learn the practices that will sustain us when we are faced with the prospect of our own death.

End-of-life care thus begins in the day-to-day life of the Christian community and not simply within the hustle and bustle and technical expertise of the medical ward at the end of our lives. End-of-life care begins where we are right now. As we concentrate on our spiritual formation in the present time, we begin to prepare ourselves for that time when suffering and pain form the tragic garland that crowns our final experience.

Theology, Medicine, and End-of-Life Care

Both medicine and theology are necessary for end-of-life care. The question is this: How can they be enabled to work together effectively in order to enhance health and well-being for people who are dying, their families, and their other loved ones? End-of-life care comprises a variety of professional practices that practitioners utilize in their quest to alleviate suffering, bring comfort, and enhance well-being in the lives of those who are dying and those who are bereaved. By introducing a theological dynamic focused on the love of God, Christian practices complement, enhance, and challenge other practices that may have a different focus.

By encouraging a reflective dialogue between the practices of medicine and Christian practices, this book, we hope, will provide a unique space within which the movement toward faithful dying can be encouraged, nurtured, and actualized. Such a dialogue between the practices of medicine and Christian practices offers the possibility of a constructive conversation that takes seriously the integrity of both disciplines and the inseparability of theory and practice. More importantly, it offers the possibility of developing practices that will help people to find hope in the midst of hopelessness, peace in the midst of turmoil, and the love of the God who promises to be with us in all things and who will never leave us (Heb. 13:5).

PRACTICES OF LIVING TO DIE WELL

CHAPTER 1

Practicing the Presence of God: Earthly Practices in Heavenly Perspective

John Swinton

> *So here's what I want you to do, God helping you: Take your everyday, ordinary life — your sleeping, eating, going-to-work, and walking-around life — and place it before God as an offering. Embracing what God does for you is the best thing you can do for him. Don't become so well-adjusted to your culture that you fit into it without even thinking. Instead, fix your attention on God. You'll be changed from the inside out. Readily recognize what he wants from you, and quickly respond to it. Unlike the culture around you, always dragging you down to its level of immaturity, God brings the best out of you, develops well-formed maturity in you.*
>
> Romans 12:1-2, The Message

Dying is a strange business. It is strange partly because it seems to run so radically counter to the thrust of our expectations and hopes for life. Death comes inexplicably into our midst and robs us of our desires for the present and our hopes for the future . . . or so our cultural narrative would have us believe. Death is also strange insofar as, within a culture that is often deeply death-denying,[1] its relationship to life is not always clear. Is death simply an aberration that needs to be avoided or battled against at all costs, or is death an aspect of living that is not only an in-

1. Ernest Becker, *The Denial of Death* (New York: The Free Press, 1973).

Unless otherwise indicated, all of the quotations from Scripture in this chapter are taken from the New International Version of the Holy Bible.

evitability but also a valuable and vital aspect of existence, a profound horizon that correlates positively with the ways in which we choose to live our lives? If death is the former, then we would be correct in utilizing every technology we have to avoid death and evade the process of dying. Within this understanding, end-of-life care would be presumed to begin as one approached the end of one's life. However, if the latter is the case — if death is in fact somehow positively correlated with life — then what we might require is a deeper understanding of the meaning of life and its relationship to death, and what it might mean to live lives that are shaped by a hopeful narrative of death.

When Does End-of-Life Care Begin?

When we think about end-of-life care, the assumption tends to be that we are focusing on a particular group of people (normally "patients" under some kind of medical care) who are currently encountering forms of illness that threaten to end their lives, sometimes prematurely. Here there is no necessary connection between the current situation and the person's previous life. End-of-life care is assumed to begin (sometimes this beginning point is quite specifically legislated by medicine, law, or insurance companies) when individuals are faced with their own mortality. Our task, then, is to provide modes of care and intervention that will enable them to die with peace, dignity, and hope. The care that is delivered tends to be primarily medical or at least clinical in origin and focus, with the resources of the health-care communities assumed to be the primary locus of care. There may be spiritual aspects to the delivery of that care, but the overall focus remains on what is happening in the present rather than on what has happened in the past or what will happen in the future.

There is, of course, nothing wrong with a clinical framework for the practices of end-of-life care. Seeking to utilize the benefits of medicine to enable and facilitate human well-being can be a very good thing to do. However, while what is occurring "in the present" for the individual is certainly vitally important, I want to suggest that what has occurred throughout a person's life is equally as important for our understanding of end-of-life care. The end of a person's life is precisely that: the *end* of that life. It is, however, crucial to bear in mind that this life which is ending – its history, narratives, experiences, and formation – is not epiphenomenal to the process of end-of-life care. Indeed, the nature of the life that an individual has lived will, to a greater or lesser extent, determine the ways in which he or she understands and faces death.

If our understanding of end-of-life care is simply confined to the end of a person's life, we will miss dimensions of the processes of living and the relationship of these processes to the meaning of dying that are of central importance. End-of-life care, therefore, doesn't begin when a person is faced with a terminal illness. End-of-life care finds its roots in the processes of formation that go on throughout a person's life and that come together in quite particular ways to produce the individual's unique experience of dying. For Christians, the place where end-of-life care begins is in the day-to-day practices of the Christian life as it is lived out in community with others.

A Christian approach to end-of-life care thus involves much more than palliation and good patient care, important as these things are. Rather, it is a formative task that finds its theological roots in Jesus' words in John 10:10: ". . . I have come that they may have life, and that they may have it *more abundantly*" (NKJV, emphasis mine). Jesus came to give us life in abundance, and as we learn what it means to live abundant lives, we are enabled to understand what it might mean to die abundant deaths. Such an approach to end-of-life care takes seriously the various approaches of dying that are available through standard health-care services, but it also assumes that what occurs at the end of our lives is profoundly influenced by what occurs throughout our lives. But what might it mean to live an abundant life or even, more oddly, to die an abundant death?

Abundant Life

Living, as many of us do, in a market-driven society, we are inevitably tempted to assume that abundant life relates primarily to the types of material goods we mark out as the signs and symbols of power and prosperity. However, the nature of abundant life that we discover in the Gospels is of a different order. In Mark 12:28-31, Jesus makes this statement:

> One of the teachers of the law came and heard them debating. Noticing that Jesus had given them a good answer, he asked him, "Of all the commandments, which is the most important?" "The most important one," answered Jesus, "is this: 'Hear, O Israel, the Lord our God, the Lord is one. Love the Lord your God with all your heart and with all your soul and with all your mind and with all your strength.' The second is this: 'Love your neighbor as yourself.' There is no commandment greater than these."

To live a life that is full and abundant is not to live a life that is void of suffering or that flees from the reality of death. Nor is it necessarily to live a life that is filled with material prosperity, as the abundant life of Jesus makes clear. Rather, life in all of its fullness relates to living our lives in ways that reveal our love for God, self, and one another in all things and at all times, including times of suffering and death. An absence of illness and disturbance may be desirable, but it is not definitive of abundant life. Indeed, those who choose to follow the crucified Savior may well find that faithfulness to that Savior involves pain and suffering. What *is* definitive of abundant life is the desire to love God in all things and at all times.

Death, Resurrection, and Eternal Hope

Within such an understanding, life is related to death in quite a particular way. No longer is death perceived as an enemy that needs to be defeated or avoided at all costs. Instead, death is radically reframed in the light of the resurrection and the promise that death has been defeated through Jesus Christ's victory on the cross. As Paul puts it in 1 Corinthians 15,

> "Death has been swallowed up in victory." "Where, O death, is your victory? Where, O death, is your sting?" The sting of death is sin, and the power of sin is the law. But thanks be to God! He gives us the victory through our Lord Jesus Christ. (vv. 54-57)

This "new fact" – that those who love God will spend eternity with God – enables people to integrate death into life in ways that are constructive, healing, and radically countercultural. Death remains painful and difficult, but it is no longer the ultimate enemy. Jesus' reaction to the death of Lazarus is informative in this respect:

> When Mary reached the place where Jesus was and saw him, she fell at his feet and said, "Lord, if you had been here, my brother would not have died." When Jesus saw her weeping, and the Jews who had come along with her also weeping, *he was deeply moved in spirit and troubled.* "Where have you laid him?" he asked. "Come and see, Lord," they replied. *Jesus wept.* (John 11:32-35, italics mine)

To live in the knowledge that one is perfectly loved by God and that death no longer has the victory is not a way of denying death or an incitement to cover one's emotions and passions and live as if death is not painful. Jesus, the one who clearly loved God in all things and at all times and who had a deeper grasp of the meaning of death than anyone around him, is deeply troubled in the face of the death of his friend. His tears resonate with the rhythms of grief that, tragically, will form an inevitable dimension of all our life songs. Likewise, his poignant lament cried from the cross — "My God, My God! Why have you forsaken me?" — provides a powerful exemplar for the role of Christian lament in the face of suffering and dying (an aspect of end-of-life care that we will explore in detail in a later chapter). The life and experiences of Jesus would indicate strongly that living life abundantly does not immunize us from the pain, suffering, loneliness, and desolation that accompanies death. But such a way of living *does* enable us to integrate death within a narrative of hope that offers the process of death and dying a radically different framework and meaning from those of our normal expectations.

Within this new narrative, death is re-imagined as an integral aspect of life, which gives meaning to both sadness and joy. Death becomes that moment when the lovers of God leave the loves of this world and take up the graceful offer to live with God and to continue to love God forever. Death is thus reconceived as an inevitable existential marking point that guides us toward a future that contains suffering, sadness, and loss, while simultaneously offering a profound promise of hope and new life. If we think about end-of-life care from this theological perspective, it becomes clear that alongside the standard modes of caring for the dying we need to think about end-of-life issues in relation to the formation of people who can hold onto the hope of the gospel and the love of God even amid the storms of illness, death, and suffering. This is not an "end of life" task; it is a "whole of life" task.

Christian practices that enable a temporal and transcendent exchange of love add an invaluable dimension to contemporary practices of end-of-life care. However, such practices do not miraculously appear as we near the end of our lives. They are the product of lives lived well — lives within which we have practiced the presence of God faithfully over an extended period of time and have come to see the gracefulness of such a way of being. It is when, in times of crisis, we draw on our memories and our history and recognize the significance of our formation that we discover we in fact have deep and resilient resources that will help us cope with our situation and continue to love God, ourselves, and those around us.

If what I have argued thus far is correct, end-of-life care begins in times of happiness, joy, and health and continues into times of illness, crisis, and brokenness. In the remainder of this chapter I will focus on the importance of spiritual formation aimed at enabling abundant life as a way of preparing and equipping us for the possibility of living well and dying faithfully. In developing this perspective, I will lay a foundation for understanding the roots and significance of the various practices that are presented in this book. Reflecting on the thinking of Brother Lawrence, a lay brother in a Carmelite monastery, I will offer a perspective on spiritual formation as an important aspect of Christian end-of-life care. This perspective locates the beginning point for all Christian end-of-life care within the day-to-day life of the Christian community as it strives to enable faithful practices and graceful discipleship.

The Practice of Spiritual Formation

Abundant life begins when we recognize the contemplative dimensions of living in the world. David Ford suggests that "the greatest mystery relates to God's love for us for our own sake and the possibility of loving God for God's own sake."[2] This is a deceivingly simple statement

2. David Ford, "What Is the Wisdom of L'Arche?" Unpublished paper presented

that takes us to the heart of the contemplative tradition. What might it mean simply to love God for God's own sake, not for what God can do for us but simply for who God is? How might such a way of being and loving be achieved? What implications would such an approach to the world have for the ways we address others and perceive ourselves? What might it mean to love others for their own sake — not for what they can do for us, but simply for who they are? These are important questions, because such a way of loving is precisely how we desire God to love us.

When we begin to think in this way, it takes us to the heart of the contemplative vocation within which one turns one's whole being toward God, not because of what one can get out of God, but for God's sake.[3] Only when we learn to love God for God's sake and to recognize that we are loved simply for our own sake can we begin to understand what it means to care for others (and for ourselves) simply for their sake. As we reflect on such a concept in the light of Jesus' threefold command about love — love God, self, and others — we discover something of the essence and goal of spiritual formation. *Spiritual formation relates to the ongoing process wherein human beings open themselves to the transforming love of God in the hope that God's love will form them into the types of people who can love God, self, and others in all times and under all circumstances.*

Spiritual formation is encouraged and enabled through engagement with particular spiritual practices — prayer, Scripture reading, meditation, lament, meeting God in worship and praise — which, through the power of the Holy Spirit, open people up to receive God's loving gifts. As we engage in such spiritual practices, we are shaped into people who, in a real sense, reveal something of the shape of the love of God. As the apostle John puts it, "No one has ever seen God; but if we love each another, God lives in us and his love is made complete in us" (1 John 4:12).

Spiritual formation is the ongoing process wherein we learn what it means to recognize the practical significance of God living within us, to live out the reality that God is love, and to recognize that our pri-

---

at a conference for theologians held at "La Ferme" in the community of L'Arche in Trosly-Breuil, France, in December 2002. (This paper is quoted with permission from the author.)

3. Ford, "What Is the Wisdom of L'Arche?"

mary calling is to love God, ourselves, and others at all times and in all circumstances.

It is important to recognize that spiritual formation is not a human achievement. Spiritual practices are not ways of making individuals spiritually stronger so that they can engage in the process of formation with more vigor and success! Quite the opposite. At the heart of the process is the recognition of the contingent nature of human beings. We are dependent on God for all things, including the formation of our spirits. As Thomas Merton puts it in his reflections on contemplation, this recognition involves "an awareness of our contingent reality as received, as a *present* from God, as a free gift of love."[4]

The practices that we utilize in spiritual formation are nothing more (and nothing less) than ways of opening ourselves to the reality of God's continuing loving presence, ways of accepting God's present of love. As we do this, we develop a fresh consciousness that allows our minds to be renewed and our perceptions of the world to be transformed as we encounter God's gracious love for the world. This is how my friend and colleague Aileen Barclay describes it:

> Spiritual formation is what God does with us and for us. God knocks on our doors until we hear; leads us to a community where we are loved; brings us to our knees where we can hear him; raises us up in new life more open to seeing his upside-down world; teaches us to recognize God in strange places; gives us friends who have also experienced despair and resurrection; journeys with us; peels off the layers (like an onion) again and again until he gets to the soft sweet place. (Lots of tears and struggles as the skin peels off.) Spiritual formation is learned through the friendships that God gives us as we live through the highs and lows of life, as we learn to live with our own brokenness. Just when you thought you'd got rid of the sin, angst, jealousy, anger, etc., God opens up another facet that you have to deal with.[5]

4. William H. Shannon, *Thomas Merton: An Introduction* (Cincinnati: St. Anthony Messenger Press, 2005), p. 75, italics mine.

5. This quotation is from personal correspondence of 5 July 2008, and is reprinted here with permission.

Attending to God in the Everydayness of Life

It is important to be clear that spiritual formation is not a task for the spiritually privileged. Jesus' call to abundant life does not set us apart from the world in an elitist sense. Rather, it is grounded deep within the world, in the everydayness of our existence. It is not coincidental that Jesus calls us to recognize the Kingdom of God as it is revealed *on earth:* "Thy kingdom come, on earth as it is in heaven." The Kingdom has not yet arrived in all of its fullness, but it has arrived. Our task is to learn to live lives that reflect this easily hidden truth. *Spiritual formation is the process wherein we learn what it means to see our earthly practices in heavenly perspective.* It occurs gradually and formatively as we learn to recognize the sacredness of our everyday lives and the subtle yet beautiful ways in which we can learn to love God in all that we do.

Spiritual formation is a continuing process wherein we learn to recognize and attend to God in the world. As we respond to God's call, our lives are transformed into the shape of the love of God. The foundational practice that underpins such an abundant way of living relates to developing the habit of reflecting on God in all things and at all times: *practicing the presence of God.* Developing our spirits is not like mastering mathematics or geography; we cannot develop our spirits through our individual intellectual endeavors. Spiritual formation is a task which requires our being mentored into the ways of the Spirit by those whose spirits have been formed by the practices of faithfulness. That being so, as in this chapter we begin to work out something of what it means to practice the presence of God in our lives, it will be helpful briefly to walk alongside a mentor on this small part of our journey. We find just such a mentor in the life and writings of Brother Lawrence, a seventeenth-century French Carmelite lay brother. In his classic work titled *The Practice of the Presence of God,* Brother Lawrence lays out a simple way of contemplation which, through a life of practice, enabled him to develop a wonderful closeness to God that stayed with him in all of the difficult circumstances of his life. His intention was to live in ways such that he noticed and attended to God in each and every aspect of his life. In living this way, he found that even the most trivial of tasks became imbued with divine meaning and love for God. For Brother Lawrence, the world was a theatre of God's grace wherein God could be found even in the most trivial of tasks:

> . . . he was pleased when he could take up a straw from the ground for the love of GOD, seeking Him only, and nothing else, not even His gifts.[6]

Brother Lawrence's approach draws us into the contemplative tradition and enables us to see the importance of learning to love God in *all* that we do, as this excerpt indicates:

> I engaged in a religious life only for the love of GOD, and I have endeavored to act only for Him; whatever becomes of me, whether I be lost or saved, I will always continue to act purely for the love of GOD. I shall have this good at least that till death I shall have done all that is in me to love Him.[7]

It is important to note that this way of being in the world does not demand that we become spiritual superstars who engage in endless rounds of spiritual exercises in an attempt to live lives that are seen to be holy. On the contrary, Brother Lawrence edges us toward the recognition that, important as formal spiritual exercises may be, we need to learn to sanctify each aspect of our everyday lives. As we draw the everydayness of our lives into the presence of God, we are sanctified not by our works – even our spiritual works – but purely by the grace and love of God:

> Our sanctification did not depend on changing our works, but in doing that for God's sake, which we commonly do for our own . . . that most excellent method he had found of going to GOD, was that of doing our common business without any view of pleasing men, and (as far as we are capable) purely for the love of GOD.[8]

In each step of Brother Lawrence's life, God became greater as he became smaller (John 3:30).

Practicing God's presence in this way is certainly a difficult discipline. Maintaining such a stance on life requires intentionality and concentration and inevitably involves disappointment and sometimes fail-

6. Brother Lawrence, *The Practice of the Presence of God and The Spiritual Maxims* (Philadelphia: The Griffith and Rowland Press, 2005), p. 7.

7. Brother Lawrence, *The Practice of the Presence of God,* p. 9.

8. Brother Lawrence, *The Practice of the Presence of God,* p. 13.

ure. But once the habit is ingrained, it becomes natural to us – the only way that we might desire to live. Brother Lawrence describes it this way:

> There is not in the world a kind of life more sweet and delightful than that of a continual conversation with God. Only those can comprehend it who practice and experience it. Yet I do not advise you to do it from that motive. It is not pleasure which we ought to seek in this exercise. Let us do it from a principle of love, and because it is God's will for us.[9]

Brother Lawrence teaches us that in order to live life abundantly, we must first learn to encounter God in the everydayness of our lives. As we learn such a practice, our motivations change from self-gratification to the desire and indeed the need to love God and to do everything for God's glory. We do our work well, we love our families well, we care for others well, we respond to illness and suffering well – all for the sake of the love of God.

Formal spiritual practices such as Scripture reading, meditation, and prayer remain significant. But now they are placed within a general context of *continuous worship,* which gives them a quite different complexion. Rather than assuming that engaging in such practices enables us somehow to leave the world of everyday experience for a different "spiritual realm," we recognize that our formal times of prayer and adoration are concentrated moments in an ongoing practice that nurtures the love and recognition of God. Brother Lawrence's experience illuminates this point:

> Prayer was nothing else but a sense of the presence of GOD, his soul being at that time insensible to everything but Divine love: and . . . when the appointed times of prayer were past, he found no difference, because he still continued with GOD, praising and blessing Him with all his might, so that he passed his life in continual joy. . . .[10]

The whole of our being and all of our experience are filled with the presence of the holy as we learn to practice the presence of God in everything that we think, say, and do.

9. Brother Lawrence, *The Practice of the Presence of God,* p. 13.
10. Brother Lawrence, *The Practice of the Presence of God,* p. 13.

The Reality of Suffering

To live in this way is not in any sense to avoid or attempt to avoid the reality of suffering. Brother Lawrence recognized the inevitability of suffering. He expected that at some point he would experience "some great pain of body or mind; that the worst that could happen to him was to lose that sense [of] GOD which he had enjoyed so long; but that the goodness of GOD assured him He would not forsake him utterly, and that He would give him strength to bear whatever evil He permitted to happen to him; and therefore that he feared nothing. . . ."[11]

Suffering is not desired, but neither is it feared in and of itself. Brother Lawrence knew that suffering was an inevitability. At some stage in his life, he would experience the pain and lostness of human suffering that is the lot of all people. But he was prepared for that event. His lifetime of attending to God had led him to a place where he saw suffering differently. Suffering remained very real; but he shifted it into a different framework. His greatest fear was not suffering per se. It was that somehow that suffering might have the power to prevent or inhibit his love for God. He was not concerned with theodicy; his only concern was to ensure that his suffering did not prevent him from continuing his devotion to God or shake his trust in God's providence:

> He expected after the pleasant days GOD had given him, he should have his turn of pain and suffering; but . . . he was not uneasy about it, knowing very well that as he could do nothing of himself, GOD would not fail to give him the strength to bear them.[12]

As we learn to practice the presence of God, we also learn to trust in the providence of God. In so doing, we begin to recognize the presence of God even in our times of suffering. We learn to "give ourselves up to God, both in temporal and spiritual things, and seek our satisfaction only in fulfilling His will. Whether He leads us by suffering or consolation, all is the same to one truly resigned."[13]

Such a way is difficult. As Therese Lysaught shows clearly in her chapter in this book, even the most faithful and prayerful Christians

11. Brother Lawrence, *The Practice of the Presence of God,* p. 11.
12. Brother Lawrence, *The Practice of the Presence of God,* p. 8.
13. Brother Lawrence, *The Practice of the Presence of God,* p. 9.

can struggle to remain prayerful when they encounter profound suffering and pain. Practicing the presence of God will not protect a person from the doubts, questions, and struggles that accompany pain and suffering. Such a way of life is not an idealistic inoculation against the spiritual consequences of suffering. Nevertheless, the core of spiritual formation that emerges from a life lived practicing God's presence at least provides a language and a worldview that enable a person to begin to make sense of his or her suffering at a time when logic easily overwhelms hope.

Faith, Hope, and Love: Living Well and Dying Faithfully

Brother Lawrence introduces us to a perspective that, if practiced faithfully, enables us to integrate our love for God into all that we think, say, and do. In modeling a way for us to live faithful lives that are dedicated to God in all of their aspects, he provides a model of spiritual formation that is vital for the practices of dying well that are laid out in the remainder of this book. As we learn to practice the presence of God, the vital foundations for end-of-life care are laid firm and dug deep.

Brother Lawrence presents us with some deeply formative insights into what it might mean to live life abundantly and according to the precepts of Jesus' threefold command about love. Following his lead, I have used this chapter to explore some foundational understandings of the practices, values, and assumptions of many of the chapters in this book. If it is true that we die in more or less the same way that we live, then learning the discipline of practicing the presence of God is a fundamental and necessary endeavor that underpins all other Christian end-of-life care practices. Living this way, learning to see all of our earthly practices in heavenly perspective, frees us from hopelessness and imbues all of our lives with deep, rhythmic meaning that will carry us when, as will inevitably be the case for us all, our time comes for suffering.

In closing this chapter, let me quote the words of Thomas Merton's prayer, which may serve as a witness to the difficulties and the joys of walking faithfully toward life's end:

> MY LORD GOD, I have no idea where I am going. I do not see the road ahead of me. I cannot know for certain where it will end. Nor do I

really know myself, and the fact that I think that I am following your will does not mean that I am actually doing so. But I believe that the desire to please you does in fact please you. And I hope I have that desire in all that I am doing. I hope that I will never do anything apart from that desire. And I know that if I do this, you will lead me by the right road, though I may know nothing about it. Therefore will I trust you always, though I may seem to be lost and in the shadow of death. I will not fear, for you are ever with me, and you will never leave me to face my perils alone.[14]

14. Thomas Merton, *Choosing to Love the World: On Contemplation* (Louisville, Colo.: Sounds True, 2008), p. 99.

CHAPTER 2

Dying Well

Amy Plantinga Pauw

Death is an inevitable part of life. There is no getting around it. This is a frightening prospect, for the specter of death destroys any illusion that we are in full control of our lives or that we are our own makers and keepers. Most of us will experience the death of someone we love dearly, and all of us must face our own. How is it, then, that some people are able to die with the assurance that death is not the final word? How is it that some are able to face the death of a loved one trusting that love is stronger than death?

The Christian answer is that we belong in life and in death to God, whose love is stronger than death. This answer is not merely a matter of interior, personal conviction. It takes concrete form through the patterned life of the Christian community, molding the way we live as well as the way we die. In the weekly rhythm of the Christian life, the community gathers to celebrate the resurrection, God's final victory over death. Every year, during the season of Lent, it focuses on Christ's death on the cross. And in other rhythms, too, the church surrounds those enduring the pain, fear, and grief of death with visible, tangible signs of assurance and hope. Through impromptu conversations and well-planned funerals, through singing, prayer, and anointing with oil, through gifts of flowers and food, the Christian community acts out its beliefs.

This essay was originally published in *Practicing Our Faith: A Way of Life for a Searching People,* ed. Dorothy C. Bass (San Francisco: Jossey-Bass, 1997), pp. 163-77. Unless otherwise indicated, all of the quotations from Scripture that appear in this chapter are taken from the New Revised Standard Version of the Holy Bible.

Those who face death experience the living presence of God through the living presence of the community that cherishes and mourns them. And the community members who cherish and mourn these deaths are at the same time preparing themselves for the deaths that will surely come to them someday. "The church has made it possible for me to face and accept death, and to hope that death does not destroy life," writes theologian William M. Shea. "The church has made it possible for me to believe that God's love is stronger than death."[1] In the Christian practice of dying well, Christian people do things with and for one another in response to God's strong love, translating into concrete acts our belief in the resurrection of Christ, and of ourselves.

Wisdom and Care for Our Time

Death stands in a continuum with other significant life passages, each of which is linked to certain Christian practices. Unlike baptism, confirmation, and marriage, however, death is universal. Death "comes equally to us all," the pastor and poet John Donne declared, "and makes us all equal when it comes."[2] Moreover, this final and momentous life passage is the one that most often leads us to confront fundamental questions about the moral and religious significance of our lives. Impending death often drives us to seek the reconciliation with others we may have been avoiding for years. It infuses our reflections on mortality and suffering, healing, and hope with new urgency. Here, at the very edges of life, the practices of the community can proclaim what we most need to hear: that even in death, we are not alone.

This is a radical assertion in a society that often isolates death and dying from the flow of daily life, unlike almost every other society in history. In modern Western society, the two institutions that have had the most influence on how people face death — hospitals and funeral homes — have altered the communal practices that once surrounded this life passage. As a result, contemporary people are especially in need of the wisdom and care that the Christian practice of dying well can offer.

1. William M. Shea, "Theologians and Their Catholic Authorities: Reminiscence and Reconnoitre," *Horizons,* Fall 1986, p. 345.

2. John Donne, "Sermon of March 8," in *Eighty Sermons* (London, 1640).

We live in a culture in which the process of dying has largely been handed over to a medical establishment reluctant to admit the limits of its life-preserving powers. The modern West is an anomaly in this regard: most ages and cultures have lived much closer to the fact of human mortality. As we live longer and tend increasingly to die in hospitals of chronic diseases, the "rescue credo" of modern medicine often interferes with our chances of dying well.

Religious convictions about the power of divine love beyond death, argued the ethicist Paul Ramsey, can provide the courage needed to recognize the limits of modern medical care. Maybe only faith in God can provide the basis for "a conscionable category of 'ceasing to oppose death,' making room for caring for the dying."[3] Contemporary Christians acknowledge what people in other times and cultures have never forgotten: that there are other kinds of hope to offer to dying persons besides the hope of elusive and high-risk physical cures. Today, many medical professionals are also seeking new avenues in curing and caring for the terminally ill, as Christian caregivers join with other concerned people to shift the focus away from the disease and back to the person. Hospice care is a growing response to this need.

Likewise, the formal acknowledgment of death and response to grief have largely been handed over to funeral homes. No longer simply providers of custodial services for the corpse, funeral homes now place ads in the yellow pages promising sympathy, care, and peace of mind "when you need us most." We may deplore the lucrative services that funeral homes have developed to meet these needs – for example, the beautification of the corpse and the use of elaborate metal caskets. But we must also notice that mourners are attracted to these services because of a genuine void in modern Western society. People yearn for communal practices that pay tribute to the dead and bring comfort to the bereaved.

Here, too, the fertile ground of Christian practice concerning death and dying may yield new fruit. The church is a community of memory in a way that the workplace and the neighborhood, much less the funeral home, are not. In worship, we regularly offer prayers of thanksgiving for the lives of those who now rest in God's mercy. As we do so, the names and faces of a few dear ones are on the minds and

3. Paul Ramsey, *The Patient as Person* (New Haven: Yale University Press, 1970), p. 156.

hearts of each worshiper. At the same time, these prayers are larger than our personal memories, and the worshiping community will continue to offer them long after our own dear ones, or even we ourselves, are remembered by name. Moreover, the Christian community can offer a depth of spiritual and practical support for the sorrowing that the funeral home can never match. Dying in its embrace, we are confident that after we die, the church will gather to celebrate our life and mourn our passing, and confident that the community will care for our family through prayers, visits, and generous hospitality.

The Many Faces of Death

The circumstances of human death vary enormously, and it is impossible to consider all of them. But we must acknowledge that Christian practices hold no magic formula for transforming premature, tragic, or unjust deaths into good deaths. We will not all die peacefully of old age, and when a life is cut short – by accident, suicide, childhood disease, or violence – Christians view it as an evil. And beyond the terrible deaths of individuals are the horrors of mass death. The twentieth century is certainly not the first century to witness them, but we have seen perhaps more than our share. The forced march of the Armenians, the Nazi death camps, the famines in Biafra, the Cambodian killing fields, and the murders of "the disappeared" in Latin America – all display cruelty beyond our ken. One source of special anguish in these kinds of death is that the victims are usually denied participation in the practices that make dying well possible. They die too young, too suddenly, too far removed from loved ones.

What does dying well mean for those who suffer "bad deaths" and for the loved ones they leave behind? Here the fact that dying well is not an individual practice but a shared one is especially significant. Death marks the end only of physical life; an individual's presence, however, extends beyond death as one's life is remembered and absorbed redemptively into the community that remains. The extent to which it is possible for the bereaved to find redemptive significance in the "bad death" of a loved one depends in large part on the practices of the community to which they belong. And the knowledge that one's life will continue to matter to the community even after one's death can be a powerful source of comfort for individuals living under the threat of sudden or violent death.

The history of Christian practices surrounding the passage of death spans more than two millennia. Christians have ministered to the dying and the dead in times of severe persecution as well as in times of strong alliance with reigning powers, in times of ecclesiastical corruption and in times of church reform, in times of communal cohesiveness and in times of urban isolation and fragmentation. An enduring and irreducible complexity seems to underlie Christian responses to the reality of death in its many forms, in many different circumstances and cultural, political, and ecclesiastical contexts. *When Christian practices are healthy, dying well embraces both lament and hope, and both a sense of divine judgment and an awareness of divine mercy.* The joining together of these diverse components reflects the variety of biblical attitudes toward death, as well as centuries of Christian theological and experiential wisdom. Each component is associated with certain shared activities of the community.

Lament

The early church inherited the Jewish community's practice of using the Bible's psalms of lament to mourn the death of the faithful. That death evokes despair and anger is not a discovery of twentieth-century psychology; it is at the heart of the practice of lament. Psalms of lament bring before God the raw intensity of the emotions evoked by death. When we pray these psalms, we expose our emotions instead of hiding them, as some Christians do when they mistakenly imagine that God will be offended by their bitterness and outrage. Jesus himself experienced great anguish in the face of death, and according to tradition, cried the bitter lament of Psalm 22 from the cross: "My God, my God, why have you forsaken me?" (Matt. 27:46). When we lament, we acknowledge the truth that God does not remove all the pain and torment of dying, either for the sufferer or for the community.

Lament needs to be an integral part of Christian practice in response to death and dying, precisely because we value so highly God's gift of earthly life. The treasured promise of Romans 8:38-39 that not even death can separate us from the love of God in Christ Jesus does not erase the fact that death does separate us from those we love on earth. Death is an irrevocable, wrenching loss for those the dead leave behind. But it is also a loss for those who die – a loss of the parts of creation they took delight in, the relationships they held most dear, and the possibilities they envisioned for the future. Particularly in the case of premature or tragic deaths, it is appropriate for Christians to adopt or develop rituals and liturgies of lament to remember those who died. Hope of everlasting life with God does not undercut Christian gratitude and concern for this life, nor deny the place of lament in Christian responses to death.

Thanksgiving and Hope

Lament must, however, be balanced by hope and thanksgiving. We are of the earth, created both good and finite. Like the flowers and the grass, we eventually wither and fade, but we may still enjoy seasons of vivid and luxuriant bloom. The approach of death can be a time of thanksgiving for all of God's good gifts during our earthly life. Christian funerals are also a time to remember the accomplishments and good efforts of the dead and to thank God for who they were and what they meant to those around them. Funerals provide a time to celebrate the gifts and the legacy of those who have died.

In addition, however, mortal life is also a place of great vulnerability and often tremendous suffering. And so Christian funerals also express hope for life beyond death, mirroring the hope that often sustains Christians before they die. In the obituary for an eighty-six-year-old man, his family celebrated the fact that "his forty-year struggle with depression has ended, and his perfect enjoyment of the beauty of God has begun." In a paradoxical way, Christians can speak about death in terms of gain as well as loss. We believe that true human fulfillment occurs only beyond this life, though our capacity to imagine life on the other side of death is a bit like a caterpillar's grasp of life on the other side of the cocoon. The fundamental Christian conviction is that, far from separating us from the love of God, death marks the point at which temporal obstacles to our experience of that love pass away. Indeed, the accounts of early Christian funerals reflect an almost defiant sense of confidence and joy. Participants in funeral processions wore white garments, sang psalms of praise, carried palm branches, and burned incense as a witness to the resurrection. Christians carried out these celebrations in the daytime as a bold, public display of hope for life beyond death. Christian funerals are always a time to celebrate both the gift of temporal life and the hope for life with God beyond death.

Yet Christian hope for life beyond death is a hope that has passed through the furnace of suffering and death. Christians affirm the good news of Easter only in the wake of the anguish of Good Friday. Our hope for everlasting life permits no evasion of death's hard reality. Jesus' response to the grieving Martha has remained one of the favorite scriptural texts for Christian funerals: "I am the resurrection and the life. Those who believe in me, even though they die, will live" (John 11:25). But in this Gospel story, Jesus proceeds to weep with Martha and her sister Mary over the death of their brother Lazarus. Indeed, even the resurrection does not erase from Christ's hands and feet the wounds of the crucifixion. Sharing the meal of Eucharist at Christian funerals is deeply appropriate, because in this sacrament, both Christ's brokenness and God's promise of new life are made vividly present.

The cross, an instrument of death, is always at the center of Christian hope. Because of this, the practice of dying well has a paradoxical quality. On the one hand, as followers of Jesus Christ, we are not to save death and dying for the end of our lives. Life in Christ requires dying now. Those who hope in God as the redeemer from death must enter into the vulnerable, suffering love that leads to the cross. The entire Christian life draws us into an ongoing "death," in which we die to everything that thwarts God's intentions for life, peace, and joy. As John Calvin summarized it, "Man dies to himself that he may begin to live to God."[4] Christians testify to hope for everlasting life with God by dying in the present to all that stands in its way. Sometimes, indeed, this leads to the premature physical death of martyrdom, as it did for early Christians who died in passive endurance for the sake of the faith and for such recent martyrs as Martin Luther King Jr. and Oscar Romero, who died in active struggles for justice.

On the other hand, Christian hope also requires a restless protest

4. John Calvin, *Institutes of the Christian Religion,* ed. John T. McNeill (Philadelphia: Westminster, 1960), 3.3.3.

against death. Death from natural causes at an advanced age or as a release from severe suffering is something to be grateful for. But the gratitude is for the gift of a long life or for the merciful end of suffering. Death, though part of our natural condition, is not something with which Christians can be fully at peace. As Paul reminds us, "The last enemy to be destroyed is death" (1 Cor. 15:26).

This is one of the places where Christian practices regarding death and dying do not fit well with contemporary cultural attitudes. Some recent self-help literature insists that there is nothing sad, frightening, or destructive about our own death; it is simply a final opportunity for personal growth or a "friendly companion on life's journey"[5] as we finally merge with the larger rhythms of the cosmos.

Christians find comfort instead in the confidence that God is actively working against the powers of death in all creation. "When the writer of Revelation spoke of the coming of the day of shalom, he did not say that on that day we would live at peace with death," notes the philosopher Nicholas Wolterstorff. "He said that on that day 'There will be no more death or mourning or crying or pain, for the old order of things has passed away.'"[6] In its power to separate and alienate, death is part of the old order. Christians who hope for the coming of God's new reign must nurture resistance to the powers of death in this world.

This facet of Christian hope is seen in the protest against unjust death that forms an integral part of some Latin American worship services. The names of the deceased are read off one by one, and at each name the congregation exclaims, *Presente!* Parents, children, relatives, and friends lifted up in this way have often died brutally and tragically. Yet the Christian worshipers refuse to accept violent death as the last word on them. As part of the "great cloud of witnesses" (Heb. 12:1), they are declared present to the living community through God's gift of life that triumphs even over the last enemy, death.

This ritual of hope in the face of brutal and unjust deaths is also done for the sake of the living. God desires a world in which peace and justice embrace. Christian hope responds as we struggle to prevent

5. Elisabeth Kübler-Ross, *Death: The Final Stage of Growth* (New York: Macmillan, 1969), p. 6.

6. Nicholas Wolterstorff, *Lament for a Son* (Grand Rapids: William B. Eerdmans, 1987), pp. 38-41, 63.

these kinds of horrible deaths in the future. This struggle on behalf of the living is at the same time an act of hope on behalf of the dead. It is the hope that their lives, and even the apparent absurdity of their deaths, will yield a new resolve to establish justice on earth.

Judgment

The complementary themes of human hope and lament are mirrored by the themes of divine mercy and judgment. These themes reflect the complexity of the Christian tradition's view of death. On the one hand, we understand death as a natural part of our finitude as creatures whose days are numbered. On the other hand, we also believe that death is intertwined with our sinfulness, with the human rejection of God's loving and life-giving intentions. Though Scripture is ambiguous about how sin originates and spreads, it is clear that sin is deadly. Left unchecked, sin pollutes, distorts, and finally destroys us. The writings of the apostle Paul in particular forged strong bonds between death and human sin in Christian reflection. Though the Bible also supports other understandings of death, Paul's notion that "death spread to all because all have sinned" (Rom. 5:12) was dominant throughout most of Christian history.

Fear of God's wrath – God's harsh judgment of our sinful lives – shaped the Christian experience of death for many centuries, and it continues as a powerful motive in some Christian communities today. Scenes of the Last Judgment, carved by artists on the doors of medieval cathedrals or presented in the books and films of contemporary Christian fundamentalists, depict the agony of those condemned to eternal fires. Fortunately, this kind of fear has given way in many Christian communities today to an understanding of divine judgment that does not deny divine love. The modern weakening of the link between death and God's wrath helps us to affirm the naturalness of death and to overcome simple formulas that claimed to understand the mysteries of God's judgment and mercy. In death and in life, we rely on God's grace, for others and for ourselves.

Still, Christians do insist that sin leads to death in a myriad of ways, and that no passage in our lives is free from sin, including death. We have lived fallen lives, and we will die fallen deaths. This means that we need to acknowledge God's judgment and seek God's forgiveness in our dying as well as in our living. Where possible, dying Christians need to seek human forgiveness as well. Confessing our sins and asking for forgiveness are regular rhythms in the Christian life. But death, as the final life passage, infuses these regular practices with a heightened urgency and significance. Though speaking of "sin" is uncomfortable for many modern people, the sense that we need forgiveness at the end of life is in our bones. This is what dying people yearn for — the opportunity to heal a breach with a sister, or to say to a son the words of love that were always so hard to speak when he was growing up. When families gather at the bedside of one who will soon die, these are the words they say: "I am sorry that I hurt you. I love you. Please forgive me." And "I understand. I forgive you. I love you too. Be at peace." In this way, we participate, however haltingly, in the reconciliation God is working in the world.

The practices of the medieval period, an age of short and unpredictable life expectancy, embodied profound insight into the fear death evokes, as well as the desire of the dying to settle accounts with God and others. The ritual of anointing with oil, used in earlier times for physical as well as spiritual healing, became a tangible way to prepare the dying soul for entrance into heaven. This provided a concrete assurance of forgiveness to people for whom words could often no longer convey meaning. Likewise, offering prayers and masses on behalf of the dead expressed concern for the bereaved and affirmed the communion of all the saints, both living and dead. In the sixteenth century, however, financial corruptions that had grown up around these rituals led Protestant reformers to repudiate them altogether. Even though this represented an important witness against manipulating the fear of death for the sake of wealth and power, the reform left Protestant Christians without adequate ways of allaying fears of God's wrath.

One of the many gains of the modern movements in Christian ecumenism and liturgical renewal has been a new willingness to set aside old theological and institutional animosities and learn from the practices of other communions. Catholic liturgies have placed renewed emphasis on the Christian funeral as a celebration of the paschal mystery of Christ's own death and resurrection. Many Protestant communions have adopted rituals of prayer for the dead and anointing for the sick. The significant convergence between the Catholic and Protestant practices of dying well is a hopeful sign for the future of the Christian community.

Mercy

Divine judgment and divine mercy, though complementary, do not have equal weight in Christian reflections on death. Judgment is the counterpoint in death's rhythm; its notes are always secondary to the dominant theme of divine mercy. We worship a God who "does not deal with us according to our sins, nor repay us according to our iniquities," but whose steadfast love is as great "as the heavens are high above the earth" (Ps. 103:10-11).

This rhythm is reflected in healthy Christian communities as well. Anointing the sick with oil and praying for the dead acknowledge the reality of divine judgment against sin and the human need for forgiveness. But these practices do not invite us to judge the dying and the deceased in God's place. Instead, they call us to acknowledge God's mercy toward the dying and to embody it through our words and actions. The fundamental way of expressing our thanks for the divine mercy that sustains us is to be instruments of that divine mercy to others.

Offering presence is the most basic way of making divine mercy actively present to a person who is dying. We need divine mercy mediated to us at every point of our lives, of course. But our need for it is especially great during the passage of death, when both our physical and our emotional resources ebb. An important way in which Christians incarnate the mercy of Jesus Christ is by loving care for the body. Dying for most of us will be a messy, painful business; we cannot expect to die well in a biological sense. But skilled and compassionate ministry to the bodily needs of dying persons can give them a profound sense of God's merciful presence. Eve Kavenaugh, a nurse who works with terminally ill patients, recognizes these deep interconnections between body and spirit. She sees her work as an opportunity to express God's mercy to the dying "by faithful and loving care of the body, which becomes increasingly more difficult to care for and often repulsive. If I remain loving and faithful to that task until the end, the patient has a new and life-giving experience of God."[7]

A phrase from the ministry to persons living with AIDS captures the importance of physical presence in caring for the dying. At the terrible last stages of the disease, family and friends embrace the dying

7. Eve Kavenaugh, "Prayer of the Flesh," *Other Side*, May-June 1993, p. 59.

person with a "care-giving surround." Christian communities can likewise embody divine mercy by a care-giving surround that aims at physical comfort and companionship for all who face death.

The Christian activity of caring presence also requires loving support of the person's spirit. Serenity and trust in God do not come easily to those whose minds are ravaged by disease and pain. Christians who continue to radiate faith and love of God through a prolonged period of dying are grace-filled teachers to the rest of the community. But dying well is not to be seen primarily as something that a dying individual achieves. A serene death is not an accomplishment by which a person must prove his or her spiritual maturity, and a difficult death is not a cause for despair.

During the last pain-racked weeks of a grandmother whose faith had long been an inspiration in her community, serenity seemed far away. Her face did not show the feelings of acceptance and calm that her loved ones so longed to see there. In some ways, they realized, she was like a baby at baptism: others must claim God's promises on her behalf. And so that is what they did at her deathbed, speaking the prayers and singing the hymns when she was too weak to do so herself. It comforted them, in the end, when she managed to let them know of her gratitude – to them, for sharing their faith, and to God, for a life of many blessings. But even if this acknowledgment had been beyond her, they would have held her in this embrace, as her parents and sponsors had done some seventy years before. Like our birth into Christian faith, our dying well draws strength from the faith of the entire community. We live by grace, and we also die by grace.

In Life and in Death, We Are God's

Some years ago, Eric Wolterstorff died in a mountaineering accident at the age of twenty-five. His father, Nicholas, has written about this tragedy in a book treasured by many people who have experienced similar losses. At the funeral, he reports, the community's actions and symbols spoke as much as the words. The cloth placed over the coffin was "simple but wonderfully beautiful," and near it burned a candle, symbolizing resurrection. The opening words recalled Eric's baptism. The music was "glorious." Together, the gathered people celebrated the Eucharist, "that sacrament of God's participation in our brokenness." They "came forward successively in groups, standing in circles around the coffin, passing the signs of Christ's brokenness to each other."[8]

The funeral did not console him for Eric's absence, Wolterstorff writes. But it did do something else. "It sank deep into me the realization that my son's death is not all there is."[9]

A Christian funeral like this one has its deepest meaning for people who have been nurtured by basic Christian convictions during the course of their lives. The same is true of the other acts of prayer and concern with which the Christian community surrounds us as we near the end of our days. Their power "cannot be instantaneously transmitted to the sick person waiting upon death whose flesh already is ravaged and mind is tormented by disease," the theologian Vigen Guroian points out. "The meaning for living and dying that faith provides must be owned by the person over a lifetime."[10] The Christian practices surrounding the passage of death echo the regular rhythms of worship and fellowship in the Christian life. Dying well grows out of the Christian community's attempts to live well before God in the present.

Dying well involves participation in complex, difficult, communal practices. But like all Christian practices, it rests on the promise that there is a divine ground beneath us in all the passages of our lives. If we manage to live well or die well, it is because we are not our own, either as individuals or as a human race. This recognition humbles us; but it also gives us hope that in our failures as well as in our successes, we belong to God. With the assurance that not even death will separate us from God's love, we can dare to nurture the Christian practices that will help each of us to embody God's mercy to one another while we live and then, when it is time, to die well.

8. Wolterstorff, *Lament for a Son,* pp. 39-40.

9. Wolterstorff, *Lament for a Son,* p. 38.

10. Vigen Guroian, "Death and Dying Well in the Orthodox Liturgical Tradition," *Second Opinion,* July 1993, p. 57.

CHAPTER 3

"Make Love Your Aim": Ecclesial Practices of Care at the End of Life

Karen D. Scheib

Shortly after I returned from the seminar on practices of care at the end of life where I first presented the material for this chapter, what had been an academic topic became personal. The small congregation I attend was shattered by the news that Lucy's cancer had returned. When the headaches came back, we all hoped this was just a side effect of the radiation. We were wrong. The tumor was active and growing. Because Lucy was an active member of our congregation as well as the pastor's wife, her dying and death affected the entire congregation.

Caring for Lucy and Ed and their children for several months shaped our congregational patterns and practices. We were drawn together and sustained by the Spirit as Lucy's death neared. The apostle Paul's images of communal ecclesial life echoed our experience: "To each is given the manifestation of the Spirit for the common good" (1 Cor. 12:7).[1] Members with gifts of leadership stepped forward to assume responsibilities and assure continuance of the church's ministry, allowing Ed and his family precious time with Lucy. Members with gifts of hospitality provided meals, and those with the gift of compassion took turns keeping watch with the family at the hospital as Lucy's death neared. We felt the Spirit move among us, binding us together as one body in prayer, grief, and love. "If one member suffers, all suffer to-

1. I am employing a devotional rather than an exegetical reading of these texts while reflecting on our congregational experience.

Unless otherwise indicated, all of the quotations from Scripture in this chapter are taken from the Revised Standard Version of the Holy Bible.

gether" (1 Cor. 12:26). We discovered that love is difficult and, at times, painful.

As we felt pulled inward by our grief, we had to remind ourselves that we were called to be in ministry not only to Lucy and Ed and their family, but to all those who entered our doors. "Make love your aim," Paul declares (1 Cor. 14:1), encouraging us to open ourselves to the greatest spiritual gift of love not meant for us alone but for "the building up of the church" (1 Cor. 13:13; 14:12). Our regular congregational patterns and practices of gathering, worship, and administration continued, yet they seemed transformed by the reality of death in our midst. Even our practices of hospitality were affected as we explained to visitors why a different person was in the pulpit each week. We managed to continue our homeless ministry and plan for another mission trip to New Orleans to help a sister church in the process of rebuilding.

I am not suggesting that our congregation was perfect in our response. What I do assert is that practices of care at the end of life are not abstract issues for any church community. Most congregations face death in some form every day. How we respond matters.

This chapter lays the groundwork for the construction of a Christian practical theology of death and dying within the context of the mainline, Euro-American Protestant tradition in the United States.[2] I move toward a Christian practical theology of death and dying by examining narratives and practices of care at the end of life within the context of the larger culture of the United States. In so doing I want to suggest that a Christian practical theology of death and dying can ground practices of care in the narratives of the community of faith in the midst of countervailing cultural narratives that perceive death quite differently.

Practical Theology

This chapter, like many other chapters in this volume, is based on the discipline of practical theology. Through practical theological reflec-

2. While the mainline or "old line" Protestant tradition is diverse, my focus is on those congregations most influenced by and reflective of the dominant Euro-American culture. Many of the issues I discuss in this chapter are either less prominent or take different form in African-American, Hispanic, or Asian Protestant churches in the United States.

tion, we seek to "make love our aim" as we fulfill the nature and purpose of the Christian community's primary goal: to share in the life and love of the Triune God.[3] Practical theology properly occurs as a communal process, the goal of which is the development of prophetic ecclesial practices that are transformative, liberative, and redemptive. I understand Christian practical theology to be *critical theological reflection on the interrelated narratives and practices of the church as they interact with the interrelated narratives and practices of the contexts and cultures in which they occur.*[4]

I include theological reflection on narratives as well as practices in my definition of practical theology because theory-laden practices are often based on interpretations of the Christian narrative, which may also be in need of critical reflection. Feminist and liberation theologies have shown us that our interpretations of Christian narratives and practices often reflect our personal and cultural biases as well as socially approved power arrangements. Critical reflection on narratives that are shaped by Scripture and tradition is a vital aspect of the practical theological task.

We have already seen in this book some of the ways in which the theological convictions and narratives of the Christian faith are necessarily and vitally embodied in and communicated through ecclesial practices – practices that are vital for the practice of dying well. Practices of care, including those that are particularly appropriate at the end of life, represent the lived theology of the church as it seeks to manifest God's love and care for the world. Christian practices are shaped by and express social processes; but they are also an expression of the divine-human relationship through which we are constituted as persons.[5]

3. The view of the church reflected here is consistent with that communion ecclesiology. See Dennis Doyle, *Communion Ecclesiology* (Maryknoll, N.Y.: Orbis Books, 2000), p. 2. See also *On the Way to Fuller Koinonia: Faith and Order Paper No. 166,* ed. T. Best and G. Gassmann (Geneva: WCC Publications, 1994).

4. My definition is quite similar to that of John Swinton and Harriet Mowat in *Practical Theology and Qualitative Research* (London: SCM Press, 2006), p. 25.

5. For a fuller discussion of this view of Christian practices, see Dorothy C. Bass and Craig Dykstra, "A Theological Understanding of Christian Practices," in *Practicing Theology: Beliefs and Practices in Christian Life,* ed. Miroslav Volf and Dorothy C. Bass (Grand Rapids: William B. Eerdmans, 2002).

Through Christian practices we respond to God's grace as we live out our convictions and commitments. Caring practices are concrete, if imperfect, ways in which the church bears witness to the divine love through which it is called into being and sustained. While practices are expressions of human activity, they are also manifestations of the gifts of the Spirit given for the life of the church and the world.

Toward a Christian Practical Theology of Death and Dying

A first step toward the construction of a Christian practical theology of death and dying requires that we take note of the particular communities and cultural contexts in which practices of care are enacted. With this is mind, I will begin by providing a brief critical analysis of some contemporary cultural narratives about death and dying that are available in the United States. It is my contention that both cultural practices and Christian practices around death and dying have been shaped by cultural narratives such as these, some of which may be in conflict with Christian narratives.[6]

The second step is a critical and constructive re-engagement with three key themes drawn from specifically Christian narratives of death and dying: (1) a definition of death as more than physical death; (2) a recovery of the rhythm of death and resurrection as the heart of Christian life; and (3) a revised concept of "the communion of saints," an often-forgotten Christian idea that reminds us that the living and the dead are connected in an ongoing community of the faithful. These three themes do not, of course, exhaust the requirements for a fully developed Christian practical theology of death and dying. They do, however, provide an important starting point for my stated task of foundation-building.

The third step toward the construction of a Christian practical theology of death and dying is the development of practices of care through which a revised theological narrative of death is embodied. I propose three sets of interrelated end-of-life practices: narrative, rela-

6. There are many other dimensions that could be examined. I have limited my analysis here due to space constraints. Our language about suffering is also critical; this is dealt with in subsequent chapters.

tional, and prophetic.[7] Through narrative practices, care providers assist persons and communities in giving narrative shape to their own experiences of living and dying. Relational practices provide a means to nurture the interpersonal, family, and communal contexts in which we live, and in which we make ethical decisions about our living and dying.[8] Through prophetic practices of care, we address the larger social and systemic forces that wound persons and inhibit care at the end of life.

Contemporary Cultural Narratives of Death and Dying

Our personal views of death and dying are influenced by cultural attitudes, language, and images. With a majority of deaths in the United States occurring in hospitals, death is commonly defined in medical terms.[9] The Uniform Determination of Death Act, based on the 1981 President's Commission Report, is now endorsed in the majority of states in the United States. The UDDA definition of death allows either "(1) the irreversible cessation of circulatory and respiratory functions, or (2) the irreversible cessation of all functions of the entire brain, including the brain stem. A determination of death must be made in accordance with accepted medical standards."[10]

Medical definitions of death are necessary and useful. Death, however, can have multiple meanings. These meanings are shaped by one's role or relationship to the deceased. The meaning of a particular death for the physician pronouncing death may be shaped both by the medical definition of death and the physician's own experience. In some instances, physicians experience death as a pronouncement of the failure

7. See Karen D. Scheib, *Challenging Invisibility: Practices of Care with Older Women* (St. Louis: Chalice Press, 2004).

8. Scheib, *Challenging Invisibility,* p. 53.

9. In 1998, this rate was 56 percent, a statistic from the National Mortality Followback Study, National Center for Health Statistics, Center for Disease Control and Prevention, 1998. This appears to be the most recent release of this data.

10. President's Commission for the Study of Ethical Problems in Medicine and Biomedical Behavioral Research, *Defining Death: A Report on the Medical, Legal, and Ethical Issues in the Determination of Death* (Washington, D.C.: U.S. Government Printing Office, 1981), cited in "Definition of Death" by B. Holly Vautier in *Dignity and Dying: A Christian Appraisal,* ed. John F. Kilner, Arlene B. Miller, and Edmund D. Pellegrino (Grand Rapids: William B. Eerdmans, 1996), p. 96.

of medical intervention. For family members, the medical definition of death is only one dimension of a multifaceted and complex experience of loss.

While serving as hospital chaplain, I saw families struggle with the medical definition of death following approval for organ donation. How does one come to terms with the death of a loved one when the skin is warm, the lungs are filling, and the heart is pumping, albeit artificially? While a medical definition of death does not fully capture the meaning of death (particularly for survivors), it nonetheless plays a prominent role in our cultural understanding of death.

Ethicist Daniel Callahan suggests that one of the cultural consequences of recent medical advances is the severing of the historic link between "our care of the dying and our stance toward death itself." On the one hand, policies that protect patient autonomy provide choices about how one dies, such as limiting aggressive treatment and receiving palliative care. On the other hand, research agendas have encouraged modern medicine "to grab death by the throat and not let it go — even as our biology one way or another continues to conspire to let us down."[11] Callahan argues that our current cultural attitudes about death go beyond "the denial of death" that Ernest Becker wrote about in the 1970s to an "incremental whittling away" at death's certainty.[12]

At the same time that the larger culture seems to deny death, it also appears to be fascinated about what might lie beyond it. Recent and current television shows offer a perspective on life after death that is quite different from the Christian witness. At the same time that such alternative cultural views proliferate, distinctively Christian understandings about death seem to have faded from the larger cultural narrative. This becomes clear when we reflect on the tendency within popular culture to view death as a personal, rather than a corporate, spiritual journey, as represented in, for example, the Christian concept of the communion of saints.

An example of this popular cultural view of death-as-a-personal-journey can be found in the television show *Ghost Whisperer*, which provides a glimpse into some current cultural images of death. In this

11. Daniel Callahan, "Death: The Distinguished Thing," in *Improving End-of-Life Care: Why Has It Been So Difficult?* (New York: Hastings Center Report, 2005), pp. 7, 9.

12. Callahan, "Death: The Distinguished Thing," p. 8.

show, death is perceived as a transition into another reality in which the person continues, relatively unchanged. Melinda, the main character of this drama, has the "gift" of seeing dead people who have not yet "crossed over." In addition to running an antique store, Melinda uses her "gift" to help these "souls" resolve unfinished tasks or attachments so that they may "cross over into the light."

I haven't watched this show enough to see if anyone ever crosses over into the darkness, but I suspect not. There is no mention of heaven, purgatory, or hell. These specifically Christian ways of talking about death and what is beyond are replaced by the more generic term "the light," which is what seems to lie beyond death. "The light" is never defined, but it appears to be available to anyone, irrespective of pre-death beliefs or behaviors. Purgatory as a place of ongoing salvation is replaced by a ghostly earthly existence where, if you're lucky, you'll get help from a therapist for the dead to work out unresolved psychological attachments.

Significantly, hell seems to disappear altogether from this image of death. The profound theological concepts highlighted in an earlier chapter by Amy Plantinga Pauw — judgment, mercy, lament, prayer, and forgiveness — have no place in this schema. Instead, death simply becomes an extension of life-as-we-know-it-now, wherein the same traumas and neuroses that people experience in this life are carried over and dealt with in the afterlife in essentially the same ways.

In another show, *Pushing Daisies,* death can be an impermanent state. A young pie-maker has a reverse Midas touch. Rather than turning things to gold, rendering them inert, if not dead, he can bring human beings and animals back to life, though a second touch reverses the process — thus the dramatic conflict at the heart of the show. He has permanently brought back his dog and his former lover, but he literally cannot get close to them. Ironically, he can bring the dead to life, but he cannot touch the loved ones he has revived. What may be reflected here is either a cultural uncertainty about what constitutes death or a belief that death is reversible, at least briefly.

In this television fantasy, resurrection is replaced by a pie-maker's touch, revealing a desire that is more prevalent in our culture. In medical dramas, "resurrection" often occurs when doctors apply electric paddles to the heart, accompanied by a shout of "Clear!" Explicit Christian understandings of death, dying, and resurrection rarely, if ever, appear in mainstream media and no longer appear to be the predominant images that shape understandings and practices of dying for many individuals and communities within the larger American (and universal) culture.

The Emergence of a New Cultural Language about Death

The death awareness movement, which emerged in the United States in the 1960s, led to a revival of interest in death and dying. A primary concern of this loosely organized social movement was to normalize and humanize death, dying, and bereavement. This movement, which included scholars, counselors, and laypersons, sought to challenge the cultural medicalization and denial of death.[13] Elisabeth Kübler-Ross is probably one of the most well-known leaders of this movement; her 1969 text *On Death and Dying* helped popularize it. This movement, which has produced many books, seminars, and how-to guides, has impacted both religious and nonreligious people in significant ways. It has raised a number of important issues, including "the right to die," "death with dignity," and organ donation. Indeed, this movement continues to influence the language of and practices surrounding death and dying in the United States.[14]

According to Lucy Bregman, author of *Beyond Silence and Denial,* the death awareness movement has led to the development of a new cultural language of dying in North America. Although this new language has overcome the "silence and denial" of earlier generations, Bregman argues that it has also played a significant role in the displacement of traditional Christian language about death and dying.[15] Two key concepts are central to the vocabulary of the death awareness movement: "death as natural" and "death as loss."[16]

13. See Kenneth Doka, "The Death Awareness Movement: Description, History, Analysis," in *The Handbook of Death and Dying,* ed. Clifton Bryant (Thousand Oaks, Calif.: Sage Publications, 2003).

14. Doka, "The Death Awareness Movement," p. 50.

15. Lucy Bregman, *Beyond Silence and Denial: Death and Dying Reconsidered* (Louisville: Westminster John Knox Press, 1999), p. 1.

16. Bregman, *Beyond Silence and Denial.* See pp. 43-76 on "death as natural," and pp. 99-132 on "death as loss."

To claim that "death is natural" is to assert that it is a natural part of human experience.[17] This assertion plays a positive role to the extent that it challenges a medicalized view of death. However, the theoretical foundation underlying the claim that "death is natural" is problematic. This claim is built on assumptions of growth-oriented psychologies and a view of nature as essentially harmonious and benign.[18]

Bregman does not believe the assertion that "death is natural" is necessarily antithetical to Christian teaching, but rather that it does not say enough about death from a Christian perspective.[19] Christian theological affirmations about death do not begin with the claim that death is natural. For example, in *Against Heresies* Irenaeus identified "sin, death, and the devil as enemies of God." Likewise, Christian theological perspectives on human beings have not assumed that moral, spiritual, and psychological maturity are inborn unfolding processes always oriented toward growth.[20] Classical articulations of the theological doctrine of justification assert that the human condition is one of radical relational brokenness that can be restored only through divine grace. The doctrine of sanctification, which describes spiritual growth, is not a naturally unfolding process but rather a gift of grace.

A second concept from the death awareness movement that Bregman analyzes is "death as loss." The positive contribution of this concept is the "recovery of loss, grief, and mourning as basic human realities." Given the centrality of these themes in the literature arising from the death awareness movement, it might be more accurate to call this movement the grief awareness movement.[21] A deeper understanding of the psychological dimensions of grief is perhaps the greatest contribution of the death awareness movement. Many contemporary Christian funeral liturgies now make more explicit reference to the experience of grief than liturgies of the past.[22] The difficulty arises when the focus on the bereaved obscures our concern for the dying person.

17. Bregman, *Beyond Silence and Denial,* p. 43.

18. Bregman, *Beyond Silence and Denial,* pp. 66-67.

19. Bregman, *Beyond Silence and Denial,* pp. 66-67.

20. Bregman, *Beyond Silence and Denial,* p. 66.

21. Bregman, *Beyond Silence and Denial,* p. 99.

22. As an example, see "A Service of Death and Resurrection," in *The United Methodist Hymnal* (Nashville: United Methodist Publishing House, 1989).

Bregman suggests that while a concern for the bereaved does not contradict Christian views of death, it does not represent the primary focus of a Christian theology of death.[23]

This shift in focus from the dying to the bereaved in Christian funeral practices is examined by homiletician Tom Long. In "Whatever Happened to the Christian Funeral?" Long reviews the history of the Christian funeral, beginning with the early church, and demonstrates the way in which Christian language and imagery have not merely been adapted in the funeral service, but replaced.[24] He describes radical changes in Christian funeral practices over the last fifty years, focusing primarily on white mainline Protestant churches.

One marked change is a shift away from an understanding of the funeral as a communal ritual with explicit Christian imagery focused on the spiritual journey of the dying person. Long asserts that funerals are now increasingly replaced by "memorial services" in which the personal life of the deceased and the immediate experiences of the bereaved become the primary concerns. The communal dimensions of death rituals have given way to an individualized experience. By examining contemporary Christian funeral practices, Long reveals the way in which the psychological needs of grievers often take center stage. "Christian death practices are no longer metaphorical expressions of the journey of a saint to be with God," Long observes. As cremation is more widely practiced and memorial services replace funerals, "the saint is not even present, except as a spiritualized memory, a backdrop for the real action, which happens in the psyches of the mourners."[25]

A cursory review of some of the recent literature in pastoral care and counseling confirms Long and Bregman's assertion that grievers often receive more attention than the dying person. In one of the basic texts I use in my introductory course on pastoral care, there is a chapter on caring for mourners, but little information on meeting the spiritual needs of dying persons.[26] A text entitled *Complicated*

23. Bregman, *Beyond Silence and Denial,* p. 184.

24. Thomas G. Long, "Whatever Happened to the Christian Funeral?" *The Cresset,* Lent 2005, Valparaiso University.

25. Long, "Whatever Happened to the Christian Funeral?"

26. Phillip Culbertson, *Caring for God's People: Counseling and Christian Wholeness* (Minneapolis: Fortress Press, 2000).

Losses, Difficult Deaths focuses entirely on the difficulty of the death for the bereaved.[27] While such a text is needed, there is nothing equivalent for the care of dying persons.

One text that does deal with ministry to the dying is *Pastoral Care Emergencies* by David Switzer. Switzer's text devotes an entire chapter to ministry to the dying. In it he identifies eight needs of the dying, but seven of these are couched in psychological language. These include "expression of feelings," "overcoming loneliness," "the need to find meaning," "the need to maintain control over one's life," and "the need to let go of life." Only in discussing "spiritual needs," which appears seventh on the list, does Switzer use any explicitly religious language. He defines this "spiritual need" in terms of finding hope, which for Christians, he suggests, is grounded in God.[28] Meeting one's spiritual needs appears to be a solitary endeavor, a matter between the believer and God. In modern contexts, this often appears to be an individualized spirituality set loose from the moorings of the death practices of traditional religious communities. The religious task of preparing the soul for the journey to God has been replaced by helping the dying come to "acceptance" of death.[29] There is little mention of the way in which the church, as the "body of Christ," might witness to or embody this hope.

Certainly care of the bereaved is an important task, and one performed regularly by pastoral-care providers. An understanding of the psychological dimensions of grief is essential for this task. However, I am not sure that Christian pastoral care to either mourners or the dying is complete if we do not provide some Christian witness to death's meaning and God's promise. The triumphant words of 1 Corinthians 15:55 – "O death, where is thy victory? O death, where is thy sting?" – are not words of comfort for mourners alone. These are words of hope for the living and the dying. Paul's reflections on the resurrection of the dead are a theological affirmation of God's power, not just words of psychological comfort. With these reflections in mind, we can now

27. Roslyn Karaban, *Complicated Losses, Difficult Deaths: A Practical Guide for Ministering to Grievers* (San José: Resource Publications, 1999).

28. David Switzer, *Pastoral Care Emergencies* (Maryknoll, N.Y.: Orbis Books, 1989), pp. 97-98.

29. This is a reference to Elisabeth Kübler-Ross's fifth step in the dying process. See Kübler-Ross, *On Death and Dying* (New York: Macmillan, 1969), pp. 112-13.

turn our attention more precisely to what a Christian theological response to this situation might look like.

A Contemporary Christian Narrative of Death

In the midst of a cultural context where traditional Christian language and imagery have been eclipsed by a new language about death, articulating a contemporary theological narrative of death is a critical task. Practices of care at the end of life occur not only in the community of faith, but also in hospitals, clinics, hospice programs, and other community settings. In these places, multiple narratives of death, dying, and the afterlife abound. Christian pastoral and practical theologians cannot engage in meaningful conversation with medical-care providers about end-of-life practices unless we have some clarity about our own distinctive perspectives and practices.

Although pastoral-care providers have benefited from a deeper understanding of the psychological and sociological dimensions of death and have incorporated these perspectives into our literature, we are sometimes confused about the uniquely pastoral dimensions of our role. The waning of specifically Christian language about death has sometimes left pastoral-care providers uncertain about how a pastoral role differs from a therapeutic one. Only as we are able to articulate a relevant contemporary theological narrative about death that takes concrete form in our practices can we productively engage in conversations about the tensions and relationships between theological and medical approaches to care at the end of life.

How might we go about this task when traditional theological images of death no longer seem easily translatable in our contemporary context? Many medical advancements in our culture, such as the increased availability of hospice and palliative care and the advent of advanced directives, are largely positive. But continuing technological advances in medicine are at times more ambiguous, both increasing life expectancy and complicating our decisions about what constitutes the end of life. What we need is a constructive retrieval and revision of concepts from the Christian tradition that can address issues in our contemporary setting.

A Broader View of Death

One of the difficulties with the concept of "death is natural" is that it provides a limited view of death as the expected biological end of a long life. In contrast, biblical images of death are complex. Death is part of creaturely and finite human existence and, at times, may be seen as a friend to the dying.[30] Death can also be the occasion for great suffering — even for Jesus, who wept at Lazarus's tomb and agonized over his own impending death. This complex understanding is lost when death is reduced only to the natural end of life.

Early Christians understood death not as a part of nature but as an inevitable consequence of creaturely existence under God's sovereignty. To see death as a part of the created order is not the same as deeming death natural. If death is natural, so is life, and both are equally a part of human experience. If death and life are equally valued as a part of the natural order, why not seek to promote or hasten death? If there is no narrative other than the one that we create for ourselves, then we have the power to determine without boundaries who should live and who should die.

Language about death as natural also appears inadequate and harsh in situations in which death is untimely. In earlier ages in the West, the death of children from disease or accident was not uncommon. Such tragedies were seen as part of the frailty of life. Unfortunately, this is still the case in many other parts of the world today. However, in the technologically developed West, the death of a child now seems "unnatural" as well as tragic. A proclamation of "death as natural" in this situation brings little comfort. This language also seems inadequate for untimely or violent death that comes about through human intention. "Death as natural" language can also suggest a fatalism about life. By contrast, a Christian theology of resurrection proclaims a sustained hope in the providence of God, who cares for us in, through, and beyond death.

A theological understanding of the relationship between sin and death has been largely lost in our culture. I am not suggesting that we necessarily retrieve classical views of death as a punishment for sin.

30. Daniel Migliore, "Death, Meaning of (Christian)," in *Dictionary of Pastoral Care and Counseling,* Rodney Hunter, general editor (Nashville: Abingdon Press, 1990), p. 261.

However, I agree with Bregman that a Christian theology of death requires some moral framework that includes God's judgment, justice, and forgiveness of sins.[31]

In building this moral framework, it is important that we distinguish between mortality as a condition of our finite existence and death that comes about through violence and intentional harm. Sometimes the death of others is a consequence of sinful human action. Such death should be seen as opposed to God's plan for life. Sometimes we are complicit in our own self-destruction, which brings with it its own judgment. We need to tread lightly here. Recovering the soteriological link between Christ's death and ours may be helpful in this regard.

At the heart of Christian faith is the affirmation that death is an enemy of God finally defeated in the death and resurrection of Christ. Our death is always linked to Christ's death. God values life over death and gives God's own life so that death may be defeated. God, not death, is the ultimate reality. When this affirmation is used glibly to encourage believers not to grieve, it is misused. It is not the immortality of the soul that we proclaim but death and resurrection. We cannot experience resurrection without encountering death. Death is real, tragic, and a source of suffering. Still, Christians affirm that nothing, including dying and death, can separate us from communion with God. Death, too, is under God's rule and is not the final reality (Rom. 8:38-39).

The apostle Paul reminds us that our lives and deaths are never our own but belong ultimately to God:

> We do not live to ourselves, and we do not die to ourselves. If we live, we live to the Lord, and if we die, we die to the Lord; so then, whether we live or whether we die, we are the Lord's. (Rom. 14:7-8, NRSV)

Because our life in God is lived out through the body of Christ, our living and dying is not a solitary journey but occurs in the company of all the faithful, both living and dead.

31. Bregman, *Beyond Silence and Denial,* pp. 183-84. See also pages 155-82 on the eschatology and the afterlife, and pp. 133-52 on death as judgment.

Recovering the Rhythm of Death and Resurrection

Reclaiming the rhythm of death and resurrection as the pattern of Christian life is a necessary step toward reformed practices of care at the end of life. Bregman states that contemporary society, not Christianity, separates death from life. She reminds us that "a more classical Christian focus links holy dying to holy living."[32] The Spirit works throughout our lives, including during the process of dying. Pastoral theologian Jean Stairs views the "rhythm of death and resurrection as a lifelong spiritual rhythm." This rhythm is reflected in both individual spiritual lives and the corporate life of the community of faith. It is a rhythm in which "the whole people of God participate." Thus the spiritual rhythm of death and resurrection need not be emphasized only at the end of life, but can provide a basis for pastoral care throughout life.[33]

The rhythm of death and resurrection points to a view of death as more than the demise of the physical body. Emotional and spiritual death can occur as well as physical death. We have all experienced the death of dreams, the end of a relationship, or the disintegration of a community. Perhaps we have experienced death in life when diseases such as Alzheimer's steal loved ones away from us even as they are in our midst. Stairs calls Christians to move death out of "the physical and private realms" to become a dimension of "public and communal" experience. Reclaiming this rhythm of death and life "means inviting people to discover death in life and life in death as well as life beyond death."[34]

The Company of the Faithful, Both Living and Dead

The "communion of saints" is a theological image that also affirms the rhythm of death and resurrection and an ongoing connection between the living and the dead. The Protestant understanding of the

32. Bregman, *Beyond Silence and Denial,* p. 186.

33. Jean Stairs, *Listening for the Soul: Pastoral Care and Spiritual Direction* (Minneapolis: Fortress Press, 2000), p. 74.

34. Stairs, *Listening for the Soul,* p. 79.

communion of saints has traditionally emphasized the Pauline use of this term as it encompasses the entire community of Christians, both living and dead. The reformers reclaimed the biblical usage of "saints" to refer to the whole community, and the creedal reference to the "communion of saints" was re-interpreted to reflect this understanding.[35]

This vision of the church, implicit in both the biblical images and the reformers' understanding of the communion of saints, has dimmed in contemporary Protestantism.[36] Some congregations do have a strong sense of corporate identity, yet for others, this is not the case. What I have often experienced and observed as both pastor and parishioner in mainline Protestant churches is what I call "saints communing" rather than a communion of saints. By this reversal of terms I mean to indicate an individualistic ecclesiology at work in which the church exists to meet personal spiritual needs. Rather than being one body with interdependent parts, the community is now a collection of seekers for whom worship and the sacraments are seen as avenues for personal and private spiritual growth, rather than as means of corporate or social transformation. The spiritual journey may occur in the company of others, but these others are often not significantly involved in one's journey. Such an individualistic ecclesiology may not be the professed ecclesiology of the congregation, but it is often the operant one.

Theologian Elizabeth Johnson revives the concept of the communion of saints through "the companionship of friends" model.[37] In this model, the communion of saints is depicted as one family dwelling in God, divided only by death. Johnson's revision of the communion of saints is a radical vision of a community marked by mutuality and equal regard for all members.[38] Johnson finds support for the "companionship of friends" model, in which the living faithful and the dead are joined in "mutual companionship in Christ," in the early church,

35. Stairs, *Listening for the Soul,* p. 109.

36. Stairs, *Listening for the Soul,* p. 114.

37. Elizabeth Johnson, *Friends of God and Prophets: A Feminist Theological Reading of the Communion of Saints* (New York: Continuum, 2000), p. 79.

38. Johnson's vision of the communion of saints can be seen as a form of communion ecclesiology. See Doyle, *Communion Ecclesiology.*

especially the writings of the apostle Paul, the Protestant Reformation, and the documents of Vatican II.[39]

In the companionship model, holiness is a communal quality that derives from the community's relationship to God, rather than being the possession of individuals. Here, relationships are structured along the lines of mutuality.[40] Johnson proposes a new metaphor, "friends of God, and prophets," drawn from Wisdom literature, to highlight the mutual and reciprocal nature of this community. This community "stretches backward and forward in time and encircles the entire globe in peace."[41]

This eschatologically oriented community is inclusive and open to persons regardless of nationality, ethnicity, sex, class, ability, age, or any other qualifier. Individuals enter into the community as they enter into a new relationship with the Holy One, who "forges bonds of connectedness throughout the universe."[42] Thus the term "saints" conveys an equality of persons "in value and religious status without discrimination"[43] – and includes both the living and the dead.

A revitalized concept of the communion of saints can help us reclaim the communal dimensions of death. Death is not simply a private matter but one that affects the entire community of faith. At the heart of the "communion of saints" is God's love, which calls this community into being. This love is not meant for this community alone, but is given for the entire creation. The inclusive nature of the communion of saints requires us to accompany all persons through the journey of death, whether it is an untimely death from AIDS or one that comes as the body fails after a long life.

Here I can provide only a preliminary sketch, not a full picture, of how we might begin to construct a contemporary Christian narrative about death. This provisional narrative seeks to broaden our view of death and to reclaim the rhythm of death and resurrection at the heart of Christian life. My hope is to highlight the relational and communal dimensions of death and dying through a reinvigorated concept of the communion of saints.

39. Johnson, *Friends of God and Prophets,* p. 79.
40. Johnson, *Friends of God and Prophets,* pp. 61, 81.
41. Johnson, *Friends of God and Prophets,* p. 41.
42. Johnson, *Friends of God and Prophets,* p. 262.
43. Johnson, *Friends of God and Prophets,* p. 61.

Practices of Care at the End of Life

Such a revised narrative of death inevitably leads to a change in our practices. A Christian practical theology of death and dying must not only attend to a revitalized Christian narrative about death and dying, but must also lead to transformed practices of care. An underlying assumption of such a practical theology, as stated earlier, is that we participate in the life and love of the Triune God as the aim of Christian life. This participation is not simply a human achievement, but rather a spiritual gift given by the Holy Spirit for the entire body of Christ. Such love calls us not only to care for those of our community but to bear prophetic witness to the larger world. Love takes concrete form through narrative, relational, and prophetic practices of care.[44]

A contemporary Christian narrative about death becomes a resource for constructing our personal and communal narratives through which we interpret experiences of death and dying. Narrative practices are the means through which we craft and share the stories about who we are as individuals, communities, and a people of faith.[45]

When we are confronted with the reality of our impending death, we may experience a conflict in our personal narrative between the future story we hoped to live and the reality of the story as it is now framed by dying. Plans we had may no longer come to fruition. Hopes of a painless death in sleep may give way to the reality of prolonged suffering.

In addition to these conflicts at the personal level, we may also experience conflicts between cultural views of death and our religious perspectives on death. Confusion or uncertainty about a Christian theology of death makes it more difficult to navigate through these conflicts. The television shows I cited earlier are replete with notions of an immortal soul and a life that continues almost unchanged in another realm after death. Death is simply a passageway to another life. Such images of the afterlife significantly contradict the Christian affirmation of the reality and finality of death. The hope of a resurrection marks the end of the power of death, not simply a passageway to an ex-

44. See Karen Scheib, *Challenging Invisibility.* I am adapting the practices initially developed in this text.

45. Scheib, *Challenging Invisibility,* p. 52. See also D. P. McAdams, *Stories We Live By* (New York: William Morrow, 1993).

tended life in a shadow realm. While we do not know the exact contours of the resurrected state, Paul proclaims that it will be both continuous with and markedly different from the life we have known (1 Cor. 15). The cultural narrative retains a remnant of this, but has no sense of the divine transformation that is resurrection.

Through narrative practices of care at the end of life with individuals and families, we assist persons in shaping narratives that provide meaning, a coherent sense of self, and a sense of belonging in the midst of chaos and confusion. Narratives always have multiple strands that sometimes cohere and at other times contradict one another. Part of our pastoral task is to help persons and communities identify the multiple, sometime ambiguous, and conflicting narratives, and assist them in constructing a hopeful "future story" shaped by the Christian tradition in the face of death.[46] The task of helping individuals construct personal narratives about death is a familiar one to parish pastors or chaplains. We are called to accompany the dying through this particular journey of life.

Pastoral care, conversation, and counsel are contexts in which personal and family narratives are reconstructed in the face of change and challenge. Care providers serve an interpretive role in the midst of life crisis. As Jean Stairs points out, the language of crisis, so prevalent in pastoral care literature, serves to mask or "even deny the reality of events that are about death and resurrection."[47] A crisis-oriented approach requires pastoral-care providers to focus on intervention, thus distracting us from our role of attending to deeper matters of the soul that life-changing events often reveal. With a narrative approach we can assist persons "to enter the heart of a crisis more fully" in order to understand it as a spiritual event and part of the rhythm of death and resurrection that marks the Christian life.[48] This interpretive task occurs in communal settings as well as in the context of individual pastoral care.

Communal narrative practices of the church include worship, preaching, and liturgy. These practices are means through which a broader view of death and the rhythm of death and resurrection are re-

46. The term "future story" is borrowed from Andrew Lester, *Hope in Pastoral Care and Counseling* (Louisville: Westminster John Knox Press, 1995).

47. Stairs, *Listening for the Soul,* p. 80.

48. Stairs, *Listening for the Soul,* p. 82.

claimed and proclaimed. Public worship can be a place where the language of death and resurrection is restored to a central place in Protestant spirituality. This happens not only through regular celebration of the Eucharist, in which this rhythm is remembered and reenacted, but also through other elements of the worship service, such as prayers, hymns, liturgies, rituals, and sermons. All of these are places in which death in all its forms can be recognized and the pattern of death and resurrection affirmed. In some Protestant traditions, however, this rhythm of death and resurrection has been relegated to Lent, Holy Week, and Easter, or to specific liturgical rites, such as baptisms and funerals.

Even when the language of death and resurrection is present in official funeral liturgies, these liturgies may be set aside in favor of a memorial service in which the life of the deceased is highlighted, often through a display of photographs, personal sharing about the deceased by those attending the service, and a celebration of life that does not adequately recognize the reality of death.[49] Pastoral-care providers and members of Christian communities can challenge these cultural practices and encourage church members to utilize liturgies that proclaim death and resurrection and reclaim the journey of the deceased toward God as the focus of the funeral. The grief of family members need not be overlooked, but that is not the primary theological message of the funeral liturgy. Contrary to the popular saying that funerals are for the living, they have traditionally been for the dead, recognizing the entrance of the deceased into the ongoing community of saints.

The rhythm of death and resurrection is at the heart of the Eucharist, but the centrality of the Eucharist in Protestant worship varies greatly. However, liturgical reform has been going on in a number of Protestant denominations over the past thirty years. Such reform has occurred in my own United Methodist tradition. As of the 2004 General Conference, with the adoption of the document titled "This Holy Mystery," the Eucharist is now officially acknowledged as the normal pattern of Christian worship, though this is not yet fully implemented in practice. To reclaim the Eucharist at the heart of worship is to place the mystery of death and resurrection at its center, a point well made by Therese Lysaught later in this book.

Living out the ongoing rhythm of death and resurrection through

49. Long, "Whatever Happened to the Christian Funeral?" p. 2.

corporate worship serves a formative function. This communal rhythm becomes a part of our internal rhythm. This does not mean that our own death may come easily to us, but it does mean that we will have a framework in which this death is a part of a larger rhythm of Christian life rather than an aberration. Death can be recognized as a difficult part of our spiritual journey, and a reality ultimately under God's (not our) jurisdiction.

Relational Practices of Care

Through relational practices of care, we tend interpersonal, familial, and communal relationships. These relationships are the context in which our sense of self is formed. Our joys and our sorrows occur in the midst of these relationships. Relational practices of care provide support for the formation of these relationships and seek to resolve conflicts within them. Relational practices of care at the end of life include remembering, accompanying, forming communal contexts for ethical decision-making, and prophecy. It will be useful to reflect on these practices in light of the framework I have outlined.

The Practice of Remembering

The practice of remembering as a relational practice of care can revive the concept of the communion of saints. Remembering the lives of ordinary and extraordinary persons of faith who have gone before, particularly those who have been marginalized or forgotten, fosters a sense of connectedness, solidarity, and empowerment. Such remembering can awaken us to resistance to oppression, and resistance to practices of care in life or at death that would reduce or minimize the humanness of the dying. We can draw strength and spiritual nourishment "by bonding in memory" with those who have gone before us.[50] We can also broaden that bond to include "all the saints," the community of living Christians and those in the liminal space between life and death. In this way we are linked in unbroken communion with all of God's faithful.

50. Long, "Whatever Happened to the Christian Funeral?" p. 2.

Remembering, as a practice of care, is not simply calling to mind, but "re-membering" – that is, reconnecting persons to the body of Christ. This remembering has particular relevance for those who are no longer able to be regularly active in a congregation as a consequence of advanced age, illness, or disability, or who are facing imminent death. This reconnection is important for the well-being of those remembered, and is also central to who we are called to be as a community of faith. To forget those among us living in the space between life and death is to forget the rhythm of death and resurrection that is at the heart of the Christian faith.

The Practice of Accompanying

Reclaiming the rhythm of death and resurrection is not only a narrative practice but also a relational practice. Accompanying persons on the journey toward death is a familiar practice in our pastoral care of the dying. We need to reclaim the theological character of this journey as a part of a lifelong movement toward God marked by the rhythms of death and resurrection. In the early church, believers carried the dead to their graves, the departure point in the next stage of their journey toward God.[51]

Reclaiming the language of the soul's journey to God shapes the relational practice of accompaniment at the end of life. Accompaniment includes a willingness to stand with persons in the liminal space between life and death. Family members cannot easily go into this liminal space with a loved one who is dying. They must come to terms with how to live in this world with the physical and emotional absence of the one who is dying. In such situations, pastoral-care providers and the community of faith as a whole may accompany dying persons on their journey. Accompanying them facilitates their being recalled by and re-membered into the community of faith in the midst of dying. Those who are dying may feel at times like they are on a solitary journey, and they may have private experiences that are not easily shared. Still, we affirm that those who are dying are not finally alone but are held in the prayers of the community and in the heart of God.

51. Long, "Whatever Happened to the Christian Funeral?" p. 15.

Willingness on the part of care providers and seekers to enter and accept "liminality" is central to the movement from life to death to life. Standing in this middle space between life and death is quite difficult and strongly resisted in our culture. This liminal experience can be a time of strong, primitive expressions of fear. Rage and anger at God may be expressed.[52] We might seek to avoid this liminal space either by taming death and declaring it to be "natural" or by rushing to the resurrection. Living in the space between death and resurrection is challenging. Even the disciples found it difficult to wait and pray with Jesus as he faced death. Yet, this is the place where much of our ministry with the dying occurs.

When death occurs in the hospital, as it often does, physicians, nurses, and other health-care providers may be those who stand in this liminal space with dying persons. Standing in this space may be particularly challenging for health-care providers, whose calling is to save lives and reduce suffering. The increasing development of palliative care practices may make this task easier, but medical language may be inadequate to describe this experience or enter into it fully. Reclaiming the language of the soul's journey can provide a way for both care providers and care receivers to talk about this passage. It is not essential that care providers share the same faith tradition with dying persons or that they speak from any faith tradition. What is important is they recognize and respect the religious and spiritual language that may be needed for the space between living and dying.

Forming Communal Contexts for Ethical Decision-Making

A third potential relational practice of care is the formation of communities of discernment as contexts for ethical decision-making at the end of life. I suggest this as a potential practice because I do not believe it is one that is yet formally developed. Some pastoral and practical theologians, such as Jean Stairs and Parker Palmer, have advocated such things as clearness committees as a means of communal discernment.[53]

52. Stairs, *Listening for the Soul,* p. 89.

53. See Jean Stairs, *Listening for the Soul,* and Parker Palmer, *The Courage to Teach: Exploring the Inner Landscapes of a Teacher's Life* (San Francisco: Jossey-Bass, 1998).

Clearness committees are usually formed in the context of an ecclesial community. They have long been used in the Quaker tradition as a means to provide a place and a process for communal discernment of the workings of the Spirit as persons face decisions about a dilemma or difficult issue. These committees follow a set of guidelines that includes confidentiality and a commitment to assist the individual who is making a decision rather than giving advice. This discernment process is based on the assumption that each of us has an Inner Teacher that offers guidance and truth as we seek to resolve our problems. This Inner Teacher is not simply our own conscience but the presence of the Holy Spirit, who provides guidance and counsel.[54]

I am suggesting an adaptation of the clearness committee as a means through which individuals and families can find support within the context of the Christian community in making decisions about end-of-life care (when time allows). Such groups might be difficult to use when decisions need to be made quickly, but they could be useful in other settings. For instance, such groups might be used in a church setting to help persons make decisions about their own end-of-life care in order to fill out an advanced directive. A clearness committee might also be an appropriate group to consider decisions about care for persons entering or residing in long-term care settings.

In the hospital setting, if there is adequate time, chaplains might assist in the formation of such committees, which could include family and church members. Chaplains frequently serve on ethics committees and assist persons and families in making decisions about end-of-life care. Clearness committees could give chaplains a way to facilitate communal decision-making, which often occurs informally. While medical-care providers are required to look to one legally designated person for a decision about end-of-life care, in reality such decisions are often made by the family. In some cultures and families, the legally designated person is not always the decision-maker. Some adaptation of the clearness committee might provide a formally recognized communal context for making a group decision that could then be communi-

54. See Jan Hoffman, "Clearness Committees and Their Use in Personal Discernment," Friends General Conference of the Religious Society of Friends, www.fgcquaker.org/library/fosteringmeetings/0208.html; and Parker Palmer, "The Clearness Committee: A Communal Approach to Discernment," The Center for Courage and Renewal, 2006, www.couragerenewal.org. See also Stairs, *Listening for the Soul,* p. 98.

cated by the legally designated decision-maker. Such groups would include family and faith narratives in the process of decision-making.

The call for a communal process of decision-making begins to move us toward the level of structural and institutional change. Narrative and relational practices can lead us to prophetic witness about the structural issues and policy issues related to end-of-life care. Reconstructing a Christian narrative about death not only impacts individual narratives but also begins to challenge the larger cultural narrative about death. Relational practices of care, such as the communal decision-making process in hospital settings, require institutional support and systemic change.

Prophetic Practices

Prophetic practices of care include advocacy and encouraging personal and communal narratives of resistance which challenge cultural narratives that deny human finitude and death.[55] Advocacy – speaking on behalf of the marginalized – may occur at an individual level, but it often occurs at the level of public policy. Prophetic practices intersect with narrative practices through the fostering of narratives of resistance. These are a means by which persons and communities develop counter-narratives to larger social and cultural narratives.[56]

The prophetic practice of advocacy requires us to examine the economics of medical care at the end of life. This includes the availability of insurance and access to medical care. Health disparities according to class and ethnicity have been well-documented by the Center for Disease Control, among others.[57] The causes of death as well as the time of death often reflect these disparities. Advocacy includes addressing these disparities so that they can be dealt with earlier in life and thus contribute to the quality of both life and death.

Dying in a modern hospital is expensive and raises the difficult question of the distribution of medical resources. How do we balance the needs of those who are dying with the needs of other acutely ill persons at other stages of life? If we take seriously the rhythm of death and

55. Scheib, *Challenging Invisibility,* p. 128.

56. Scheib, *Challenging Invisibility,* p. 55.

57. Access this information at www.cdc.gov/omhd.

resurrection, might this change our attitudes and practices concerning the nature and intensity of care provided at the end of life? How do we ensure that care for the dying is not deemed too expensive while at the same time challenging a tendency in medicine to see death as a failure?

Narrative practices and prophetic practices intersect in the development and encouragement of narratives of resistance.[58] Narratives of resistance emerge in the midst of conflicts between cultural narratives and personal and communal narratives. Christian narrative practices that affirm the ongoing rhythm of death and resurrection in the midst of a culture that denies death are narratives of resistance. A personal narrative that sees the process of dying as a time of spiritual growth rather than only as a time of unending loss is a narrative of resistance. When health-care providers challenge the hegemony of the medical view of death and encourage the consideration of alternative narratives of death, including religious ones, they are engaging in narratives of resistance.

Conclusion

Many of the ecclesial practices of care that I have proposed might appear best suited for the interior life of the church and best performed during its services of worship or through one-on-one pastoral care with church members. However, I reassert my opening claim that ecclesial practices are a means by which the church manifests God's love to those outside its walls as well as within them. The construction of a contemporary Christian narrative about death and dying and the proposed ecclesial practices of care through which this narrative is expressed enable conversation between pastoral-care providers and medical-care providers as together we seek to improve care at the end of life.

Many health-care providers are themselves persons of faith who may feel a medical narrative of death by itself is inadequate to address the deep mystery of death. But such professionals are often at a loss for alternatives. Steeped in the language of science and rational discourse, they may be more comfortable with paradigmatic ways of knowing. Such ways of knowing are crucial for the diagnosis and treatment of disease, but may be less well-suited to describing the journey of the

58. Scheib, *Challenging Invisibility,* p. 142.

soul from life to death. This task requires a narrative way of knowing, which is communicated through stories.[59] This has been a primary mode for communicating the Christian faith.

The task of articulating a Christian narrative of death and dying is the responsibility of the religious community. Only when this narrative is clearly articulated can it be proposed as an additional narrative alongside the medical narrative. An articulation of a Christian narrative can also foster the recognition that there are many possible religious narratives of death and dying. Jewish, Hindu, Muslim, Buddhist, and other religious and cultural narratives about death also exist. At times the medical narrative may need to take precedence, particularly when treatment is needed. At other times, religious narratives, which seek to find meaning in the midst of suffering and death, may be better able to describe experience.

An articulation of ecclesial practices of care can also clarify the pastoral role in caring for the dying. The pastoral role includes interpretive intervention in which the rhythms of death and resurrection are named and entered into more fully. It also includes accompanying persons through the liminal stages of dying, neither denying death nor rushing toward resurrection. Accompaniment may be a communal journey, including health-care providers who also inhabit the liminal space with persons facing death. Clarity about the pastoral role is essential for chaplains working in medical settings, since they may be pressured to adopt procedures defined by standard medical practice. This clarity of roles can also be helpful in forming partnerships with medical-care providers who recognize the religious and spiritual needs of dying persons, but may be unable — because of role, training, or ethical limitations — to directly address these needs.

In prophetic practices of care, common cause can be found with those in health-care professions seeking policy changes to improve care at the end of life. We can encourage the narratives of resistance of those in the health-care professions who are calling for changes in medical practice that recognize the communal, religious, and spiritual dimensions of death and dying. Theologians, pastoral-care providers, and medical-care and health-care providers can make love our aim and thus seek "a more excellent way" to care for persons at the end of life.

59. Jerome Bruner, *Acts of Meaning* (Cambridge: Harvard University Press, 1990).

PRACTICES OF FAITHFUL SUFFERING

CHAPTER 4

Suffering in Communion with Christ: Sacraments, Dying Faithfully, and End-of-Life Care

M. Therese Lysaught

In his autobiography *The Gift of Peace*, Joseph Cardinal Bernardin recounts his losing battle with pancreatic cancer. Like many patients, Bernardin finds himself thrown into the world of medicine. One week he knows himself to be a perfectly healthy sixty-seven-year-old man, one of the most powerful prelates in the United States; the next week he finds himself waking up after surgery in a cancer hospital. In recounting his journey from first symptoms to surgery, he tells a relatively typical story: the operation is scheduled for early in the morning; he is nervous but attended by friends; the doctor is running late; the procedure goes well; and so on. But he makes this powerful observation:

> I spent only one night in the intensive care unit. Then they brought me back to my own room, where I experienced the discomforts one normally encounters after going through extensive surgery. I wanted to pray, but the physical discomfort was overwhelming. I remember saying to the friends that visited me, "Pray while you're well, because if you wait until you're sick you might not be able to do it." They looked at me, astonished. I said, "I'm in so much discomfort that I can't focus on prayer. My faith is still present. There is nothing wrong with my faith, but in terms of prayer, I'm just too preoccupied with pain. I'm going to remember that I must pray when I am well!"[1]

1. Joseph Cardinal Bernardin, *The Gift of Peace* (Chicago: Loyola Press, 1997), pp. 67-68.

His friends are astonished, because they know the Cardinal to be a man of prayer. *The Gift of Peace* opens with a section in which he recounts how, at the age of forty-five and already an archbishop, he was taken to task by his priest-comrades for neglecting his own prayer life, a chastisement he marks as a turning point in his life. From this moment on, he began to devote the first hour of his day to prayer. Twenty years later, when he is diagnosed with pancreatic cancer, his daily prayer has come to shape his life in significant ways. Yet now, in the throes of post-operative pain, the pain of what will prove to be a terminal illness, he discovers that prayer comes only with difficulty, even to one well-practiced in prayer!

I open with this story for two reasons. First, those who are interested in faithful dying and end-of-life care will find few better exemplars than Cardinal Bernardin.[2] His story certainly is one that illustrates what dying faithfully might look like. Just as importantly, throughout his illness, he remained a priest – Cardinal Archbishop of Chicago, one of the largest Catholic dioceses in the United States – as well as a figure of national stature.[3] Thus, as we will see, his story is equally a story about one way to faithfully care for the dying.

Second, I open with this story because I want to reflect on the sacraments as a way of sustaining faith in times of suffering and death. In particular, this chapter seeks to trace connections between sacramental practices and faithful dying as well as faithful end-of-life care. Bernardin's story illustrates the shape of these connections in a clear and powerful way. Yet, as his observations on prayer above suggest, his story may well confound how we normally think about the relationships between sacramental practices and end-of-life care. A major argument of this chapter is, to paraphrase the Cardinal: *Participate in the sacraments while you're well, because if you wait until you're sick, it might be too late.*

2. Elsewhere I have argued that Bernardin's story provides a model for rethinking bioethics as Christoform. See "Love Your Enemies: Toward a Christoform Bioethic," in *Gathered for the Journey: Moral Theology in Catholic Perspective,* ed. David Matzko McCarthy and M. Therese Lysaught (Grand Rapids: William B. Eerdmans, 2007), pp. 307-28.

3. Notably, the title of the third chapter of *The Gift of Peace* is "Priest First, Patient Second." He clearly intended to witness – first in his life, then through his book – not only to his diocese but also to the larger Catholic community, and to the larger non-Catholic community, to the possibilities for a different way of thinking about and approaching dying.

The power and importance of sacramental practices lie, in other words, not solely or primarily in their utilization in the immediate context of end-of-life care. Rather, I will argue that the power and importance of sacramental practices for end-of-life care lie in the ongoing, lifelong immersion of Christians in these practices in the context of the church. Sacramental practices serve to form congregations and worshipers – in an ongoing, continuous, recursive way – to be the body of Christ in the world in their living, their working, and their dying. And it is only in this way that they can begin to make sense within the context of medical care.

Rethinking Sacraments and Health

Before turning to the question of sacraments and the end of life, let us begin with the question of the relationship between sacraments and health or healing. In April 2006, Herbert Benson and his colleagues published a study on the therapeutic effects of intercessory prayer in cardiac bypass patients, a study that made the front page of *The New York Times*.[4] Confounding previous studies, Benson and his colleagues found that patients who were prayed for, and who knew that they were being prayed for, had worse outcomes than patients who were not being prayed for. Prayer, it seems, might be bad for one's health, or at least for one's heart.

We could reach this conclusion, I would submit, without the benefit of any multicenter, randomized clinical trial. All we need to do is to look back over the past two thousand years of Christian history. Here – in a retrospective rather than prospective analysis – we could single out a group of over ten thousand people (a good enough sample size for statistical analysis, if we could gather the right comparison and control group) who themselves participated almost continuously, nonstop, in sacramental practices. These study subjects prayed, worshiped, confessed their sins, and immersed themselves in the Eucharist to a degree far beyond that of their contemporaries. Yet time and again, as we

4. Herbert Benson et al., "Study of the Therapeutic Effects of Intercessory Prayer (STEP) in Cardiac Bypass Patients: A Multicenter Randomized Clinical Trial of Uncertainty and Certainty of Receiving Intercessory Prayer," *American Heart Journal* 151, no. 4 (April 2006): 934-42.

read the stories of their lives, we find them racked with the most awful diseases. They die young. In fact, it seems quite often that their morbidity and mortality are (not in every instance, but statistically speaking) far worse than those of the average, everyday Christian.

This group is, of course, the saints.[5] If we were going to look for a relationship between sacramental practices and health, the saints would be the place to start. But what we find there confounds. Consider, for example, St. Francis. Granted, he did not eat well, and he adopted a rather extreme lifestyle. But bracketing that, he certainly was devoted to the Eucharist and assiduous in prayer. What is more, after praying for weeks at a point when his health was not so good, not only did he not get healed – he got the stigmata! While that might not be entirely a health issue, it certainly was physically burdensome. This saint who got so close to Christ that even during his life people began to refer to him as *alter Christi,* "another Christ" – he meets the end of his life at a relatively young age (forty-five), blind, with dropsy and a variety of other ailments.

Or consider St. Thérèse of Lisieux, "the greatest saint of modern times," as she has been proclaimed, and a doctor of the church. This Carmelite, whose autobiography glows with love for the Eucharist and whose life was a constant prayer, died of tuberculosis at the age of twenty-four. Similarly, there is St. Bernadette Soubirous, blessed with visions of the Holy Mother, whose digging unearthed Lourdes, the most visited site for healing pilgrimages in the world. For years she suffered from the most painful form of tuberculosis – tuberculosis of the bone – before dying. More recently, we watched John Paul II, who is not yet a saint but whose canonization is not far off, during his decades-long battle with Parkinson's. In a slight variation on the theme, there are those like Blessed Damien of Molokai, who, after serving lepers in Hawaii for thirty years, contracted the disease himself. Or we have Cardinal Bernardin, who, after a life of immersion in prayer and the sacraments, finds himself struck not only by one of the most malignant and fast-moving forms of cancer, but also by extraordinarily painful spinal stenosis.

5. According to the non-authoritative Web site Catholic Online, "There are over 10,000 named saints and beati from history, the Roman Martyrology and Orthodox sources, but no definitive 'head count'" (http://www.catholic.org/saints/faq.php).

This litany could continue, but I think even this short list makes it clear: one cannot draw a direct, positive correlation between sacramental practices and health. If we could, these people – of all people! – would have lived to be as old as Methuselah without a pain or a creak. But this is not the case. In fact, the hagiographic record – not unlike the Benson study – at least suggests that there might rather be an inverse relationship between the two. And that is significant. For the saints help us get past an instrumental view of sacramental practices – the assumption that the sacraments are or should be oriented toward some outcome external to the liturgy itself. The data they provide suggest that a different dynamic is at work.

Instrumental Sacramentality

Before unpacking this alternative dynamic, let me say a few words about what I mean by an "instrumental" view of the sacraments. Let me begin by describing one standard way of talking about the relationship between a sacramental practice and healing. I take as my example the sacrament of anointing the sick and the problems one finds particularly (though not exclusively) in the literature from my own Roman Catholic tradition. Here the link between sacraments, healing, and health – if there is one – should be most apparent. But if we read most of (the little) that has been written about the practice, we run almost immediately into a perplexity. From Peter Lombard in the twelfth century to some of the most recent post-Vatican II publications, there has been no little consternation about the "proper effects" of the sacrament. Is the "effect" of the sacrament physical or spiritual? Is it "primarily" one or the other?

Many pages of ink have been spilt wrestling with this question. And the source of the consternation is the fact that, well . . . the sacrament of anointing does not always seem to "work." In other words, people get anointed, and they do not get better. Often they die. (Wouldn't it be interesting to do a Benson-like study on the sacrament of anointing? What would we do if we discovered higher rates of morbidity and mortality among those anointed? Would we stop anointing people?) But if anointing is a sacrament – a visible means of invisible grace – it must have some "effect."

Therefore, the tradition has finessed the answer to the question: Since there must always be an effect, but we cannot always see it, the "primary" effect – the one that happens every time without question – must be spiritual; anointing provides "spiritual healing" or cleansing of the remnants of sin or preparation of the soul for the final journey, or something in that genre. Physical healing has become a "secondary" effect – we cannot say physical healing is not an effect of the sacrament, but this outcome is determined by whether or not physical healing will serve to further the work of God in the world, so we cannot always count on it.

Implicit in this way of thinking about the anointing of the sick are a number of problematic assumptions about grace, sacraments, and the Christian life, assumptions that plague how we think about the range of liturgical practices. First, it is premised on an extraordinarily individualistic account of the sacraments. Sacraments here are actions of God (grace) directed at and effective in and for particular individuals. Individuals are the primary – and sometimes only – beneficiaries of the sacramental action. When the sacrament has done its particularly delimited work on the individual, it is finished – the vector from God to the recipient is unidirectional and terminal, ending in an indelible mark or some predictable therapeutic intervention on the soul of the recipient.

Consequently, the view of grace operative here is almost "medicinal." Sacraments dispense discrete "dosages" of grace, quanta that have particular benefits for the soul of the recipient depending on which intervention is being done (baptism, reconciliation, Eucharist, anointing), analogous to the ways in which medicinal interventions benefit the body of the patient.

This individualistic model generates a mechanistic yet spiritualized account of how grace operates in the world. In other words, one can more or less precisely trace out the mechanism by which grace operates (i.e., God, through particular materiality, formed by the right words, said by the right person, results in a particular change in the soul of the recipient), but the operation of grace is largely (if not entirely) restricted to the spiritual plane, which itself is located either in some ethereal transcendence or in the ultimately private space: the individual soul.

In other words, despite all protestations to the contrary, this approach to sacramental practices presumes and reinforces a dualistic conception of the human person, an unbridgeable bifurcation between soul and body. While problematic for a whole host of reasons, for our purposes such dualism is a problem because of what it says and does about God. It presumes either that God can or would choose to act on our souls without touching our bodies, or that God does not or cannot really affect our bodies.

This particular problem within Catholic sacramental theology is often reinforced by a general philosophy of pastoral care — at least as it has developed over the past twenty years, particularly within hospice and end-of-life care. While pastoral care is often celebrated among Christians as keeping the "spiritual" dimension alive within modern medicine, it tends rather to relativize Christianity (and all religious traditions). In my experience with hospice and hospital care, the chaplain members of the interdisciplinary care team are the only members that are optional; if patients are not interested in addressing the spiritual dimensions of their illness or dying process, they are not required to do so. Imagine a patient trying to forego interaction with the physician, nurse, or social worker in the same way! This ambiguous space of "spirituality" within medicine and even hospice has led to at best a "generic," customized (almost commodified or consumerist) approach to religious practice.[6] Any and all religious or spiritual practices are deemed equivalent in the medical context because they express the patient's own particular, individual spiritual preferences.

Such an approach cannot help but deform Christian sacramental practices. Not only does it abstract them from their proper theological context, thereby rendering them largely unintelligible. More problematically, sacramental practices become located within the modern dualist and empiricist assumptions that shape medicine, a view of the world in which medicine — because it deals with the quantifiable — can make claims about knowing the truth and being effective, while faith — being entirely subjective, personal — cannot. We accept a Cartesian view of the world that neatly divides science and religion into two opposing camps, and locates the "real" objective world and "real" objective healing squarely on the side of "science." Medicine is given — by Christians

6. I thank Andrew Lustig for this way of phrasing it. See his "Prescribing Prayer?" *Commonweal,* April 23, 2004, p. 7.

no less than non-Christians – enormous power and normative status because of the illusion that it can exhibit mastery and control over all disease. When it comes to healing and health care, medicine sets the agenda, defines the terms, creates the spaces, licenses the personnel, holds the authority. Medicine is deemed scientific, objective, and effective, and it provides descriptions of "reality" into which "faith perspectives" must fit themselves. Faith perspectives must accommodate themselves to modern medicine if they are to gain permission to operate within its jurisdiction.

In this way, Christian healing practices have become defined relative to the world of modern medicine. Theologians are permitted to make a space for faith within that reality – to open up conversations on "spirituality," to work on the virtues of the physician, to get some spiritual-assessment questions included on an ethics consult form, or to make a space for religious practices within the hospital setting. But when Christian practices are "inserted" into such a context, they risk being reduced to "health technologies"[7] – truthful if they produce a clinically measurable benefit, but since they often do not "work" (especially in the hospice context), then they become simply a means of comfort, rituals that provide "meaning," or it is suggested that they "heal" metaphorically, effecting their changes on the spiritual side of the divide.

To be clear, I have no wish to deny that individuals benefit from sacraments or that God can work through sacramental practices even in the least ideal of contexts. But if we are to even begin to understand the witness of the saints, or if we want to understand how, exactly, practices like the sacraments might make a crucial difference for care at the end of life, we must push beyond this sort of instrumentality. For not only does such an account render the sacraments increasingly random and the saints increasingly odd; the theological account required for an instrumental account of the sacraments evacuates grace of its real power. It compartmentalizes the work of God in the world, cordoning it off to the "spiritual" plane and minimizing how grace – God's ongoing action – might effect concrete, real change in the world.

7. Again, see Lustig, "Prescribing Prayer?" p. 7.

Ecclesial Sacramentality

As a corrective to this instrumental sacramentality, let me propose what we might call an ecclesial account of sacramentality. For liturgical practices are just that – ecclesial. As the Constitution on the Sacred Liturgy from the Second Vatican Council notes, liturgical actions embody and intend the church as a whole:

> Liturgical services are not private functions but are celebrations of the Church. . . . Therefore, liturgical services pertain to the whole Body of the Church. They manifest it and have effects upon it.[8]

In other words, liturgical practices concern not first and foremost individuals, but rather the church.

This offers two important correctives to the sacramental theology outlined above. First, it recognizes that sacramental practices do indeed work on, in, and through "bodies" – but the primary body through which they work is the body of Christ, the church. It is only as our bodies, the bodies of Christians, become part of the church and its practices that the sacraments come to work on, in, and through individual bodies as well. Sacraments, or liturgical practices more generally, are actions that constitute and sustain the church itself. They are not, as often described, rites of passage marking important milestones and transitions in the lives of individuals, or ritualizations of liminal experiences by which individuals negotiate "meaning."[9] Sacraments are, instead, actions intended to make the church (baptism), renew the church (Eucharist), heal breaches within the church (reconciliation), structure the life together of the church (marriage, orders), and so on. As liturgical practices, sacraments pertain primarily to the church.

Not only do sacramental practices have effects on the body of Christ; as the Council noted, they also "manifest it." For liturgical celebrations are nothing less than Christ's own offer of praise, adoration, and thanksgiving to the Father. As actions of grace in the world, litur-

8. Vatican II, Constitution on the Sacred Liturgy (Sacrosanctum Concilium), no. 23. This can be accessed via the Vatican Web site: http://www.vatican.va/archive/hist_councils/ii_vatican_council/documents/vat-ii_const_19631204_sacrosanctum-concilium_en.html.

9. Such an account is more indebted to ritual studies than to theology.

gical practices are acts of the Trinitarian God, acts in which the Three Persons continue their ongoing, eternal perichoretic dance. Insofar as we participate in the body of Christ, we become able – through and with Christ – to participate in the life of the Trinity, to adore and praise God with Christ. Sacramental actions are thus not about discrete dosages of grace that temporarily restore the state of an individual soul. Sacramental practices are expressions of adoration and love for God. They are, in short, *worship.* The sacrament of anointing, to return to my earlier example, is not an instrumental intervention designed to invoke the thaumaturgic power of God to heal a sick person. The sacrament of anointing as a liturgical practice is an act of worship – of praise, adoration, and overflowing love for the God who first loved us. As an act of Christ's body, the sacrament of anointing must always reflect Christ's work, which was to relentlessly point to and draw us to the Father.

It is for this reason that the center point of Christian worship is the Eucharist. From the Eucharist, all liturgical practices gain their intelligibility. From the Eucharist, they gain their shape. All the time, they move us *toward* the Eucharist. When we come together for worship, we stand again and again at the foot of the cross. And the body on the cross, this incarnate Jesus crucified, teaches us who we were meant to be. Too often, Christians mistakenly identify some human character trait as the "image" of God in us – for example, our reason or free will or creativity. The early church theologian and bishop Athanasius, however, reminds us that the true "image of God" is Jesus Christ. To be the "image" of God is to be like Christ, he who "suffered death on the cross."

Liturgical practices, then, serve to shape us (corporately and individually) into the body of Christ. Paul Wadell, a Roman Catholic theologian, reminds us that although we have learned to approach the liturgy as something safe and comfortable and constantly reassuring, we ought rather to understand it as something terribly dangerous.[10] We risk becoming the bread of life whom we eat. We risk becoming the body of this Christ who lived and ministered in a particular way, and who was crucified and died for us. In partaking of Christ's broken

10. Paul Wadell, *Becoming Friends: Worship, Justice, and the Practice of Christian Friendship* (Grand Rapids: Brazos Press, 2002), p. 16.

body and poured-out blood, we are changed – as Augustine and Aquinas held – into Christ.[11] We become a new creature.

This is not to suggest, of course, that this is automatic – that if we go through the motions of sacramental practices, we will be transformed. Clearly not. If, however, we enter into sacraments as worship and open ourselves in adoration to God's presence, it will be hard to remain unchanged. As we listen to God's Word in the Scripture, we learn again and again to see our lives and the world within God's story, learning to see and judge the world as God does – which is most often the opposite of how we are inclined to see it. We train our bodies to live as he lived – to pass peace, to keep silence and listen attentively to God, to give abundantly of our gifts. We are formed in the habit of being receptive to God's action in the world, of pointing always to God. We come to know the fullest vision of "the good life," or God's life with us, standing at the gates of heaven – as Alexander Schmemann describes the liturgy – never forgetting that the shape of the Christian life this side of the gate is the cross.

One might say that through liturgy the church comes to be a place that embodies a different "politics," a different way of living together. The New Testament provides different images of this life together – in the Acts of the Apostles, for example, or in Paul's somewhat cryptic insights into how life within the body of Christ (and the Kingdom of God) ought to operate with different rules than those that govern the world – that at least within the space of the body of Christ, the last shall be first, we should forgive seventy times seven, and so on.

Again, such formation is not automatic. As long as sacramental practices are seen as individual-centered therapy for the soul, without regard for their practical, material, corporate nature, they will be limited in their ability to do their work. But all is not lost. Lots of seed will fall on rocky, thorny, even shallow soil. But where God's gift of worship falls upon rich dirt, both congregations and congregants will find themselves increasingly formed as the ongoing, public incarnation of the body of Christ in the world.

11. Paul Wadell, "What Do All Those Masses Do for Us? Reflections on the Christian Moral Life and the Eucharist," in *Living No Longer for Ourselves: Liturgy and Justice in the Nineties,* ed. Kathleen Hughes and Mark R. Francis (Collegeville, Minn.: The Liturgical Press, 1991), p. 167. See also St. Thomas Aquinas, *Summa Theologiae,* III.79.3.

"Go in Peace to Love and Serve the Lord"

It is in this public incarnation that sacramental practices can begin to meet healing and the end of life. In his first encyclical, entitled *God Is Love (Deus Caritas Est),* Pope Benedict XVI states this pointedly:

> Faith, worship, and ethos are interwoven as a single reality which takes shape in our encounter with God's agape. Here the usual contraposition between worship and ethics simply falls apart. "Worship" itself, Eucharistic communion, includes the reality both of being loved and of loving others in turn. A Eucharist which does not pass over into the concrete practice of love is intrinsically fragmented.[12]

Worship, in other words, enables the church to act as the body of Christ in the world. The love celebrated in worship – God's love for us and our return of that love in thanksgiving and adoration – necessarily spills out beyond the time and space of liturgy itself. Receiving the gift of God's love in sacramental practices, we carry it into the world in our everyday lives. The Orthodox refer to this as "the liturgy after the liturgy," to signal that worship does not end (nor do we cease being church) when we leave the building. If it does, something has gone wrong. As Benedict notes, "A Eucharist which does not pass over into the concrete practice of love is intrinsically fragmented."

For the church lives as a "new creation" not for its own sake, but – following Christ – for the sake of the world. We carry God's love into the world because we believe that God's redemption is real, that it is possible for the politics we meet and learn in the liturgy to become equally as tangible, obvious, incarnate, and experienced in our day-to-day lives. God not only has made us for God's self, to echo Augustine, but has made all of reality for this beatific end. God longs for all of the world to rest in him.

Worship becomes the place and time from which God works to transform the world. Aquinas noted that *caritas,* charity, is the shape of the Christian life.[13] Although we too often use the word *charity* to refer

12. Benedict XVI, *God Is Love (Deus Caritas Est),* §14. The encyclical can be accessed online at http://www.vatican.va/holy_father/benedict_xvi/encyclicals/documents/hf_ben-xvi_enc_20051225_deus-caritas-est_en.html.

13. Aquinas, *Summa Theologiae,* II-II.23.8.

to donations of money, or even the uncompensated dollars spent by not-for-profit health-care institutions in providing health care in their communities, for Aquinas and the Christian tradition, the word means, rather, love. To be a person of charity is to be a person who loves. In particular, the word intends the kind of love manifested by God – not just a love that gives but a love that gives all, that creates *ex nihilo,* that gives abundantly, a love that by giving the self "empties" one of one's self. This is the love we see displayed in the life of Christ from the Incarnation to the cross. In theological language, this love is called kenotic.

As we meet this love in the Eucharist and the sacraments, we are – by grace – transformed (act by act by act) into the image of Christ so that we, too, can incarnate that kenotic love in the world. God's love is to become the shape of our lives. This is a love that not only gives money or things but rather exemplifies itself in solidarity, in face-to-face personal interaction. Thus, Christian charity is less about giving money than it is about being with others, spending time with them, especially the poor, the sick, the enemy, the dying. As Stanley Hauerwas and Samuel Wells have noted, "Christian witness will continue to be identified not by those to whom Christians give money but by those with whom Christians take time to eat."[14]

The End of a Sacramental Life: The Witness of Joseph Cardinal Bernardin

These very sensibilities shape Joseph Cardinal Bernardin's work in *The Gift of Peace.* Here we see how sacramental practices have the power to transform those who worship into the image of Christ, to carry on Christ's work in the world. Bodies so formed cannot help but be bodies that approach the end of life differently, for the center of the Gospels is the story of dying faithfully. We might say that sacramental practices enable the church to embody in the world a different politics of dying. In simply doing this, they can make possible the in-breaking of God's powerful, life-changing, world-changing grace. Bernardin is one who,

14. Stanley Hauerwas and Samuel Wells, *The Blackwell Companion to Christian Ethics* (New York: Blackwell, 2004), p. 42.

through lifelong immersion in sacramental practices, embodies in his very body kenotic *caritas* and who therefore practices a different politics of the end of life.

As mentioned earlier, Bernardin opens *The Gift of Peace* with a reflection on how he learned to make daily prayer a priority. This is no idle introduction: he returns to this story in the middle of his narration of his battle with cancer. As an insanely busy Cardinal Archbishop, he promises God and himself that he will "give the first hour of each day to prayer."[15] Such prayer could, of course, take many forms. Bernardin's choice – the Liturgy of the Hours and the Rosary – reflects his ecclesial and Christocentric convictions. The first, as the prayer of the church, connects him daily "with all the people, especially clerics and religious, who are reciting or praying the Liturgy of the Hours throughout the world."[16] The second, through the Joyful, Sorrowful, and Glorious Mysteries, connects his prayer and consciousness to the Paschal Mystery celebrated daily in the Archdiocese in the Eucharist. His prayer connects him daily to the Gospel stories and the cross.

Although some might see these prayer forms as repetitive or rote, Bernardin makes clear how such a practice is at the same time deeply personal. Through this practice he comes to identify those elements of his own character that most inhibit him from becoming conformed to Christ. His major struggle he names "letting go," and he acknowledges that learning to do so has been a lifelong discipline:

> Letting go is never easy. I have prayed and struggled constantly to be able to let go of things more willingly, to be free of everything that keeps the Lord from finding greater hospitality in my soul or interferes with my surrender to what God asks of me. . . . But there is something in us humans that makes us want to hold onto ourselves and everything and everybody familiar to us. My daily prayer is that I can open wide the doors of my heart to Jesus and his expectations of me. I have desperately wanted to open the door of my soul as Zacchaeus opened the door of his house. Only in that way can the Lord take over my life completely. Yet many times in the past I have

15. Bernardin, *The Gift of Peace,* p. 97.
16. Bernardin, *The Gift of Peace,* p. 98.

> only let him come in part of the way. I talked with him but seemed afraid to let him take over.[17]

Why this fear? Because, he acknowledges, he is a man of power. He writes this book as the leader of one of the largest archdioceses in the country, as a major public figure, and a man of national reputation. He notes that he wanted to succeed and to be acknowledged as a person who had succeeded; he wanted to control things, to make them come out "right"; he feared that God's will might be different than his, and that following God's will rather than his own might lead to criticism; that following God's will might lead to sacrifices he didn't want to make; or perhaps it was simply pride.[18]

Bernardin's honest confessions here may well resonate with many who work in health care. Not only can the urgency of the work – saving lives, attending to suffering – make it difficult to make a practice like prayer part of one's daily life, but it seems a luxurious indulgence or (perhaps) not the best use of limited time and resources. As Bernardin's story unfolds, however, we see that this seemingly "useless" practice proves essential for his ability to do the work God has given him to do. Not only does it shape the way he sees the world, enabling him daily to locate his work and the events of his life within the contexts of the Gospels and Paschal Mystery; it also forms him, over time, to be one who with his body lives and acts as Christ. It forms him to be one who particularly in the face of crisis remains receptive to God's presence and continually points toward God.

Most importantly, we see how this lifelong immersion in sacramental practices enables him to embody God's *caritas* kenotically. As he tells the story:

> God speaks very gently to us when he invites us to make more room for him in our lives. The tension that arises comes not from him but from me as I struggle to find out how to offer him fuller hospitality and then to do it wholeheartedly. The Lord is clear about what he wants, but it is really difficult to let go of myself and my work and trust him completely. The first step of letting go, of course, is linked with my emptying myself of everything – the plans I consider the

17. Bernardin, *The Gift of Peace,* pp. 7-8.
18. Bernardin, *The Gift of Peace,* pp. 8-9.

> largest as well as the distractions I judge the smallest — so that the Lord can really take over.[19]

His sacramental practice of prayer, in other words, enables him to act as the body of Christ in the world, to embody a very different politics, especially in the face of the end of life.

Kenotic *Caritas:* Forgiveness and Reconciliation

This different politics becomes apparent in the first chapter of *The Gift of Peace,* where Bernardin narrates his experience of being falsely accused of sexually abusing a seminarian.[20] I will not rehearse the details of this part of the story here (though I would encourage all to read it), but a few key elements are important. As with crisis situations in medicine, the accusation came out of nowhere and was devastating. Bernardin's world was, in many ways, turned upside down. The accusation struck at one of the key centers of his identity: his chastity. Because he was Cardinal Archbishop of Chicago, this was news, and that meant that instantly millions of people knew about the charge and most likely believed it to be true. He was startled, devastated, angry, bewildered at who could possibly launch such a false charge against him, and deeply humiliated. "As never before," he notes, "I felt the presence of evil."[21] Here a destructive power was at work, bearing down on him, threatening everything he held valuable — his life's work, his deepest convictions, his personal reputation, his position as Cardinal of Chicago.

Yet at the same time he felt equally sustained by the conviction that "The truth will set you free" (John 8:32). He knew almost tangibly the presence of the God he had come increasingly to know in prayer. And the habit of prayer he had learned through ordinary days and years now became crucial. Before facing hordes of reporters the day after the accusation became public, he prayed the rosary early in the morning,

19. Bernardin, *The Gift of Peace,* pp. 15-16. As he continues, he cites Philippians 2:6-8 to make clear that what he means by "emptying oneself" is Christic kenosis.

20. Given that *The Gift of Peace* is such a short book, Bernardin clearly sees this story and the story of his battle with cancer as linked. Those interested primarily in questions at the end of life would do well not to skip or skim over this part of the narrative.

21. Bernardin, *The Gift of Peace,* p. 23.

meditating on the Sorrowful Mysteries, and later spent an hour by himself in prayer and meditation. While he felt very much akin to Jesus and his experience of aloneness in the garden during his own Agony, he equally knew that it was God's grace, strength, and presence that enabled him to face the reporters, to stand calmly in the face of evil, and to speak the truth in love and peaceableness.

Moreover, from the beginning, he found himself overwhelmed with a sense of compassion for his accuser. A few days after the filing of the charges, he noted, "I felt a genuine impulse to pray with and comfort him."[22] He almost immediately wrote a letter to the man, asking if he might visit him to pray with him. The man's lawyers never delivered the letter. The case eventually unraveled on its own, and the charges were eventually dropped as the "evidence" proved to be fabricated. Bernardin could have simply rejoiced in his vindication, or he could have brought counter-charges for defamation of character. But this is not the road he chooses. Rather, eleven months after the suit was dropped, he again tried to contact his accuser. This time he was successful. In the end, he met with him and – beyond what would be wildly imaginable – was reconciled with him.

Here, in other words, the Eucharist spilled over into a concrete practice of love. Out of compassion and a self-emptying love, Bernardin sought out a face-to-face meeting with his accuser, with his enemy, in order that they might be reconciled. Through his person, Bernardin embodied Christ to this man, Steven Cook, a man we soon discover is dying.[23] And the reality of Christoform love made real in this encounter led them to celebrate the sacraments. Bernardin brought to this encounter two gifts, gifts of Christ's presence,[24] gifts he was not sure would be well-received:

> I hesitated for a moment after that, unsure of how he would react to the gift I removed from my briefcase. I told him that I would not

22. Bernardin, *The Gift of Peace,* p. 25.

23. Steven Cook suffered from AIDS, which in 1993, before the invention of antiretrovirals, meant he was a man with a terminal illness. Bernardin learned this in the course of this experience. Thus, in his reaching out to Cook, he knew he was also caring for the dying.

24. These gifts were, indeed, the gift of Christ – the Word (Scripture) and the Word (body and blood).

> press the issue but I did want to show him two items I had brought with me. "Steven," I said, "I have brought you something, a Bible that I have inscribed to you. But I do understand, and I won't be offended if you don't want to accept it." Steven took the Bible in quivering hands, pressed it to his heart as tears welled up in his eyes. I then took a hundred-year-old chalice out of my case. "Steven, this is a gift from a man I don't even know. He asked me to use it to say Mass for you someday." "Please," Steven responded tearfully, "let's celebrate Mass now."[25]

Together with their friends, they celebrated Mass and the anointing of the sick. Certainly, the rites were personally meaningful to the parties involved. But Bernardin's story equally makes clear that, more importantly, they renewed the church. They renewed the relationship between two members of the church, as the Cardinal notes:

> Then [during the anointing] I said a few words: "In every family there are times when there is hurt, anger, or alienation. But we cannot run away from our family. We have only one family and so, after every falling out, we must make every effort to be reconciled. So, too, the Church is our spiritual family. Once we become a member, we may be hurt or become alienated, but it is still our family. Since there is no other, we must work at reconciliation."[26]

Bernardin and Cook became friends, such that six months later, when Bernardin was diagnosed with pancreatic cancer, one of the first letters he received was from his former accuser. And through this encounter, Cook, who had long been alienated from the church, returned to the church and remained so until the end of his life eight months later.

Bernardin makes clear that it was only by becoming open to the presence and grace of God in his life, an openness given by God and cultivated through the practice of prayer, that he was enabled to embody a different politics. Through the practice of prayer, Bernardin learned to love God and to let go of the god of self-love. He developed the virtues necessary to be able to love one who was clearly his enemy,

25. Bernardin, *The Gift of Peace,* pp. 38-39. Just prior to the offering of these gifts, Cook declined Bernardin's offer to celebrate Mass together.

26. Bernardin, *The Gift of Peace,* pp. 39-40.

the person who he states had inflicted upon him the most damage, in the most vicious manner, that he had ever experienced.

What does such love look like? It is nonviolent – the Cardinal made clear to his advisers and attorneys at the outset of the crisis that there would be no scorched-earth countersuit to beat the enemy down. It is compassionate – it feels the pain of the other, even of the enemy. It is reconciling – it seeks not to obliterate the enemy but to overcome the enmity between them through reconciliation. It reaches out to the enemy, in order both to create community with the enemy and to do the work of God's love in the world.

To this extent, it is Christoform – Bernardin makes clear that such is the nature of Christian love, rooted in the person of Jesus. Through his practice of prayer, tied in to the larger sacramental life of the church, he has come to know Jesus as a fully human person, one who experienced pain and suffering and yet "transformed human suffering into something greater: an ability to walk with the afflicted and to empty himself so that his loving Father could work more fully through him."[27] And it is this Jesus that Bernardin meets through his practice of prayer that increasingly becomes the One who shapes his life.

Kenotic *Caritas:* Dying Faithfully

This experience becomes the prelude to the final chapter of Bernadin's story: his struggle with terminal pancreatic cancer complicated by painful spinal stenosis, osteoporosis, and curvature of the spine. In his narrative, we watch as he uses the tools of medicine to resist the growth of cancer in his body. We watch as he wins a short-lived remission, and then how the cancer returns with renewed virulence. But importantly, the autobiography of his illness is not primarily about his illness – it is instead about what it means to die faithfully. In the interest of space, I will point to four key aspects of his story.

First, Bernardin is very conscious about "dying publicly" (the subtitle of one of the last sections of the book). When his cancer returns and he realizes that his situation is now terminal, he tells the media, "Probably the most important thing I could do for the people of the

27. Bernardin, *The Gift of Peace,* p. 46.

Archdiocese – and everyone of goodwill – would be the way I prepare for death."[28] This witness is not solely individual; he knows well that as Cardinal Archbishop, he represents the church. In his actions, he embodies its truth, its convictions, its politics. And he knows that the church's approach to dying is different.

For example, while acknowledging the centrality of the notion of confidentiality within contemporary medicine, from the start he waives his right to this; he asks his medical staff not only to not keep his condition confidential but in fact to hold a press conference! His corporate, ecclesial sense of the church as members of one another means that "they have a right to know, and I have an obligation to tell them."[29] Further, he notes, he needs their prayers. This is a pattern he continues throughout: "My decision to discuss my cancer openly and honestly has sent a message that when we are ill, we need not close in on ourselves or remove ourselves from others. Instead, it is during these times when we need people the most."[30]

Second, rather than drawing inward, as illness tends to make us do, Bernardin, shaped by a lifelong immersion in Christoformative practices, does the opposite: He begins a new ministry – to cancer patients. It starts out seemingly accidentally. While he is in the hospital recovering from his surgery, he begins to walk the halls of the hospital (part of his therapy). He visits the other patients on his floor. By the time he leaves the hospital, he discovers that God has given him a new ministry: "Following my first round of chemotherapy and radiation treatments, I told my advisors that I now had a new priority in my ministry: spending time with the sick and the troubled."[31] In the fifteen months before his death, he finds himself regularly corresponding with, visiting, and praying for more than seven hundred people! Just as importantly, they pray for him.

But of course, this was no accident. Because he was formed through a lifetime of prayer and sacramental immersion, visiting the sick on his hallway comes "naturally." Opening himself up to these and others becomes the most "obvious" thing to do. It is his own sense that

28. Bernardin, *The Gift of Peace,* p. 136.

29. Bernardin, *The Gift of Peace,* p. 63.

30. Bernardin, *The Gift of Peace,* p. 94.

31. Bernardin, *The Gift of Peace,* p. 89.

without his formation of the preceding twenty years, he would have been no different than others who experience illness: "It draws you inside yourself. When we are ill, we tend to focus on our own pain and suffering. We may feel sorry for ourselves or become depressed."[32] It is not that he does not feel these things, but rather that they are located within a larger context of embodying Christ even in the face of his own illness and suffering. He continues this ministry until his death.

Third, his sacramental formation leads him to a new understanding of death. The final chapter in his story he entitles "Befriending Death." As the phrase suggests, he comes to regard "death not as an enemy or threat but as a friend."[33] The re-orientation is first suggested to him by his friend Henri Nouwen, who learned it during his ministry among persons with disabilities when he lived in the Daybreak Community of L'Arche. Nouwen reminds him of something that he has long known intellectually but that he has lost sight of through the exhausting regimen of radiation treatments:

> It's very simple. If you have fear and anxiety and you talk to them as a friend, then those fears and anxieties are minimized and could even disappear. If you see them as an enemy, then you go into a state of denial and try to get as far away as possible from them. People of faith who believe that death is the transition from this life to eternal life, should see death as a friend.[34]

32. Bernardin, *The Gift of Peace,* p. 71.

33. Bernardin, *The Gift of Peace,* p. 126.

34. Bernardin, *The Gift of Peace,* pp. 127-28. In learning to love our enemies, do they necessarily remain such — namely, enemies? The Gospel does not promise that if we love our enemies, such enmity will disappear. In fact, it seems to promise that habits of loving one's enemies may well multiply them or lead to crucifixion or martyrdom. Alternatively, Pope Benedict XVI, in his most recent encyclical, suggests that Christians might see death as a gift: "Perhaps many people reject the faith today simply because they do not find the prospect of eternal life attractive. What they desire is not eternal life at all, but this present life, for which faith in eternal life seems something of an impediment. To continue living for ever — endlessly — appears more like a curse than a gift. Death, admittedly, one would wish to postpone for as long as possible. But to live always, without end — this, all things considered, can only be monotonous and ultimately unbearable. This is precisely the point made, for example, by Saint Ambrose, one of the Church Fathers, in the funeral discourse for his deceased brother Satyrus: 'Death was not part of nature; it became part of nature. God did not decree death from the beginning; he prescribed it as a remedy. Human life, because of sin . . . began to experience the burden

Nouwen's insight resonates with Bernardin's life, shaped as it was by practices of "letting go," giving God Lordship over his life, forgiveness, and ministering to others who were sick and dying. Liberation from the tyranny of suffering and death, reconciliation with death, and learning to love the enemy death to the point of calling it "friend" are for Bernardin the fruits of a worshipful life lived amid the community of the broken. This, he believes, is "God's special gift to us all: the gift of peace. When we are at peace, we find the freedom to be most fully who we are, even in the worst of times. . . . We empty ourselves so that God may more fully work within us. And we become instruments in the hands of the Lord."[35]

Such peace, of course, is the peace of Christ. Even though Bernardin comes to refer to death as his friend, he continues to understand his journey as one that enters into Christ's Passion. As he moves into the final phase of his illness, he notes, "The cross has become my constant companion."[36] As such, Bernardin's re-reading of death is clearly Christoform – shaped by a Christ-like self-emptying, death, and resurrection. The love he gains for this enemy, death, is Christian love – *agape,* God's love for us – which is embodied most completely on the cross. Here and elsewhere, loving one's enemies means forgiving the real injuries, pain, and suffering they cause us. It means being reconciled to the presence and reality of the other. It means foregoing the fantasy that we "win" by eliminating or defeating them with violence. It might mean that we are rightly to "resist" their attempts to have power over us, to govern our lives with fear, to determine our actions.[37]

---

of wretchedness in unremitting labour and unbearable sorrow. There had to be a limit to its evils; death had to restore what life had forfeited. Without the assistance of grace, immortality is more of a burden than a blessing.' A little earlier, Ambrose had said: 'Death is, then, no cause for mourning, for it is the cause of mankind's salvation.'" (*Spe Salvi,* no. 10. See http://www.vatican.va/holy_father/benedict_xvi/encyclicals/documents/hf_ben-xvi_enc_20071130_spe-salvi_en.html).

35. Bernardin, *The Gift of Peace,* p. 153.

36. Bernardin, *The Gift of Peace,* p. 129.

37. In many ways, it ought not be surprising that Bernardin was able to embody such a counter-intuitive approach to death. For importantly, he was also a first-order Franciscan oblate. This distinctive attitude of peace and reconciliation in the face of death finds a new form in the work of St. Francis of Assisi. St. Francis, that most popular saint of all times, is particularly noted for his deep devotion to Jesus and how closely his life conformed to that of Christ in the Gospels. Two years before his own death, St.

Finally, as with Bernardin's reconciliation with Steven Cook, the sacraments become part of his ministry to cancer patients and sustain the church as his life comes to an end. As he meets face-to-face with so many people with cancer, the sacrament of anointing becomes almost a constant rhythm in the final part of the book. When he receives his final diagnosis, he is in the middle of three weekly communal anointing services that he had scheduled. He emphasizes how powerful he finds it to receive "this sacrament in the company of so many members of this local church."[38] He presides over the second, and now is himself anointed as well as being one who anoints others. One letter he receives after that service (which is included in the book) indicates that the sacrament drew to the church yet another man who, like Steven Cook, had fallen away.

Bernardin's deeply sacramental sensibilities become evident not only in these events but also in his choice to close the book by returning to sermons he preached during the Masses surrounding his installation as Archbishop and Cardinal in 1982. When he knows he has only a short time to live, one way he begins to bring closure to his life and

---

Francis retreated to a mountaintop hermitage in La Verna, Italy. There, in the course of intense prayer, he received the stigmata, the marks of Jesus' Passion, in his hands, feet, and sides. The pain of the stigmata was compounded over the next two years by additional painful conditions, including blindness. And yet he continued to be filled with joy, his enthusiasm bursting forth now in one of his most classic prayers, The Canticle of Brother Sun. Here, as Francis praises the Trinitarian God in each element of God's magnificent creation, he culminates with death: "Praised be you, my Lord, through our Sister Bodily Death, from whom no living man can escape." Francis greets death, in other words, not only as a friend but as a sister, and what is more, as that through which God can be praised. Thus, via Francis and others, the Christian tradition acknowledges the reality of death — that it is, indeed, the greatest of human enemies — but at the same time, from the beginning and at many points thereafter, the tradition witnesses that the distinctive Christian response is to approach it by saying "Peace be with you"; "Praise you, Lord, for our sister bodily death."

This Franciscan attitude pervaded Bernardin's life. It is reported that when Bernardin, as Cardinal Archbishop of Chicago, faced what he knew would be a particularly difficult or contentious meeting, he would open the meeting with St. Francis's classic peace prayer that begins, "Lord, make me an instrument of your peace. . . ." It is also not coincidental that the last initiative he started was the Catholic Common Ground Initiative, designed to try to foster reconciliation among the increasingly polarized factions in the Catholic Church.

38. Bernardin, *The Gift of Peace,* p. 131.

his work is by celebrating Mass with his fellow priests. In Italy, in Chicago, he gathers with his brothers to celebrate the Paschal Mystery, to enter into it during a time of pain, suffering, illness, and sorrow, but by so doing to witness to our conviction that it is Christ, not us, that makes and sustains the church.

Conclusion: Suffering in Communion with the Lord

Bernardin makes clear that those who follow the Lord will, like all human persons, know pain and suffering. But, he argues, "there is a decisive difference between our pain as disciples and that experienced by those who are not the Lord's disciples. The difference stems from the fact that, as disciples, we suffer in communion with the Lord. And that makes all the difference in the world!"[39] Correlatively, there will be – or ought to be – a decisive difference between how Christians, formed through lifelong participation in sacramental practices, approach the end of their lives and end-of-life care. For we are all called to be saints.

We are all called, in other words, to immerse ourselves daily in the sacramental life of the church in order that kenotic *caritas* becomes the shape of our lives. We are called, through the sacramental life of the church, to become Christoform in our caregiving and our dying. As we enter ever more deeply and unceasingly into the worship of the Triune God, we risk becoming ever more transformed into the image of the crucified Christ. The question is not "What role can the sacraments play in end-of-life care?" but rather "How do the sacraments shape our lives now, day-to-day, that they may transform Christian approaches to the end of life?"

I submit that those so formed may well find, as Bernardin did, how necessary such sacramental formation is for the very ability to do their work and to do it faithfully. Indeed, it may lead them to transform not only their day-to-day work but their very discipline.[40] Bernardin's story

39. Bernardin, *The Gift of Peace,* pp. 46-47.

40. Those who know the story of Dame Cecily Saunders will know how critical such a sacramental infrastructure was to her ability to conceive of what became the hospice movement. She traces her inspiration for developing the hospice movement to her meditation on Psalm 37. She sought to design St. Christopher's Hospice with the chapel in the center of the building so that visually, structurally, and infrastructurally, the Eu-

illustrates the seemingly ironic truth that the more we become immersed in Christ, the more unique (in many ways) our own form of discipleship will become. Those who care for the dying may well ask themselves "With whom do we eat?" Those who are dying might learn to see themselves not (solely) as patients but in fact as persons called to a new ministry. As Bernardin remarks, "I came to believe in a new way that the Lord would walk with me through this journey of illness that would take me from a former way of life into a new manner of living."[41] Not all dying persons are positioned, as Bernardin was, to minister to more than seven hundred cancer patients. But it may well be that dying faithfully, in the image of Christ, might mean finding the particular way in which each person might embody kenotic *caritas* at the end of his or her own life.[42]

Certainly, this account of sacraments and end-of-life care does not mean to dismiss the use of the sacraments for those who have been away from the church, or for those whose lives have not been so shaped in Christoform ways. God's grace will always abound. But as in the case of Steven Cook, I hope Bernardin's story suggests how the "clinical" use of the sacraments, especially in end-of-life contexts, ought rightly be understood. Rather than medicinal or miraculous interventions-of-last-resort, the sacraments are rightly celebrated in those contexts where the embodied action of Christ-bearers has made real the in-

---

charist would be at the center of their lives and work together and "Christ's victory over pain and death" could "radiate out from the Chapel into every part of the corporate life." The centrality of the Eucharist is further indicated in a letter she wrote early after the opening of St. Christopher's. She notes, "Today we are having our first Communion service, with two patients down from the ward in their beds, so we have really gone straight on with the important things." See David Clark, *Cicely Saunders — Founder of the Hospice Movement: Selected Letters, 1959-1999* (New York: Oxford University Press, 1995), p. 122.

41. Bernardin, *The Gift of Peace,* p. 109.

42. Such an idea has a long history in the Christian tradition. Before the Enlightenment and the development of modern medicine, when the sick were tended to in the contexts of monasteries and religious hospices, the sick were understood to be Christ himself and were to be approached as such by the monks and sisters who tended them. At the same time, those who were sick were understood to have the responsibility, as images of Christ, to pray for their caregivers and for those whose financial resources supported the monasteries. See Guenter Risse, *Mending Bodies, Saving Souls* (New York: Oxford University Press, 1999), Chapters 2 and 3.

breaking of Christ's presence into the world. And at all times, sacraments must be understood as actions whose fundamental purposes are Christological – the building up of the body of Christ, the church, and the ongoing formation of those who worship as embodied images of Christ.

Nor, clearly, does a sacramental approach to end-of-life care minimize the important role of medicine. Bernardin's story, however, illustrates what it means to approach medicine under the aegis of faith rather than approaching the sacraments as an instrument of medical care. Throughout, Bernardin is entirely positive about the fruits and usefulness of medicine as well as the professionalism and faithfulness of the medical staff that cares for him. He makes use of the tools of modern medicine as befits Christian commitment to life. When he is diagnosed, he undergoes surgery, chemotherapy, and radiation. He dutifully makes all his follow-up appointments. He schedules surgery for his back. When his cancer returns, he again begins chemotherapy and radiation. But when he realizes that the cancer is advancing, he discontinues treatment, cancels the surgery, and prepares to die.

Yet his participation in medicine becomes an opportunity to live differently within the world of medicine – to witness, for example, how odd the notion of confidentiality should sound within the body of Christ. It equally becomes an opportunity to locate medicine within the larger context of faith. His own hospital appointments become a chance to begin and continue a new ministry; his own illness becomes an opportunity to witness to his faith in Christ. Medicine becomes a vehicle for advancing the gospel. And the grace of his witness affects even the medical staff.

Bernadin recounts what was clearly for him one of the most powerful moments in his own story. Just weeks before his death, Loyola Medical Center (where he had been receiving care) dedicated a new cancer center in his honor. He was able to attend this event, though he was greatly fatigued. Apart from the public festivities, he offered some impromptu remarks to the medical staff, thanking them for the wonderful care they had provided to him. Being who he was, he gave them his blessing, "and then I was very moved as all of them raised their hands and voices to bless me."[43]

43. Bernardin, *The Gift of Peace,* p. 145.

Blessing, reconciliation, worship, ministry, care for the sick, care for the dying, love, joy, and the gift of peace – in this one story, not only are these the ways that the sacraments sustained faith in the context of suffering and pain; these are the ways that one sacramentally formed son of the church made God's transformative power real in Chicago, real in medicine, real in the world through his care for the terminally ill and, indeed, his own dying. May we follow his example, as well as those of the saints, and immerse ourselves in the sacraments, that we might become increasingly Christoform and, in the context of end-of-life care, become vehicles through which God's redemptive presence is made real in the world.

CHAPTER 5

The Practice of Prayer and Care for the Dying

Allen Verhey

A wise and wonderful teacher once told me that through prayer we not only commune with God but find new strength for daily life. I won't tell you whether that wise and wonderful teacher was my mother or a theologian, but that teacher's line is something like the text for these remarks about the practice of prayer and the practice of care for the dying.

I simply want to take this reminder of the significance of prayer to the hospital, to the nursing home, to the hospice, and to all the places we endure and care in the face of sickness and suffering, pain and death. I simply want to echo my wise and wonderful teacher: In prayer we may find new strength – new virtue – for dying and for caring for the dying.

I say "simply," but the task I undertake in this chapter may seem daunting and unpromising. In our culture, dying has become a medical matter, and care for the dying has been assigned to those skilled in medicine. Modern medicine, moreover, seems thoroughly and deliberately "religionless." A technologically well-equipped hospital is emblematic of a "world come of age." The practices of piety seem to have been pushed to the margins of medical care, retreating more and more as the knowledge and power of medicine advance, surviving only in a bad joke now and then, as when the doctor told her patient that the only thing left to do was to pray, and the patient replied, "Is it that bad, then?"

In this context the practice of prayer seems to have no place, unless, of course, as Therese Lysaught noted in the previous chapter, it can be shown by empirical research to be effective therapeutically. But I am with Therese in believing that when prayer is rendered a technology in the service of medicine, when it is authorized or judged in terms of its therapeutic effectiveness as an alternative or supplementary medical technology, then it is corrupted. Then it is no longer a practice of piety in the ways that perhaps Thomas Merton and Brother Lawrence would assume, but rather it has become a practice of medicine, attentive not to God but to something other than God, something for which God and prayer may (or may not) be useful. When this happens, the practice of prayer can hardly be expected to reform dying or our care for the dying. Instead, we will judge God and prayer in terms given by our current practices and expectations.

We may nevertheless take courage for this daunting task from the fact that prayer is as commonplace in hospitals as bedpans – indeed, as commonplace in hospitals as it is in churches. Think of it: As noisily secular as modern medicine is, this practice of piety is commonplace. When people hurt and suffer, when they face death, we are not surprised to find them under the care of a physician and in a hospital. And we are not surprised to find them praying. (Perhaps that is why some seem intent upon co-opting prayer, rendering it serviceable to the therapeutic ends of medicine.) To be sure, sometimes such prayers seem to regard God as a divine last resort, a heavenly pharmacopeia. But the simple fact that prayer is commonplace suggests that it is not unreasonable – and may even be important – to ask how a faithful practice of prayer can and does and should guide and challenge the ways we endure suffering and the ways we attend to the sick and dying.

The question is not whether prayer is medically useful (neither for the sake of co-opting a practice of piety for the practice of medicine nor for the sake of providing an apologetic for prayer as a technology). The question is whether the practice of prayer can guide and govern our dying and our care for the dying — whether we can set medicine within the practice of prayer, not prayer within the practice of medicine.

When we would seek to guide and govern medicine, we are in the arena of medical ethics. And our task can seem daunting and unpromising not only because of what medicine has become but even more because of what medical ethics has become. Contemporary medical ethics is frequently no less self-consciously and deliberately secular than medicine. Medical ethics has paid very little attention to prayer (in spite of its frequency in hospitals), except as a possible violation of patient autonomy. I hope to remedy that a little, for medical ethics has neglected the practices of piety to its great loss. At the very least, ethicists should find it curious that large numbers of patients (and large numbers of doctors and nurses, too) keep calling on God for guidance rather than on the experts in medical ethics.

This brings us back to the beginning, the notion stolen from a wise and wonderful teacher that in prayer we not only commune with God but find new strength – new virtue – for daily life. How might the practice of prayer govern and guide our dying and our care for the dying in daily life?

Prayer as the Crucial Element: A Story

It is conventional in medical ethics that there be consideration of a case. So, consider this: In his Harvard Diary,[1] Robert Coles tells the story of a friend of his, a physician who knows his cancer is not likely to be beaten back; he is also a Christian who knows that the final triumph belongs to the risen Christ. The dying man was visited by a hospital chaplain, who asked how he was "coping." "Fine," he said, in the fashion of all those replies by which people indicate that they are doing reasonably well given their circumstances and that they would rather not elaborate just now on what those circumstances are. But this chaplain was unwilling to accept such a reply. He inquired again about how the man was feeling, how he was managing, how he was dealing with the stress. Relentlessly he pressed on to questions about denial and anger and acceptance. But finally he gave up with the suggestion that, when the man was ready to discuss things, he should not hesitate to call.

After the chaplain left, Coles' friend did get angry, not so much about his circumstances or his dying, but about the chaplain. The chaplain, he said, was a psycho-babbling fool. And Coles, the eminent Harvard psychiatrist, agreed. What his friend needed and wanted, Coles says, was someone with whom to attend to God, not someone who dwelt upon the stages of dying as though they were "Stations of the Cross."

1. Robert Coles, "Psychiatric Stations of the Cross," in *Harvard Diary: Reflections on the Sacred and the Secular* (New York: Crossroad, 1990), pp. 10-12.

Coles' friend was not finished with the chaplain. He called for the chaplain to return; there were some ideas, he said, that he wanted to bring up "for discussion." When the chaplain returned, Coles' friend had his Bible out, with the bookmark set to Psalm 69, and he simply asked the chaplain to read. Coles quotes the opening verses of Psalm 69. It is a prayer, a lament: "Save me, O God, for the waters have come up to my neck. . . . I have come into the deep waters. . . ." Coles might have read a little further. The chaplain, at least, was probably instructed to continue. It is an imprecatory psalm, after all, and the curse on the enemy may be no small part of the reason this dying man chose this particular passage for this particular representative of the church. "I looked for sympathy," it says, "but there was none, for comforters, but I found none. They put gall in my food, and gave me vinegar for my thirst. May the table set before them become a snare; may it become retribution and a trap."

Coles' friend, with his complaint about gall in his food and vinegar for his thirst, was not, of course, complaining about hospital food. He was complaining about a chaplain who had emptied his role of the practices of piety, who neglected prayer and Scripture, and who filled his visits to the sick with the practices of psychotherapy. And the curse upon the table set before him, I suppose, was not intended to suggest that the skills and language of psychology are useless, but rather to remind the chaplain that at the table set before us we may eat and drink judgment on ourselves if we forget or ignore the gifts of God for the people of God, which surely include not only bread and wine, but all the practices of piety, including prayer.

My worry, however, is not only that the church or its representatives will forfeit their inheritance for a mess of psychology. My worry is also that in medical ethics Christians will ignore or neglect the practices of piety for the sake of an impartial point of view and the generic principles favored by secular medical ethics. Just imagine for a moment that the chaplain who visited Coles' friend had been enlisted on the hospital ethics committee and there taught to respect and protect a patient's autonomy, to regard human relationships as contracts between self-interested and autonomous individuals, to speak a universal moral language.

Then perhaps you can imagine Coles' friend being visited by this chaplain again, now trained as an ethicist rather than as a psychological counselor. The chaplain turned ethicist might still be just trying to be tactful and helpful, still be struggling to find work and words appropriate to his role in the "world come of age" called a hospital, still be embracing perhaps some notion of a "religionless Christianity" and "religionless" work and words in that secular world called medicine. But the chaplain turned ethicist would now be concerned not so much with psychological states and stages as with not interfering with the patient's rights, including, of course, the right to be left alone.

This visit might begin with an inquiry about whether the patient understood the consent form he had refused to sign and continue with a question about whether he had signed a living will or assigned durable power of attorney for medical decisions. The chaplain turned ethicist might be no less relentless than before, but now pressing toward the goal of respecting and protecting the so-called autonomy of this patient. Indeed, the chaplain turned ethicist might now resist with still more resolve praying and reading Scripture with the patient, for such activities come dangerously close to a violation of privacy and surely substitute a particular vision of human flourishing for the impartial and universal perspective regarded as important by philosophers and ethics committees. His enthusiasm for a common moral language, for the kind of "Esperanto" that ethicists like to speak, will make him hesitate to speak in a distinctively Christian voice, hesitate to use and to offer the gifts of prayer and Scripture when people are dying or suffering and face hard medical and moral decisions.

If you can imagine all of that, then you can also imagine that after this visit of the chaplain turned ethicist, Coles' friend might complain no less bitterly about gall in his food and curse the ethicist no less legitimately. He might call this ethicist back with the bookmark placed at Psalm 69. Again, the point would not be that philosophical skills or generic moral principles are useless. But Coles' friend still needs and wants hard praying, not just to have his "autonomy" respected and protected. He still needs and wants someone with whom to attend to God and to the ways of God, not a conversation in moral "Esperanto," a language he little understands and doesn't really care to learn, not now as he lies dying, at any rate. He has decisions to make, to be sure, hard medical and moral decisions about what should be done and what should be left undone, but he wants to make them oriented to God by the gifts of God, by the practices of piety, and not just with impartial rationality.

Now imagine something more: Imagine that this chaplain turned ethicist returns to his office after reading Psalm 69. Imagine that he wonders whether there had been some test of his theological and religious integrity in that hospital room. And imagine that he decides he did not pass this test. He sees that he was not altogether faithful to his identity as a Christian pastor and Christian ethicist. His agenda as a medical ethicist had left no room for the possible contribution of activities central to Christian piety. He had presumed that the practices of piety were irrelevant to discernment. He had condescendingly interpreted the disposition to pray either as a slothful refusal to do the hard intellectual work necessary for discernment or as a proud claim to have some magical access to the right answers.

"A patient might legitimately expect more from a representative of the church, even in this secular world of medicine and medical ethics," he might say to himself, resolving to make one more visit to the room of Coles' friend, there perhaps to learn something from the pious sick that he had forgotten under the instruction of medical ethicists, something of how the practices of piety might still form and inform the practice of medicine and our care for the dying.

Let's go with him. "We have come to pray," we say, "for we know 'the LORD hears the needy'" (Ps. 69:33), hoping he will recognize the citation of Psalm 69. He welcomes us, and the hint of a smile suggests that he did in fact recognize that we had continued to read the psalm that contained his complaint and his curse. Before we begin to pray, however, we ask why prayer is so important to him.

His reply, I imagine, would go something like this: "It is important because I am a Christian and because I long to live the Christian life, even in the dying of it, and prayer is part of the Christian life. Indeed, it is, as John Calvin said, the most important part, 'the chief exercise of faith.'[2] Moreover, it is a part of the whole Christian life which cannot be left out without the whole ceasing to be the Christian life. The Christian life is a life of prayer. It is, as Karl Barth said, a life of 'humble and resolute, frightened and joyful invocation of the gracious God in gratitude, praise, and above all petition.'"[3] Well, perhaps his response

2. John Calvin, *Institutes of the Christian Religion,* ed. John T. McNeill, trans. Ford Lewis Battles (Philadelphia: Westminster Press, 1960), 3.20.1.

3. Karl Barth, *Church Dogmatics: The Christian Life,* IV/4, trans. Geoffrey Bromiley (Grand Rapids: Eerdmans, 1981), p. 43.

wouldn't go exactly like that. Not many people quote Calvin and Barth in their hospital rooms.

Perhaps his reply would instead go something like this: "Prayer is important to me because it is a practice of piety. As you know, chaplain, Alasdair MacIntyre defined a practice as a 'form of socially established cooperative human activity through which goods internal to that form of activity are realized in the course of trying to achieve those standards of excellence which are appropriate to, and partially definitive of, that form of activity with the result that human powers to achieve excellence and human conceptions of the ends and goods involved are systematically extended.'"[4] Well, OK, probably not.

But even if he has not memorized an important and difficult passage from MacInyre's *After Virtue,* even if he has never read a philosopher or a theologian, he may still make a reply to which Calvin, Barth, and MacIntyre would nod their heads and say, "Yes, that's what I meant." He is a Christian. He has learned to pray in the Christian community. And in learning to pray, he has learned as well the good that is intrinsic to prayer. He has learned to attend to God, to look to God. And he has learned it not just intellectually, not just as an idea. In learning to pray, he has learned a human activity that engages his body as well as his mind, his affections and passions and loyalty as well as his rationality, and that focuses his whole self on God.

Attending to God is not easy — or painless. And given our inveterate attention to ourselves and to our own needs and wants, we frequently corrupt it. We corrupt prayer whenever we turn it to a means to accomplish some other good than the good of prayer, whenever we make of it an instrument to achieve wealth or happiness or life or health or moral improvement.

In learning to pray, Coles' friend has learned to look to God and, after the blinding vision, to begin to look at all else in a new light. In prayer he does not attend to something beyond God, which God or prayer might be used to reach; he attends to God. That is the good intrinsic to prayer, the good "internal to that form of activity."

In learning to pray, he has learned as well certain standards of excellence that belong to prayer and its attention to God, that are "appro-

4. Alasdair MacIntyre, *After Virtue: A Study in Moral Theory* (Notre Dame: University of Notre Dame Press, 1981), p. 175.

priate to" prayer and "partially definitive" of prayer. He has learned reverence, the readiness to attend to God as God and to attend to all else in his life as related to God. He has learned humility, the readiness to acknowledge that we are not gods, but the creatures of God, cherished by God, but finite, mortal, and, yes, sinful creatures in need finally of God's grace and God's future. He has learned gratitude, a disposition of thankfulness for the opportunities within the limits of our finiteness and mortality to delight in God and in the gifts of God. Attentive to God, he has learned care, growing attentive to his neighbor as related to God. He has learned to care even for those who are least, to care especially for those who hurt and cry out to high heaven in anguish. Looking to God, he has learned hope, a disposition of confidence and courage that comes not from trusting oneself and the little truth one knows well or the little good one does well, but from trusting the grace and power of God.

These standards of excellence form virtues not only for prayer but for daily life. The prayer-formed person – in the whole of her being and in all of her doing – will be reverent, humble, grateful, caring, and hopeful. One does not pray in order to achieve those virtues. They are not formed when we use prayer as a technique. But they are formed in simple attentiveness to God, and they spill over into new virtues for dying and caring for the dying in daily life.

"That's why prayer is so important to me," Coles' friend might conclude. "That's why I called it the 'chief exercise of faith,'" Calvin might say. "That's why I said the Christian life was 'invocation,'" Barth might say. "That's what I meant by a 'practice,'" MacIntyre might add. And if I may add my own word here, that's how we can begin to see the links between this practice of piety and the practice of medicine, between our praying and our dying and our caring for the dying. We can try to envision the prayer-formed physician and the prayer-formed patient and the prayer-formed community that supports and sustains them both.

Prayer as Invocation

We are ready at last to offer prayer with Coles' friend. "And how should we begin?" we ask, and he replies, "With invocation, of course, for prayer is to call upon God and to adore God as the One on whom we depend." To call upon God is to recall who God is and what God has done. It requires remembrance, for we invoke not just any old god, not some nameless god of philosophical theism, not some idolatrous object of someone's "ultimate concern," but the God remembered in religious community and in other practices of piety, especially the practice of reading Scripture. Invocation is remembrance, and remembrance is not just recollection but the way in which identity and community are constituted. So we invoke the God made known in mighty works and great promises, and as we do, we are oriented to that God and to all things in relation to God.

We invoke God as creator; and as we do, we learn to make neither life nor choice an idol, for nothing God made is God. That is a good and simple gift to medical ethics, when talk of "the sanctity of life" would sometimes require our friend to make every effort to preserve his life, and when "respect for autonomy" would prohibit every moral question besides "Who should decide?" We invoke God as creator; and as we do, we learn as well not to turn our back to life or to choice; for all that God made is good. That, too, is a good and simple gift to medical ethics, when a "compassionate" doctor would kill, or when another would exercise some arbitrary power to keep Coles' friend alive. We invoke God as creator; and as we do, we learn to refuse to reduce the embodied selves God made either to mere organisms or merely to their capacities for agency. Resistance to both forms of reductionism is a gift to medical ethics both at the beginnings and at the endings of life, and in all the care between as well.

Next, we invoke God as the provider. We do so in remembrance that God has heard the cries of those who hurt – that God has cared. We do so in remembrance of the One who suffered and died, and we attend to that cross as the place where the truth about our world was nailed. The truth about our world is the horrible reality of suffering and death. The truth about our world is the power of evil in the story of the cross and in the myriads of sad stories others tell with and of their bodies. The truth about our world is dripping with blood and hanging on a cross, but the same cross that points to the reality and power of evil also points to the real presence of God and to the constant care of God.

So, in invocation and remembrance we learn again that in spite of sickness, in spite of cancer, in spite of death's apparent triumph, God's care is the world's constant companion and our friend's constant companion. Invocation and remembrance do not deny the sad truth about our world or about our friend; they do not provide any magic charm against death or sickness; they do not provide a tidy theodicy to "justify" God and the ways of God. But by attention to this God we may learn that God is present in spite of sickness and death. We may know that God cares, that God suffers with those who hurt, even in places no medicine can touch. Then our friend – and every patient – may cry out, "God, why?" and still be assured that he is not abandoned by God. And the rest of us (including physicians) may be formed by such a prayer and by such a providence to embody care even when medicine cannot cure, to be present to the sick even when our powers to heal have failed, to resist the temptation to abandon the patient who reminds us of our weakness and the great weakness of our great medical powers.

Such prayer is not an alternative to medicine, "not a supplement to the insufficiency of our medical knowledge" and skill. Rather, it forms and sustains a standard of excellence in medical practice that insists on simple presence to the sick and a refusal to abandon the hurting to their pain. Such invocation and such a prayer-formed medicine will not always triumph over disease or death, but they will always gesture care in the midst of them and in spite of them.

We will return to these themes of lament and care before we are done, but for now note that we invoke God also as redeemer and healer. We make such invocation in remembrance of Jesus and, indeed, in the name of Jesus, hoping for the good future that Jesus announced and made real and present by his works of healing and his words of blessing, the good future that God made sure by raising him from the dead. As we invoke this God, as we attend to the redeemer and healer in prayer, we orient ourselves and our lives and our medicine – along with our prayers – to God's promises and claims. So a prayerful people and a prayer-formed medicine will celebrate and toast life, not death, but also be able to endure even dying with hope. A prayerful people and a prayer-formed medicine will delight in human flourishing, including the human flourishing we call health. They will not welcome the dwindling of human strength to be human, including the loss of strength called sickness, but they will be able to endure even that in the confidence that God's grace is sufficient.

A prayer-formed community will not despise medicine, as if to turn to medicine were to turn against God and God's grace. Medicine is a good gift of God the creator, and a gracious provision of God the provider, and a reflection and servant of God the redeemer. To condemn medicine because God is the healer would be like condemning government because God is the ruler, or condemning families because God is "Abba."

Of course, if medicine presumes for itself the role of faithful savior or ultimate healer, then its arrogance may be and must be condemned. One cannot invoke the one true God and take a presumptuous medicine too seriously (or a presumptuous state or a presumptuous parent). Perhaps Coles' friend, like other good and honest doctors, is less tempted to this sort of idolatrous and extravagant expectation of medicine than many other patients who sometimes enter the hospital speaking some version of this line from Auden: "We who must die demand a miracle."[5]

But when we invoke God as redeemer, we are freed from the vanity and illusion of wielding human power to defeat mortality or to eliminate the human vulnerability to suffering. An honest prayer could "let the air out of inflationary medical promises"[6] and restore a modest medicine to its rightful place alongside other measures that protect and promote life and health, like good nutrition, public sanitation, a clean environment, and the like. One thing more here: A prayer-formed people, celebrating life and health as the good gifts and wonderful promises of God, will acknowledge in remembrance of Jesus that a life oriented to the kingdom may be shorter and harder, for there are goods more important than our own survival, and there are duties more compelling than our own ease.

Prayer as Confession

Having made invocation, we pause to ask whether we should continue. Coles' friend says "Yes," and we ask, "How?" "With prayers of confes-

5. W. H. Auden, "For the Time Being," in *Religious Drama,* ed. Marvin Halversin (Cleveland: Meridian Books, 1957), p. 17.

6. William F. May, "Images That Shape the Public Obligations of the Minister," *Bulletin of the Park Ridge Center* 4/1 (Jan. 1989): 25.

sion, of course," he says, "for those who have invoked God can make no pretense to be worthy of God's care and presence. Those oriented to God are re-oriented to all else; it is called, I think, *metanoia* – a turning, repentance."

It seems obvious to us that we have no major-league sinner here, but we humor him. "What would you confess?" we ask. "Are you a smoker?" "That, too," he says, "but I see a reflection of my life in my doctor, and I don't like it. I've been where she is, angry at the patient who refuses another round of therapy, angry at my powerlessness to save him, eager to use my authority as a physician to convince him to try again, and eager to avoid him when he refuses to try again or dies before we can. It is no great callousness that I confess; it is the failure to acknowledge the fallibility and limits of medical care.

"And now I find myself where my patients have been, and I don't like it much better – angry at the doctor who cannot deliver a miracle, judging her much too quickly and severely, angrier still that she would try to tell me how to live while I am dying, and eager to render her still more powerless and optionless. It is no great callousness that I confess here, either; it is the failure to acknowledge the fallibility and limits of my own autonomy."

Confession is good for the soul, of course, but it is also good for medical ethics. It helps us see the fallibility of both medicine and patients. It helps us recognize the evil we sometimes do in resisting evil, the suffering we sometimes inflict in the effort to banish suffering and those who remind us of it. A prayer of confession, this form of attention to God, may help the dying to turn from despising the doctor because the doctor is a reminder of his sickness and mortality. And it may help the doctor to turn both from the disposition to abandon the patient because he is a reminder of her powerlessness to save him, and from any readiness to eliminate suffering by eliminating the sufferer.

A prayer of confession may form the possibility of a continuing conversation. Where assertion of authority by a physician would ordinarily have put a stop to an argument and reduced the patient to manipulable nature, a prayer of confession may enable the conversation to continue. And where the assertion of autonomy by a patient would ordinarily have put a stop to a discussion and reduced the physician to an animated tool, a prayer of confession may enable the conversation to continue. We may at least talk together longer and listen to each other better if in confession we turn from the pretense of being either final judge or final savior, for we are formed by prayers of confession to be critical without condescension and helpful without conceit. And that is a good and simple gift to medical practice and to medical ethics.

Prayer as Thanksgiving and Lament

"There are prayers of thanksgiving to be made as well," our friend says, and he begins to mention gifts great and small. And not the least among the gifts for which he gives thanks are opportunities to fulfill some tasks, great and small. He thanks God for a little time to be reconciled with an enemy and for enough relief from pain for the tasks of fun with the family. He gives thanks for the opportunity and the task of being a witness, a "martyr," he says, to demonstrate even in his dying that there are things more important than mere survival, and that many things are more to be feared than death. There is a gift here to medicine and to medical ethics in the simple and joyful acknowledgment that the sick and dying are still living, that they may not be reduced to the passivity of their sick role. Moreover, their choices may not be regarded simply in terms of the arbitrary self-assertiveness of their autonomy. The sick and dying have tasks and opportunities that must be considered both by themselves and by their caregivers.

Then our friend mentions one more gift for which he is thankful. He gives thanks to God, he says, that he does not always have to give thanks to God. He is grateful, he says, that he does not always have to be grateful. The psalms of lament have been a gift, he says, and he follows them by attending to God sometimes in the form of lament, crying out to God and against God in anger and in anguish.

The first gift, he says, was simply noticing that they are there, included in that songbook of the second temple. In ancient Israel the practices of faith allowed not only for the expression of praise and joy but also for the expression of grief and doubt and fear and anger. They not only acknowledged the reality of such emotions; they gave them social sanction. The community of faith gave the suffering a voice, and lament gave the voice of the sufferer form and direction.

In contemporary liturgical practices, however, one seldom finds lament. We make little room for the cry of anguish in our prayer books.

Even our funeral liturgies rush to talk about the life and the light that death and darkness cannot overcome. Little wonder, I suppose; lament is hardly "good news." Little wonder, but still a pity, for we neglect the cry of anguish to our harm and to the harm of our communities. When we leave aside the language of lament, we obscure the hurtful realities of human experience and drive both suffering and response to suffering outside the practice of our faith. Thus we marginalize not only suffering but also sufferers. When we make so little room in liturgy for lament, then in their hurt and their anger and their sense of absurdity, sufferers think they sit alone in the congregation. They must struggle to lift themselves by their bootstraps to the heights of some triumphant liturgy. When we neglect lament, we alienate the suffering from worship and from community precisely when they need both the most. Lament had a place in ancient liturgies. Where is it in ours?

If we retrieve lament, we may again give the suffering voice and preserve for them a place in the community. Those who suffer might realize that they may cry out to God in anger and in anguish and that, when they do, they are not alienated from the community. If we retrieve lament, the rest of us gain some leverage against our triumphalism. We are always tempted by a spiritual triumphalism which supposes that righteousness and faith can provide a charm against sickness and sadness and that prayer works like magic to end our suffering and to ensure our flourishing. But there is also our medical triumphalism that supposes some new piece of medical wizardry will finally rescue us from the human condition, with its vulnerability to death and suffering. If we retrieve lament, we may also renew our capacity for genuine compassion, for we may learn again to give the suffering a voice, to preserve for them a place in community, to be present to them.

In lament, suffering finds a voice looking heavenward. By its attention to God it may be contrasted to a dirge. In a dirge, notably in David's dirge at the death of Saul and Jonathan in 2 Samuel 1:19-27, God is not addressed or even mentioned. The dead are eulogized, but the decisive feature of this and every dirge is the contrast between past glories and present misery. In its refrain and conclusion – "How are the mighty fallen!" – there is a sharp and total contrast to the remembered glories of Saul and Jonathan. Once they were "swifter than eagles, . . . stronger than lions," but now "how are the mighty fallen!"

The tragic reversal of the dirge moves from glory to shame, from strength to powerlessness. It is suffering finding a voice. But in lament, in this form of attention to God, there is a reversal of the reversal. Looking heavenward, lament moves from distress toward wholeness, from powerlessness to the certainty of a hearing, from anger toward confidence in God's justice, from guilt toward the assurance of God's forgiveness. The distress and powerlessness and anger and guilt are still there, still finding voice, but the very form of the lament moves the sufferer toward his share in Israel's faith that the saving reversal, not the tragic reversal, is the pattern of their existence.

Attention to God allows the pattern to change, but it does not disallow the sorrow. Looking heavenward in lament helps the sufferer both to find words that express the pain and to find hope for a saving reversal, to find words and works that nurture the reconstruction of a faithful identity, a faithful direction.

There is no pretense here, no denial, no withdrawal to some otherworldly consolation. Lament calls faith and worship to deal with life as it comes to us. To look to God is not to look away. Moreover, the psalms of lament show clearly that biblical faith is, without embarrassment, communal. The ones who suffer have to do with God, and God has to do with them. The ones who suffer have to do with the community, and the community has to do with them. The ones who lament know that they need not fake it or be polite in the presence of God and of God's people,[7] and they know that they need not face the hurt alone. They may also know that God does not neglect their cry. Christ weeps in their tears. They believe the reversal of the reversal.

But even if they cannot get so far, even if they do not share just now the faith of the church, even if they have no certainty of a hearing (like the author of Psalm 88, the saddest of the laments), still they may know that the community accepts their cry as their own cry, that the community believes for them even in their doubt, that the community keeps faith with them — and for them — even in their lack of faith just now.

7. To be sure, the lament gave both form and limits to the venting of emotions. Indeed, if there were no forms and limits for the expression of rage and sorrow, then perhaps politeness would be reasonably preferred. The forms and limits not only make the venting of emotions communally manageable, however; they also help, as we have seen, to give direction to the sufferer, to help encompass the hurt within a faithful identity.

Prayer as Petition

There is little time when we turn finally from lament to petition, and we apologize a little, but our friend will have no apologies. "Prayer is not magic," he says. "It is not a way to put God at my disposal. It is the way to put myself at God's disposal. It is not a technique to get what I want, either a fortune or fourteen more healthy years. It is not a spiritual technique to be pulled out as a last resort when medical technologies have failed. What was that bad joke you told earlier? Prayer is not a means, not even a 'means to make God present.' It attends to God; and as it does, it discovers in memory and hope that God is present. To treat prayer as a means to some other good than the good that belongs to prayer makes prayer a superstition and trivializes God into some 'great scalpel in the sky.'"[8]

"May we not then make petition together?" we ask, a little shocked.

"Of course we can," he says, "but carefully; for here it is easy to attend to ourselves rather than to God, and to our wishes rather than to God's cause."

So we form our petitions on the model of the One to whom we attend. We pray — and pray boldly — that God's name and power may be hallowed, that God's Kingdom may come, that God's good future will be established "speedily and soon" — in this man's own lifetime. And because that good future is already established, we pray — and pray boldly — as the Lord taught us, for a taste of that future, for a taste of it in such ordinary things as everyday bread and everyday forgiveness, in such ordinary things as tonight's rest and tomorrow's life, in such mundane stuff as the workings of mortal flesh, and in the healing of our embodied and communal selves. But because that good future is not yet — still sadly not yet — we may continue to make lament and to pray no less boldly for the presence of the one who suffers with us, the one who made the human cry of lament his own cry, the one who hurts in our pain. We pray no less boldly for that than for the power of the one who promises in God's good future to raise us up and heal us: "the redemption of our bodies" (Rom. 8:23).

We do not, and I think we may not, pray for death. Death is not the

8. William F. May, *The Physician's Covenant: Images of the Healer in Medical Ethics* (Philadelphia: Westminster Press, 1983), p. 60.

cause of God. In the good future of God, death will be no more. Attending to God rather than to ourselves, to God's cause rather than to our own wishes, we are unlikely to bring a petition for death to our lips. Until that good future comes, however, there will sometimes be good reasons to cease praying for a patient's survival. Attending to God in confident hope of God's final triumph frees us from desperately holding onto this life, frees us to let go of it, leaving it in the hands of the One who can be trusted.[9]

Perhaps only a prayer-formed person will see clearly that there is an important moral difference not only between praying for someone's death and ceasing to pray for someone's survival but also between killing and letting go of a desperate hold on life. At least it seems increasingly difficult to make that distinction in moral "Esperanto," whether the language chosen is one of utility or autonomy.

Doctors and nurses make intercession, too, of course. They make petition for those for whom they care, and over whom they exercise responsibility. The conscientious caregiver, especially the one who takes himself too seriously and the one who regards herself messianically, will be tempted to make prayer a means again, a supplementary technology, to ensure the effectiveness of their own work. But such a prayer is no less corrupted into superstition because the petitioner is a medical practitioner, and "God" is no less trivialized as "the great scalpel in the sky" because the bloody hands of a surgeon are lifted up in such a prayer.

Looking Heavenward

"There is a petition I saw chiseled on an urban cathedral once that might be good for those who care for the sick and dying," Coles' friend remarks. "'Christ, look upon us in this city. And keep our sympathy and pity fresh and our faces heavenward, lest we grow hard.'"[10] It can

9. Incidentally, these questions of what we may pray for are interesting and illuminating moral questions. They are found in the Talmud and in the early theologians of the church, but they are not found in the recent literature on medical ethics. I suppose medical ethics does not really need any additional interesting questions right now, but it is poorer for its failure to attend to prayer. It is poorer for its failure to attend by prayer to God.

10. Bernard O. Brown, "The Problem of Compassion," *Criterion,* Winter 1990, p. 24.

happen, as even the softest heart knows. Why is it that we grow hard? Why is it that compassion withers and hearts harden? And how might looking heavenward help? How might prayer strengthen and enliven and direct compassion?

There is, first, sometimes something about those who suffer that makes our hearts shiver and shrivel and makes our eyes look away. And sometimes the thing about those who suffer that makes our eyes look away is simply and precisely their suffering. How can "looking heavenward" help? Let it be said again, first of all, that "looking heavenward" is not finally to look away. Looking heavenward, we call upon One who hears the cries of those who hurt and One who calls people to something like the same uncalculating compassion. Looking heavenward, we name a risen Lord and remember that his wounds were raised with him. Looking heavenward, we see enthroned the One who says, "Inasmuch as you have not been kind or considerate or even moderately helpful to one of the least of these, you were not kind or considerate or helpful to me." Looking heavenward directs our eyes back to those who suffer, and we see their weakness and vulnerability, their hurt and pain, their loneliness in a new way – as the very image of the Lord we serve.

We stand there sputtering and stuttering, "Do you mean to say that that was you, Lord? That that fat old fart was you, Lord? That irritating fool was you, Lord? She surely had a rough life. And she was you, even so? Do you really mean that that broken body was your spiritual presence?" The answer is always "Yes," and that answer calls for a kind of reverence in response, relating to the sufferer as the sufferer is related to God.

Then, still looking heavenward, we may intercede for the suffering. When we pray, "Please be with that fool," we cultivate a readiness to be with him ourselves. And if, looking heavenward, we can identify why it is important for God to be present to this person, we will have made some progress toward compassion and found some direction for it. For example, "Please be with her because she is tired of being probed and poked and prodded and has forgotten the power and pleasure of a genuinely human touch." Or, "Please be with him because he is accustomed to commanding his world of subordinates, and now the humblest subordinate, his own body, seems to be in revolt." Or even, "Please be with him because . . . well, because you are the sort of God who loves even fools like me and him."

Sometimes, however, what makes our hearts grow hard is not something in "them" but something in us. Fear, for example, is fertile soil for hard hearts. Compassion for a person with AIDS still takes some courage. If fear is the soil, pride is the seed of hard hearts. Not many of us are enormous egotists – not like the character who turns to his dinner companion and says, "But look, I've been talking about myself long enough. What do you think of me?" But all of us know how self-absorbed we can be and how difficult it is then to be really attentive to another's suffering. Compassion takes not just courage but humility. And guilt can make compassion wither, too. If some preoccupation or carelessness of ours gets in the way of compassion in a first encounter with the one who suffers, it is often very tempting not to notice the person's suffering in subsequent encounters.

But how can "looking heavenward" help? Looking heavenward, we are reminded that we rely on a grace that we should not be reticent to share. Looking heavenward, we find ourselves in the presence of One who is present to our weakness and our horror no less than to the weakness and horror of the sick and dying. Looking heavenward, we may even discover that, if our embodied self is identified with Christ, then our integrity is threatened not so much by hurt as by the failure humbly to share the suffering of another. Looking heavenward, we may learn courage and humility. And when we are feeling guilty, we may, looking heavenward, form a prayer of confession; and in forming a prayer of repentance, we may also form the self, freeing the self from being fated by that first careless and self-absorbed encounter. We may learn of turnings and new beginnings in repentance. It is not magic, of course, but to look heavenward can help reconstruct a compassionate self in spite of fear, pride, and guilt.

Another reason that compassion sometimes withers is this. Suffering is always individual: it differentiates and it alienates. Compassion, on the other hand, is always communal: it shares and it unites. Jesus said, "It is more blessed to give than to receive" (Acts 20:35), but he might have added that it's a lot easier, too. To receive care is to be reminded of one's suffering, and in a culture that values independence as much as this one does, it can add to one's suffering. To experience the kind, good works of a friend (or a nurse) is sometimes to experience the hard division of the human race (and a hospital) into two groups: the relatively self-sufficient benefactors and the needy beneficiaries — and to be reminded of the side of that divide that one inhabits. To receive care graciously is hard work, and where it is not received graciously, compassion becomes hard work, too.

And how can "looking heavenward" help? Prayers of thanksgiving help provide a different picture and different relations, a world — and a hospital — in which each is a recipient of gifts, in which human giving is set, as Bill May says, in the context of primordial receiving.[11] Looking heavenward, sufferers may be reminded that dependency and indebtedness do not alienate them from the human condition or from the other dependent and indebted humans who care for them. Prayers of thanksgiving can commend and form in doctors and nurses and all of us simple works of mercy, not as a self-important conceit of philanthropy but as small deeds of kindness, which are no less a response to gift than the prayers of thanksgiving themselves.

Finally, compassion withers when we expect too much from it or from ourselves. When compassion simply arms itself with artifice and not with wisdom, it can self-deceptively lose sight of the limits of technology. In the context of the extravagant modern expectation that technology will deliver us from our mortality and from our human vulnerability to suffering, it may be little wonder that we suffer "compassion fatigue," for we expect so much, so limitlessly much from ourselves and our tools. In the context of the failure of such expectations, compassion withers. Indeed, caregivers who make it their identity and purpose to eliminate mortality or suffering will experience the death or suffering of one for whom they care as a threat to their identity; they will suffer.

And how can "looking heavenward" help? Looking heavenward can remind us of our limits. Doctors and nurses and parents and friends who look heavenward and make petition for the sick and suffering may, of course, be tempted to corrupt and trivialize prayer by making it into a means, a supplementary technology, an old and desperate artifice, to ensure the effectiveness of their own work. On the other hand, looking heavenward, attending to God in the form of a petition for the one who suffers, may form an altered (and an "altared") sense of compassion.

In petition, doctors and nurses and all of us hand the one under our care over to the hands of God. Looking heavenward, we are re-

11. May, "Images That Shape the Public Obligations of the Minister," p. 28.

minded that we need not anxiously substitute for an absent God; we learn again that we are not Messiah and that we need not accept that intolerable burden. But there is a Messiah, and the Messiah can be trusted. When we hear again the always stunning "Inasmuch . . . ," we are reminded that, if anyone is to be counted Messiah in our encounters, the one who suffers is. Looking heavenward, we will provide the best care we can, but we can let go of the anxious control we had conscientiously assumed. We can take ourselves a little less seriously. We can freely acknowledge the limits of our tools and our own limits. We can learn again a more carefree care.

A Final Word

"One final word," Coles' friend might say. "We said before that a prayer-formed people will not despise medicine. It may also be said that a prayer-formed people will not despise medical ethics, either. Only let them pray now and then. Prayer is not magic for decisions either, of course. It is not a technique to get what I want, even when what I want is an answer or a solution to a dilemma rather than a fortune or fourteen more healthy years. It is not a technology to be pulled out as a last resort when medical ethics has failed to tell us clearly what we ought to do. It does not rescue us from moral ambiguity. Part of what we know to be God's cause may still conflict with another part of what we know to be God's cause. You will still have to work hard, attending to cases, sorting out principles, identifying the various goods at stake, listening carefully to different accounts of the situation. Prayer does not rescue you from all that, but it does permit you to do all that in ways that are attentive to God and attentive, as well, to the relations of all that to God.

"In prayer," he says, "we not only commune with God but find new strength – new virtue – for daily life and for dying and caring for the dying. A wise teacher once told me that."

CHAPTER 6

"Why Me, Lord?": Practicing Lament at the Foot of the Cross

John Swinton

For a long time I have been fascinated by the question of human suffering. There is a sense in which the gospel is defined by suffering, both human and divine. Suffering sits at the heart of our redemption and at the center of our practices of faithful discipleship. Suffering and responding to human suffering are basic constituents of faithful discipleship and mission. The church is redeemed by a crucified God who suffers in and for the world God created (John 3:16). The church that is formed on the rock of a suffering savior is empowered to live out a story within which it is called to share in the sufferings of Christ (Col. 1:24). The church is sent out into the world to address suffering in all of its dimensions of ministry (Ps. 147:3). In terms of my own discipleship as someone whose vocation and ministry is to take on the responsibility of being a teacher, a preacher, and a theologian, I am called to use my pastoral and theological skills to enable the church to fulfill this fundamental missiological task creatively and faithfully.

Having said all of that, my interest in suffering is quite specific. I am not so much interested in asking and seeking to answer the apparently obvious question of why suffering exists, a question that I have argued elsewhere is unanswerable.[1] Rather, I am drawn to the wider

1. For an extended discussion on theodicy and human suffering, see John Swinton, *Raging with Compassion: Pastoral Responses to the Problem of Evil* (Grand Rapids: William B. Eerdmans, 2007).

Unless otherwise indicated, all of the quotations from Scripture in this chapter are taken from the New International Version of the Holy Bible.

and I think more pastorally important question of what we as Christians are meant to *do* with suffering. Our tradition informs us that suffering is with us and that it will always be with us until the Lord returns and ends all suffering and death (James 5:8-9). Suffering is thus not simply a dislocated theoretical question or an intellectual problem that needs to be solved. Rather, the problem of suffering is a deeply practical one that requires responses of a particular shape and kind. Christians are called not to try to *explain* the existence of suffering, but to *respond* to suffering in ways that mirror God's ongoing response to suffering as revealed paradigmatically in the life, death, and resurrection of Jesus and the continuing practices of the church. God does not promise freedom from suffering, at least not in this life. But God *does* promise to give suffering a shape and a context that are potentially transformative.

Suffering Faithfully

One of the key observations of this book is that Western culture's understanding of suffering, particularly around end-of-life issues, has been significantly medicalized. It is difficult if not impossible to think of death, dying, and suffering without bringing medicine to mind. This is not in itself necessarily a problem. Nevertheless, valuable as medicine is, it can only answer *some* questions and offer relief within certain areas. The experience of suffering stretches the language of medicine and science to a point where it simply cannot contain the experience. And yet, the power of medical discourse continues to shape and form the experience of suffering for individuals and communities in significant ways.

Often the only language available to us when we encounter our sufferings is the language of diagnosis, treatment, and prognosis, which tends to point us away from the inevitability of death and the possibility that the suffering which Christians experience may be shaped by another story and may have quite different meanings and expectations attached to it in terms of a hoped-for outcome. The suggestion that runs throughout this book is that the key task for Christians is not to avoid suffering and death. Rather, the key task is to learn how to face such things faithfully and with the assurance that God is with us and for us even as we suffer. Of course, this sounds more than a little strange to ears that are attuned to the curative expectations that we tend to place on medicine. Nevertheless, if the Westminster Catechism is correct when it states that "The chief end of man is to glorify God and enjoy Him forever,"[2] then surely the chief end of end-of-life care must be to enable people to glorify God and to enjoy him and his consolation even in the midst of suffering. As I put this point earlier in Chapter One, the goal is to live abundant lives even in the shadow of death. If this is so, then a primary task of end-of-life care will inevitably be *theological.* Medicine, of course, has an important part to play, but that part can only be played faithfully and effectively if it is enlisted in the theological task of ensuring that human beings can glorify God now and forever, quite apart from the limits placed upon them by suffering and impending death. Such a suggestion may sound like foolishness in a highly technologized medical setting where it is not always obvious that end-of-life care might and should be a locus for theological activity. But the apostle Paul has already warned us that we are called to a ministry of foolishness, so I imagine such dissonance is to be expected (1 Cor. 1).

In this chapter I would like to offer a theological challenge – or, better, a theological opportunity – to the providers and the recipients of end-of-life care. Using Luther's theology of the cross as a critical hermeneutic, I will offer a challenge and a possible alternative to the cultural triumphalism that is attributed to medicine and medical technology. In so doing I will call on Christian physicians and Christian patients to take seriously the resources of their tradition and to begin to recognize the potential of that tradition for creating a different yet complementary paradigm within which we can understand and respond to suffering and dying. This new paradigm does not in any sense exclude current end-of-life care practices. It is not intended as an attack on medicine. It is, however, intended as a significant challenge to medical *ideology*[3] – as it is shared by professionals and laypeople alike – that draws its self-understanding from dominant

2. The Westminster Shorter Catechism. This can be accessed online at http://www.reformed.org/documents/WSC.html.

3. That is, a position that favors one point of view above all others and that adheres to this point of view no matter what. The ideologue sees the world from a single point of view, and can thus "explain" it and attempt to "change" it.

cultural assumptions and expectations about health, suffering, and dying. Through critical theological reflection on the practices of medicine in the context of end-of-life care, I hope to offer a paradigm within which we can understand and begin to reframe the role and the goals of medicine in light of the mystery and power of the cross. Let us begin with a story: Lisa's story.

Lisa's Story

Dr. Daniel Rayson tells a story of a disturbing and, for him, profound encounter he had early on in his career with a young cancer sufferer.[4] Rayson was in the first year of a hematology/oncology fellowship when he met a young woman named Lisa. She was twenty-six years old and lived in Madison, Wisconsin. Lisa suffered from an aggressive adenocarcinoma. The cancer had "ravaged the left side of her pelvis [and had] caused cutaneous nodules to appear over her abdomen, and sprayed her lungs like buckshot." She had had various forms of chemotherapy and radiation treatment, but the indications were that none of it was working. Lisa was on "oxygen at 2 liters per minute continuously and . . . she took long-acting morphine, 60 mg, three times a day."[5] Lisa was the mother of two young children: a two-year-old boy, James, and a four-year-old girl, Chelsea. On paper, the future didn't look good.

None of this clinical and demographic information prepared Rayson for "the bubbly, bald woman who bounced across the room much as Tigger in the Winnie the Pooh stories. She skillfully managed not to trip over her oxygen tank, grabbed my hand with a firm grip, and laughed out, 'You must be Doctor Dan. I'm Lisa.'"[6] Precisely what Rayson had expected isn't clear, but it certainly wasn't this! Perhaps he had expected Lisa's mood to match the seriousness of the clinical diagnosis? But there was a lot of joy left in Lisa's life. The conversation continued:

4. Daniel Rayson, "Lisa's Stories," *Journal of the American Medical Association* 282, no. 17 (1999): 1605-6.

5. "Lisa's Stories," p. 1605.

6. "Lisa's Stories," p. 1605.

> "I hope you have some tricks up your sleeve because I have a feeling things aren't going as well as people tell me they are."
>
> "What do you mean?" I asked innocently.
>
> "Well, my hip pain is worse, and these lumpy-bumpies are getting bigger."
>
> She yanked up her T-shirt to demonstrate the purplish nodules that served as our barometer of the disease that was slowly eating away at her. Dutifully I took out my tape measure and noted the sizes, comparing them to what was found one month ago – all larger.[7]

Despite Lisa's flagging a real and growing concern that things were not going as well as she had hoped, Rayson's gaze remained firmly fixed on the pathology of the situation. Perhaps he assumed that he would be able to confirm or disconfirm her fears (i.e., offer hope) by measuring the size of the nodules and communicating the implications of their size to Lisa in terms of present and future treatment possibilities. But Lisa was not prepared to allow him to remain at a distance:

> In the midst of my measuring she started laughing again. "You look like a tailor with that old measuring tape, not a doctor. Every time my lumpy-bumpies get measured it reminds me of lining up my kids against the kitchen wall to see how tall they're getting. I use a red crayon for Chelsea and a blue one for James. At least they're growing faster than these things!"[8]

In drawing her family into the clinical encounter, Lisa opened up the wider dimensions of the meaning of her illness. Now the illness was more than measurable "cutaneous nodules." These symptoms began to take the shape of a family. Lisa's "lumpy bumpies" suddenly gained new meaning, and two of the things that provided that meaning had names: Chelsea and James.

Rayson focused on the clinical implications of the size of the nodules; Lisa drew her doctor close and reminded him that these nodules had implications that stretched far beyond the accuracy of his clinical diagnosis. But he didn't "hear" her. He assumed that hope – true,

7. "Lisa's Stories," p. 1605.
8. "Lisa's Stories," p. 1605.

meaningful hope – would be shaped and defined by his ability to identify and select the appropriate form of medical intervention. He was, of course, not wrong. Indeed, Lisa shared his faith in the promises of medical technology. It is certainly true that the cancer was progressing and that there was a need for a change in medical action. But that was not the only change that was required.

In the eyes of both the doctor and the patient, hope was not lost as long as there was the possibility of another intervention. Hope was defined in terms of technology rather than theology. Rayson continues:

> I left the room to confer with a number of senior staff. Their subtle shaking of heads filled me with foreboding, but as I reviewed her past therapies, I realized that one of the new drugs that was active in a number of different types of cancer had not yet been tried. The staff agreed it was worth a shot and I re-entered the examination room with a new sense of optimism. I explained the details of the medication's administration, the potential adverse effects and ways we would try to prevent them, as well as my hope that we would see the long-sought-for response that might begin to heal her.
>
> "Any questions?" I asked.
>
> "Let's get on with it, Doctor Dan. Sounds good to me. Can I get it today?"[9]

All was not lost. Hope was still possible. Lisa remained happy to allow her faith to remain with the doctor. But she did have one question:

> She started toward the chemotherapy unit, then stopped, turned, and laughed again. "You know, my best girlfriend said the weirdest thing last week. She told me about a girl she knew who died of leukemia. This girl had a couple of kids and she had written a bunch of stories for them to remember her by. My girlfriend said that I should do the same thing for my kids, but I don't think I'm that far gone, am I, Doctor Dan?"
>
> There was a moment of stunned silence. The clinic was busy, and I couldn't possibly talk to her in the hall about death and dying. I had attended many lectures on the importance of breaking bad news and the methods of doing so. None had prepared me to handle such

9. "Lisa's Stories," p. 1605.

a critical question posed as a seeming afterthought. Her smile was radiant.

"No, Lisa, I don't think you're at that point," I replied. "I'm hopeful that this new treatment will work and that you will be able to spend a lot more time with your kids."

"That's what I thought, Doctor Dan. Thanks. Now on to round three."

As she limped off to the chemotherapy suite with her oxygen tank trailing behind her, she again turned briefly to flash me that huge smile, gave a quick thumbs-up, and was gone.

Two weeks later, Lisa was dead.[10]

Lisa's story raises in a very vivid manner some key issues regarding the way in which those of us who uncritically share in the worldview of medicine can tend to frame and respond to issues of disease, dying, and death. In this case, rather than seeing serious illness as a polyvalent event that may not simply be a locus for the practice of restorative treatments, Rayson focused his clinical gaze on Lisa's pathology. This is not a personal criticism of Rayson as a physician. The overwhelming desire to cure and to prevent death is shared by many of us who have been deeply influenced by medical models of health and health care that dominate the worldview of much of Western culture. Nevertheless, in Rayson's encounter with Lisa there were strong indications that she wanted to move beyond the physiology of her condition and begin to explore the deeper meanings of her illness and how these meanings related to her life and to her dying. But Rayson and Lisa's optimism, spawned by faith in the power of technological intervention to save the day, took priority over the possibility that death may not merely be a medical failure and that enabling a good and meaningful death might in fact be a primary task.

The roots of the problems that Rayson and Lisa encountered go far deeper than inadequate skills of communication. What we have here is a fundamental clash of worldviews — a clash between what the patient sees as foundationally important and what they both assume to be the goals of medicine. This should not be interpreted as a clash between patient and doctor. The tension here is much more subtle. Rayson's

10. "Lisa's Stories," p. 1605.

faith in medicine to help Lisa was clearly matched by her own expectation and faith that he could do what she assumed medicine could do. True, Rayson did not pick up on the subtleties of Lisa's introduction of the importance of meaning beyond her immediate suffering, but Lisa also seemed to have perceived it as being of secondary importance. The outcome, however, was that Lisa never got the chance to write her stories, and a vital aspect of her process of dying well was lost for her and for her family. In narrowly questing after cure and the relief of suffering as defined by the goals of medicine,[11] both of them missed a vital opportunity to explore crucial areas of Lisa's living and her dying.

Narratives of Restitution

Arthur Frank notes the ways in which contemporary Western culture's expectations regarding health and disease tend to be driven by what he calls "narratives of restitution." Restitution narratives have a basic story-line that goes something like this:

> "Yesterday I was healthy, today I'm sick, but tomorrow I'll be healthy again." This story line is filled out with talk of tests and their interpretation, treatments and their possible outcomes, the competence of physicians, and alternative treatments. These events are real, but also they are metaphors . . . of enacting a story line of restoring health.[12]

The restitution narrative finds its institutional voice in the practices of medicine and the rapidly growing expectations and faith that all of us have in medical technology to facilitate our movement from illness to health (with health understood primarily in terms of the absence of illness). This narrative finds its personal embodiment in the hopes and expectations that we have regarding the power of medicine to make us well. We turn to medicine when we want to understand

11. For a related discussion on the nature of the goals of medicine, see Eric J. Cassell, *The Nature of Suffering and the Goals of Medicine* (New York: Oxford University Press, 2004).

12. Arthur W. Frank, *The Wounded Storyteller: Body, Illness, and Ethics* (Chicago: University of Chicago Press, 1995), p. 77.

what disease is and how we should deal with it in terms of treatment and recovery. The fact that suffering and death constantly defy and confound the practices of medicine is not something that we really want to spend time reflecting on. The illusion of immortality and the omnipotence of medicine are powerful culturally ingrained myths that sustain us, often even up to the point of our demise. Gary Myers notes how end-of-life medicine has a tendency to be driven by narratives of restitution that obscure end-of-life realities:

> When physicians use a strategy of restoration to respond [to patients' pleas for help], this ritual may initially organize and comfort patients by focusing them on available treatments, but it often delays or entirely prevents dying patients from receiving the prognostic information that they need in order to come to terms with their approaching death and to plan their end-of-life care.[13]

According to Myers, such narratives of restitution, particularly within end-of-life care, can easily "support patients' formation of optimistic illusions about the effectiveness of treatment and the possibility of cure."[14] The brief excerpt from Lisa's story offers a rather tragic example of the practical and personal implications of such a focus on restitution. Myers, reflecting on Lisa's story, puts the point thus: "Sadness, grief, anxiety, and despair are managed by ritualizing Lisa's dying as a treatable illness. Optimism is maintained at the cost of human significance."[15] If people are constantly told that there is a possibility of restoration and that hoping for such restoration is the most appropriate way to deal with their experiences of illness, how and where will they get the opportunity to think about what it might mean to tell other stories, including the story of dying well?[16] Where can a person find the

13. Gary E. Myers, "Restoration or Transformation? Choosing Ritual Strategies for End-of-Life Care," *Mortality* 8, no. 4 (2003): 376.

14. Myers, "Restoration or Transformation?" p. 376.

15. Myers, "Restoration or Transformation?" p. 379.

16. This criticism is not, of course, confined to medicine. Precisely the same arguments can be made against certain forms of Christian healing that clearly have drawn from cultural and medical assumptions with regard to expected outcomes and the assumption that "healing" and "cure" are the same thing. The problem is not medicine per se but the cultural assumptions that work themselves out unnoticed within healthcare (and Christian) practices.

resources that will enable her to encounter death and dying with a faith and a hope that are not dependent on the limited claims of human knowledge? Where can both physician and patient find the resources to begin to rethink and to challenge the culturally popular but theologically and practically problematic narratives of restitution? How can we be enabled to think about what it might mean to develop a different theory – or, perhaps better, a different theology that will bring with it a narrative of transformation that respects the importance of restitution but refuses to be bound or defined by it?

From a Narrative of Restitution to a Theology of the Cross

In reflecting theologically on the issues raised thus far, I find myself drawn to the significance of Martin Luther's theology of the cross as a critical theological hermeneutic that will help us understand something of the dynamics of the issue at hand. In reflecting on end-of-life care in light of the theology of the cross, we will be pointed toward revised and faithful practices which hold the potential for developing narratives of restoration that are cross-shaped and that have practical utility for both Christian practitioners and Christian patients. In what follows, I will begin by outlining Luther's theology of the cross and then draw out in more detail its implications for the way in which we imagine and reshape end-of-life practices.

Luther's Theology of the Cross (Theologia Crucis)

In his Heidelberg Disputation of 1518,[17] Luther outlined his understanding of "true theology" as being a theology of the cross. *Theologia crucis* assumes that the whole of human experience should be perceived as cruciform. Jesus is not encountered in a triumphalist escape from suffering. He is found, instead, in the midst of human suffering, paradigmatically on the cross, but contemporarily in all suffering. In a fascinating reversal of expectations about God and God's power, the

17. Gerhard O. Forde, *On Being a Theologian of the Cross: Reflections on Luther's Heidelberg Disputation, 1518* (Grand Rapids: William B. Eerdmans, 1997).

theology of the cross informs us that God's glory is revealed in precisely the places where we least expect God to be.[18]

Such a theology makes futile all human attempts to comprehend God through reason and logic. It points out that one of the problems for theology is that it looks for God in all of the wrong places. Luther's *theologia crucis* points us away from the places where reason assumes God to be and toward the hiddenness of God, which is revealed in strange places. Luther puts it this way:

> That person does not deserve to be called a theologian who looks upon the invisible things of God as though they were clearly perceptible in those things that have actually happened [Rom. 1.20]. . . .
>
> That person deserves to be called a theologian, however, who comprehends the visible and manifest things of God through suffering and the cross.[19]

Luther contrasts the theology of the cross with its opposite: the theology of glory. The theology of glory assumes that God is made manifest in acts of power and in systems (political and ecclesiological) that are perceived as strong and powerful according to human standards and definitions of such terms. A theology of glory has a similar premise to what Ernest Becker has described as "the denial of death."[20] A theology of the cross sees that we must go through death to receive the gift of new life.[21] While the theology of glory has always been attractive to the church, and to Christians, it is through a theology of the cross that we are enabled to move beyond our mistaken assumptions about who God is, how God manifests his power, and what the shape of true Christian discipleship actually is.

Working against the Theology of Glory In formulating the theology of the cross, Luther's initial target was medieval systems of theology

18. See 1 Corinthians 1:18-19: "For the message of the cross is foolishness to those who are perishing, but to us who are being saved it is the power of God. For it is written:

> "I will destroy the wisdom of the wise;
> the intelligence of the intelligent I will frustrate."

19. Forde, *On Being a Theologian of the Cross,* pp. 72, 77.
20. Ernest Becker, *The Denial of Death* (New York: Collier-Macmillan, 1973).
21. Forde, *On Being a Theologian of the Cross,* p. 18.

that sought, through the use of human reason, to claim an understanding of God and God's glory that was, in their perception, worthy of the name "God." As Robert Kolb explains, "These scholastic theologians sought to fashion . . . a God worthy of the name, according to the standards of the emperors and kings, whose glory and power defined how glory and power were supposed to look."[22] The systems of thought and the practices that emerged from them taught a form of glory that was drawn from human definitions of the term and that focused on such things as worldly success – human, ecclesiological, and political power, with *power* being defined primarily in terms of the ability of one group to dominate another and impose their will upon them.

Most troubling for Luther was the underlying assumption within such theologies that through the proper use of reason God could in some sense be "discovered." Not surprisingly, the god that theologians "discovered" in this way tended to bear a remarkable resemblance to those who were seeking after such a god, and this god's aspirations bore a remarkable resemblance to their political and ecclesiological aspirations! As Paul Althaus correctly points out,

> Natural theology and speculative metaphysics which seek to learn to know God from the works of creation are in the same category as the works righteousness of the moralist. Both are ways in which man exalts himself to the level of God. . . . Both use the same standard for God and for man's relationship to God: glory and power.[23]

Reason thus creates a god of glory made in the likeness of human beings or at least human aspirations. This god of glory is then used triumphalistically to shape the church and model the actions and practices of Christians.

Championing the Theology of the Cross The theology of the cross stands in opposition to the theology of glory. For the theologian of the cross, God is known in a different way:

> The theology of glory seeks to know God directly in his obvious divine power, wisdom, and glory; whereas the theology of the cross

22. Robert Kolb, "Luther on the Theology of the Cross," *Lutheran Quarterly* 16 (2006): 446.

23. Paul Althaus, *The Theology of Martin Luther*, trans. Robert C. Schultz (Philadelphia: Fortress Press, 1966).

> paradoxically recognizes him precisely where he has hidden himself in his sufferings and in all that which the theology of glory considers to be weakness and foolishness. The theology of glory leads man to stand before God and strike a bargain on the basis of his ethical achievement in fulfilling the law, whereas the theology of the cross views man as one who has been called to suffer.[24]

The theology of the cross finds God in exactly the opposite place from where theologians of glory might expect to find him. As Walter Von Loewenich puts it, "God reveals himself in concealment, God's wisdom appears to men as foolishness, God's power is perfected in weakness, God's glory parades in lowliness, God's life becomes effective in the death of his Son."[25]

The invisible things of God are hidden within or beneath their opposite, according to Douglas John Hall: "God's glory is indeed revealed in Jesus the Christ, but it is revealed as something completely antithetical to our preconceptions of divinity and glory."[26] God is both revealed and hidden, according to Robert Kolb:

> God is to be found precisely where theologians of glory are horrified to find him: as a kid in a crib, as a criminal on a cross, as a corpse in a crypt. God reveals himself by hiding himself right in the middle of human existence as it has been bent out of shape by the human fall.[27]

Most importantly for our purposes, Luther realized that earthly definitions of power, glory, suffering, and death were not definitive or prescriptive for Christians. The cross of Christ points toward a radical new reality and a profound reframing of power, glory, suffering, and death. God's glory is manifested in the mercy and love he shows for sinners on the cross. The chief goal of human beings is not to escape suffering and death, but to understand them differently and to become and remain reunited with God, who dwells in the midst of suffering. In Christ's

24. Althaus, *The Theology of Martin Luther,* p. 27.

25. Walter Von Loewenich, *Luther's Theology of the Cross* (Minneapolis: Augsburg Press, 1976), p. 11.

26. Douglas John Hall, *The Cross in Our Context: Jesus and the Suffering World* (Minneapolis: Augsburg Fortress Publishers, 2003), p. 5.

27. Kolb, "Luther on the Theology of the Cross," p. 449.

sufferings we discover a redemptive identification of God with suffering humanity. The shame and foolishness of the cross are the salvation of human beings.

The Cross as a New Reality

The theology of the cross provides us with a new and challenging understanding of the nature of reality. Despite appearances, the world does not really work the way our society and culture tell us it does:

> True reality is not what the world and reason think it is. The true reality of God and of his salvation is "paradoxical" and hidden under its opposite. Reason is able neither to understand nor to experience it. Judged by the standards of reason and experience, that is, by the standards of the world, true reality is unreal and its exact opposite is real. Only faith can comprehend that true and paradoxical reality.[28]

The eyes of faith challenge the seemingly self-apparent reality of the empirical world and call the Christian to trust in that which is hidden and contradictory. Everyday reality does not cease to exist. Christians still suffer and die. However, the meaning of suffering and dying is transformed by the knowledge that God in his true power suffers with and for humanity and incessantly calls humanity back to God's self, even in the midst of suffering:

> A theology of the cross . . . insists that God, who wills to meet us, love us, redeem us, meets, loves, and redeems us precisely where we are: in the valley of the shadow of death.[29]

In opposition to theologies that look through and beyond the cross to see what lies behind it and what underpins it (e.g., atonement theologies), the theology of the cross looks at the cross and there discovers God.

28. Althaus, *The Theology of Martin Luther,* p. 32.
29. See Hall, *The Cross in Our Context,* p. 34.

The Theology of the Cross and End-of-Life Care

Luther's theology of the cross can be enlightening in at least three ways with regard to our current discussion of end-of-life care:

1. First, it challenges Christian patients and health-care practitioners to reflect on the theological assumptions that may implicitly be embedded within their own practices and approaches to end-of-life care. Are we driven by an implicit or even an explicit theology of glory that focuses primarily on narratives of restitution and a particular, worldly understanding of medical power, or are we guided and challenged by a theology of the cross which focuses on the possibility not only that suffering may have deep meaning, but that it might in fact be a place where we encounter Jesus in new ways?
2. Second, it provides us with a powerful tool for constructive, critical analysis of the goals and practices of end-of-life care. This analysis will enable us to uncover aspects of contemporary popular assumptions about medical practices which, when challenged theologically and practically, become problematic.
3. Third, the theology of the cross points us toward a particular form of language that can facilitate the process of suffering faithfully and help us to continue to love God, self, and others and, perhaps, to praise God even in the midst of the most terrible storms.

As we look back on Lisa's story, it is not difficult to sense important resonances between the triumphalism of the theology of glory that Luther describes and the expectations that we as a society tend to place on the practices of medicine, particularly in its more technologized forms. The "glory" that we ask medicine to reveal does not, of course, require the presence of God for its achievement. In our expectations, the role of God is replaced by the role of the physician, with her practical wisdom and the armory of medical technology that is available to her. For current purposes I will refer to this implicit theology of glory as "glorious medicine."

The Wrongheadedness of "Glorious Medicine"

Glorious medicine is an approach to the medical task and to medical technology that can be shared by physicians and patients alike. It reflects an attitude, a hope, and an expectation that may be implicit in either particular medical attitudes or practices or in public expectations of what such practices can and should do in the face of serious illness. Such an approach is based on narratives of restitution, and accordingly it places great emphasis on the power of medicine to overcome illness and suffering and, by implication, death. Glorious medicine assumes that through the appropriate application of reason and technology it will be possible to progress toward the development of a cure for all diseases and the elimination of all suffering, perhaps not now, but certainly in the future. Like James and John wrestling with the other disciples in order to sit by Jesus' right and left hand in glory (Mark 10:35ff.), glorious medicine strives to use human power and reason to gain victory over death and to end suffering, tasks which theologically, of course, can only ever be achieved by God alone.[30]

Such an ideology of medical glory leads practitioners to engage in, and patients to expect, the utilization of various technological practices designed to initiate a particular and narrow perception of healing primarily centered on curative actions embedded within various narratives of restitution. Glorious medicine thus walks in parallel with the position and the assumptions of theologians of glory: *If human beings use their own powers well enough, all will be well.*

Changing the Subject This narrative of restitution assumes that the only truly glorious outcomes of a person's encounter with disease and suffering are cure and restoration. Anything less is implicitly or explicitly perceived as a failure. The inevitability of death is avoided by ascribing medical technology with endless salvific possibilities. In order to sustain its worldview, glorious medicine can only allow itself to see and respond to the signs and symbols that indicate victory over the enemy of disease, death, and suffering. This is at least partly why it is sometimes difficult to persuade the medical professions of the importance of the rather less tangible and noncurative aspects of care such as spirituality and spiritual care.

End-of-life care can therefore raise some difficult issues for those

30. See Isaiah 25:8 (KJV): "He will swallow up death in victory: and the Lord God will wipe away tears from off all faces; and the rebuke of his people shall he take away from off all the earth: for the Lord hath spoken it."

influenced by the worldview and expectations of glorious medicine. Because the perceived failure of death and the sought-after glory of medical intervention do not sit well together, glorious medicine needs to *change the subject* when it encounters the "failure" of terminal illness and the inevitability of death. Pain, suffering, fear, chaos, and confusion are certainly acknowledged as real. However, the way that pain, loss, fear, and confusion are interpreted and dealt with in a clinical context often draws the theological and spiritual sting out of their challenge by shifting the language from personal narratives of human experience to the rather more impersonal narrative of diagnostic criteria.

Glorious medicine takes the complex and messy experience of suffering and dying and re-forms it into a set of clinical categories that can effectively be managed through the use of reason and technology. Instead of developing a grammar of suffering that might enable clinicians to face such experiences head on, glorious medicine re-narrates the patient's experience and changes it into its own terms. As Gary Myers correctly observes,

> In order to provide comfort, physicians expropriate prognosis and curative treatments from their normal scientific function to construct a ritual that reframes the terrifying and helpless experience of dying into the more hopeful and manageable experience of fighting against a serious but potentially curable disease.[31]

The raw and disturbing language of suffering becomes translated into the language of diagnoses, signs, symptoms, and curative actions. Pain becomes a symptom; fear, confusion, and chaos become things to be medicated; the deep significance of the desire to write stories for one's children is overridden by the search for restitution. Rather than telling it like it is — "Yes, Lisa, you might die, and it may be worthwhile to start thinking about writing your stories" — the glorious physician draws the patient into a medical world that is full of promise and optimism. The patient's narratives of anger, hurt, confusion, and chaos are muted and distilled into a smooth set of procedures designed to restore, fix, and mend. The patient, of course, is not an unwilling participant in this kind of medicine. In fact, it is what most of us have come to expect

31. Myers, "Restoration or Transformation?" p. 381.

and indeed to desire. The problem is that often none of the hoped-for solutions are possible. Sometimes death is inevitable. But the loud voice of glorious medicine and the accompanying cultural expectations of the patient mean that this reality is easily sidelined and/or avoided. "That's what I thought, Doctor Dan. Thanks. Now on to round three!"

Striving to Be Strong As I have already suggested, a theology of glory is a theology of the strong. It assumes that God is powerful and glorious in the same way that human beings strive to be powerful and glorious. It looks for God only in places where God's glory is revealed in ways that match human assumptions about strength, power, and glory. It also assumes that the task of human beings is to strive for similar ways of being like God. That a similar process goes on within glorious medicine is witnessed to by the various military metaphors that are used to describe how medicine should interact with and respond to disease and death.[32] By framing disease and death as enemies to be battled against (e.g., the *war* against AIDS; the *battle* against cancer; the *fight* for life), glorious medicine shapes the experience of suffering and death into its own image and according to its own assumptions of how illness should be responded to. It calls for patients to be strong and stoic and suggests that they respond to illness in ways that are in line with its glorious intentions. As Deborah Erwin, reflecting on the experience of cancer, correctly observes,

> The medically militarized attitudes and norms which . . . [culture] . . . sanctions for patients and families in this assault to counter the cancer adversary are those of a stoic, brave, loyal, and romantically optimistic soldier. Even if death is the final outcome, Americans illustrate that they want and expect dignity, and maybe even glory.[33]

The patient and the physician are perceived as glorious warriors standing in solidarity with one another as they battle against the intruding forces of illness:

32. Susan Sontag, *Illness as Metaphor* and *AIDS and Its Metaphors* (New York: Picador, 2001).

33. Deborah Erwin, "The Militarization of Cancer Treatment in American Society," in *Encounters with Biomedicine: Case Studies in Medical Anthropology,* ed. H. A. Baer (New York: Gordon & Breach, 1987), p. 207.

> Cancer is an insidious enemy, perceived as an intruder from a foreign source (chemicals, pollutants, etc.) or a traitorous rebel trying to lead some kind of insurgency against the normal cells and tissues within the body. . . . A female patient with thyroid cancer refers to the cancer cells as "black, greedy little things that eat up everything in reach." Patients say that the cancer "preys on the weakest part of the body," and could "just lay dormant in your blood, then come back at you again."[34]

When suffering is understood as an assault to be defended against with all of one's power and strength, there is little room for the weakness, fear, lament, anger, and confusion that mark many people's experiences of death and dying. Instead, the patient is encouraged to stand shoulder to shoulder with the bearers of glorious medicine in the hope of a valiant death or, even better, a glorious healing: "Thanks. Now on to round three. . . ."

But death is rarely valiant, and healing often never comes. Pain is painful, suffering is real, and death is frightening. Glorious medicine cannot tell the truth and still retain its power. It has no narrative that might transform suffering without eradicating it. True, medicine has great power, and that power can be used to bring healing and the relief of suffering. However, that power is frequently revealed as foolishness in the face of the reality of death and the process of suffering and dying. We need something more than earthly power alone can offer.

The Wisdom of a Practical Theology of the Cross

The theology of the cross stands against glorious medicine in ways that allow us to enter the situation of the sufferer at a different level and view things from a different perspective. This new perspective is not an alternative to medicine. It is, however, a clear statement against the impingement of glorious medicine on both the doctor and the patient. The theologian of the cross (or perhaps we could even stretch that to the "physician of the cross") learns to discover God's glory in strange places. In faith she recognizes that while suffering can be a place of horror, it is also a place where Jesus is and can be found. The physician

34. Erwin, "The Militarization of Cancer Treatment in American Society," p. 207.

of the cross recognizes that suffering and death have transformed meaning in light of the cross and the resurrection. In so doing, she begins to see that a primary healing task is to enable suffering, dying people to know that God has not abandoned them. In the crucifixion, human beings paradigmatically abandoned God to suffering, shame, and the horrors of death on the cross. But the theology of the cross draws our attention to a profound reversal: On the cross humans abandoned God, but God refused to abandon human beings. The presence of the crucified Lord saturates human suffering; Jesus refuses to return the abandonment that humans inflicted on him.[35] This recognition transforms the goals of end-of-life care.

Because God is in the suffering (as opposed to only in the cure), the physician of the cross begins to notice aspects of her current practice that are problematic. Jesus sits in the midst of suffering, seeking to reconcile the sufferer with God and to sustain that relationship through suffering solidarity and the hope of redemption. The physician of glory battles to prevent and avoid death and suffering without actually looking at them. She therefore sees some things and misses others. The physician of the cross sees suffering as a place for practical theological reflection and action with a view to redemptive transformation; the physician of glory sees it as a locus for the practice of her restorative skills. Neither perspective is necessarily wrong. Indeed, both may be necessary. Nonetheless, knowledge of the latter without knowledge of the former leads to care that is seriously lacking in insight and healing potential. The physician of the cross sees that it is not possible to care fully for persons who are suffering and dying without recognizing the presence of Jesus with them.

The presence of Jesus with us in suffering is not simply a passive solidarity in the midst of trials and tribulations. If a man falls down a well, he does not want his "rescuer" simply to jump down into the well and sit beside him! The theology of the cross is first and foremost a theology of reconciliation and redemption. The cross reminds us that all is not well between human beings and God, and there is nothing we

35. Indeed, God's abandonment of Jesus on the cross is indicative of his presence with us. If sin causes Jesus' abandonment by God, and if Jesus' abandonment was vicarious (for us), then we can be assured that God will never abandon us, because sin has been effectively dealt with through the sacrifice of Jesus.

can do to fix the breach. Only the cross of Christ, a beautiful and startling act of divine grace, can achieve such a task. The fragmentation of the Fall is overturned at the foot of the cross. The disobedience of human beings finds its reply in the suffering obedience of Jesus. He is with us and for us in our suffering, seeing our brokenness and leading us back into right relationship with God even in the midst of tribulation. In other words, Jesus' presence within suffering is proactive, not passive. It is aimed at facilitating the redemption of the sufferer. *Jesus inhabits suffering for the sake of redemption.*

The recognition of the reality and purpose of Jesus' presence in suffering challenges the reductionism of glorious medicine and opens up the possibility that theological encounter and reflection in end-of-life care might be more than "an option," or a task that the physician automatically turns over to the chaplain. It may form a vital but often forgotten dimension of the clinical process — a dimension that patients often point us toward, but that we can easily miss when we fail to look at suffering. As Matthew 25 reminds us, ministering to the sick and dying is ministry to Jesus.

In a paradoxical way, the theology of the cross turns out to be a narrative of restitution. But the meaning of restitution in light of the cross is quite different. While not letting go of the hope and possibility of physical restoration, the theology of the cross is comfortable with acknowledging the situation as it is: death is death, and suffering is suffering. *The comfort and consolation of the theology of the cross comes not from naïve optimism or malignant stoicism, but from the knowledge that where there is suffering, there is God. And where God is, there is the hope of redemption.* A key task for physicians of the cross will be to recognize the presence of Jesus in the midst of suffering and to allow that knowledge to reshape and reframe their clinical encounters.

The Psalms of Lament as a Language of the Cross

Our reflections on the practices of "glorious medicine" in light of the theology of the cross have raised some important issues for the practice of medicine in general and in particular for Christians who seek to practice end-of-life medicine faithfully. To become a physician of the cross is to allow the knowledge of the presence and purpose of Jesus in suffering to draw one's attention to the hidden practical theological dynamics that are a vital dimension of all clinical encounters. Thus far we have begun to indicate how the theology of the cross might function as a transformative theological underpinning for Christians working in end-of-life care situations. But what about patients? In what way might the theology of the cross be significant for Christians who are suffering and dying? In seeking to answer this question, I want to focus on a form of practice which is implicit in the narrative that we focused on earlier in this chapter and which emerges in an interesting way from our discussion of the theology of the cross: *the practice of lament.* In the closing sections of this chapter I will argue that lament, understood within the framework of the theology of the cross, offers a powerful pastoral practice that can bring healing and hope for those encountering the closure of their lives.

How Can We Sing the Lord's Song in a Strange Land?

In Psalm 137 the psalmist cries out from a situation of exile in Babylon: "How can we sing the Lord's song in a strange land?" God's apparent abandonment of the people of Israel draws out a deep lament that is marked by both faithfulness and real pain. Jerusalem seems a long way away. As he sits beside the rivers of Babylon, the psalmist longs for home, not knowing if he will ever again see it:

> By the rivers of Babylon we sat and wept
> when we remembered Zion.
> There on the poplars
> we hung our harps,
>
> for there our captors asked us for songs,
> our tormentors demanded songs of joy;
> they said, "Sing us one of the songs of Zion!"
>
> How can we sing the songs of the LORD
> while in a foreign land? (vv. 1-4)

This is a profound question that has important implications for end-of-life care.

In her book *Illness as Metaphor*, Susan Sontag observes, "Health and illness are like two different countries. If we are lucky, we spend most of our time dwelling in the first, though nearly all of us are, at some time or other, passport holders of both domains."[36] There is a tantalizing analogy between the situation of the psalmist and the situation of the one experiencing terminal illness. Both cry out to the Lord, "How can we sing the Lord's song in a strange land!?" One is exiled to Babylon; the other is forced to sing songs of worship in the strange country of illness. In both situations the idea of praising God in the midst of suffering and exile appears to be foolishness.

And yet, that is precisely what we as Christians are called to do. Furthermore, we are not only called to sing the Lord's song in strange lands; we are instructed to do so at all times! In Ephesians 6:18 the apostle Paul urges us to pray at all times, irrespective of our circumstances: "And pray in the Spirit on all occasions with all kinds of prayers and requests. With this in mind, be alert and always keep on praying for all the saints." In Psalm 34:1-3, the psalmist instructs us to praise the Lord at all times and in all circumstances:

> I will extol the LORD at all times;
> his praise will always be on my lips.
> My soul will boast in the LORD;
> let the afflicted hear and rejoice.
> Glorify the LORD with me;
> let us exalt his name together.

Like the theologians of glory, Paul and the psalmist urge us to focus on the glory of God. Unlike the theologians of glory, however, they do not see God's glory as relating to human power and wisdom or freedom from suffering or the struggle to avoid death. God's glory is to be acknowledged in prayer and praise, even amidst the ravages of suffering, affliction, and exile. Put slightly differently, Christians are called to worship, pray, and find solace in Jesus *in the midst of their suffering*, even when liberation and healing may not be possible. Both Paul and the psalmist point toward a theology of the cross wherein God is recognized by the sufferer in the midst of suffering in ways that enhance,

36. Susan Sontag, *Illness as Metaphor* (New York: Farrar, Straus & Giroux, 1978), p. 1.

support, and restore his faith and initiate an experience of the intimate presence of God. In praise and prayer God continues to call this person back into right relationship with him.

At one level this appears to be a ridiculous and unattainable goal. How can we be expected to pray and praise when our world is being undone by suffering, pain, and the threat of impending death? How can we praise God when all we really want to do is cry out in pain and agony for that which we have lost or are in the process of losing? It is precisely as we begin to ask these questions that we find ourselves intuitively drawn toward the psalms of lament.[37] In light of the suggestion that God is with us in our suffering, it is clearly not coincidental that God has also provided a language for expressing our suffering as we seek to encounter Jesus, who resides in the midst of our suffering.

Put simply, a lament is a cry or a repeated cry of pain, rage, sorrow, and grief that emerges in the midst of deep pain, suffering, and alienation. Lament suggests that the person who is lamenting has a genuine grievance. She feels that she has been done wrong and that the way she has interpreted God's promise and covenantal responsibility is not consistent with the way that things actually are. But lament is much more than complaint or catharsis. Lament is first and foremost a powerful form of prayer. It is a heartfelt cry to God to enter into the situation and bring about change. It is not an act of disbelief or faithlessness. Quite the opposite: Lament is directed to a God who is perceived as very real and who is worthy of both faith and praise.

Lament is faithful prayer. It is, however, a very particular form of prayer that is not content with soothing platitudes or images of a God who will only listen to voices that appease and compliment. Lament takes seriously the fact that God is the creator and that everything that happens in his world has divine significance and is a worthy subject for prayer. The practice of lament takes the brokenness of human experience into the heart of God and demands that God answer. *"How long will the wicked, O Lord, how long will the wicked be jubilant?"* (Ps. 94:3).

When it comes to suffering, disease, and dying, the psalms of lament tell it like it is. Psalm 6:1-7 is a striking example of that directness:

37. For a more complete development of this perspective on lament, see Swinton, *Raging with Compassion,* Chapter 5.

O Lord, do not rebuke me in your anger
or discipline me in your wrath.

Be merciful to me, Lord, for I am faint;
O Lord, heal me, for my bones are in agony.

My soul is in anguish.
How long, O Lord, how long?

Turn, O Lord, and deliver me;
save me because of your unfailing love.

No one remembers you when he is dead.
Who praises you from the grave?

I am worn out from groaning;
all night long I flood my bed with weeping
and drench my couch with tears.

My eyes grow weak with sorrow;
they fail because of all my foes.

Here we see the psalmist addressing head on the radical dissonance that is caused by disease, suffering, and the threat of death. He expresses surprise, dismay, and disappointment; he never expected this to happen to him! Lament allows the honest expression of pain, anger, sadness, and confusion. It provides a language for suffering that does not attempt to placate, avoid, or look past suffering. The psalmist looks suffering straight in the face in Psalm 69:3 and rages,

I am worn out calling for help;
my throat is parched.
My eyes fail,
looking for my God.

Importantly, lament enables us to know that we are not alone and that ultimately God has covenantal responsibility for our situation. Only God can save us – and he will, according to Psalm 69:29-36:

I am in pain and distress;
may your salvation, O God, protect me.

I will praise God's name in song
  and glorify him with thanksgiving.

This will please the LORD more than an ox,
  more than a bull with its horns and hoofs.

The poor will see and be glad –
  you who seek God, may your hearts live!

The LORD hears the needy
  and does not despise his captive people.

Let heaven and earth praise him,
  the seas and all that move in them,

for God will save Zion
  and rebuild the cities of Judah.
  Then people will settle there and possess it;

the children of his servants will inherit it,
  and those who love his name will dwell there.

Lament provides us with a language of hurt, pain, and outrage that speaks against the way that things are, but always in the hope that the way things are just now is not the way they will always be. Lament is thus profoundly hopeful. That is clear at the end of Psalm 13:

> How long, O LORD? Will you forget me forever? How long will you hide your face from me? How long must I wrestle with my thoughts and every day have sorrow in my heart? How long will my enemy triumph over me?
>
> Look on me and answer, O LORD my God. Give light to my eyes, or I will sleep in death; my enemy will say, "I have overcome him," and my foes will rejoice when I fall. But I trust in your unfailing love; my heart rejoices in your salvation. I will sing to the LORD, for he has been good to me.

Engagement in such a process of lamentation is a powerful healing practice that enables us to hang on to our humanity in the midst of apparent dehumanization and to emerge from the silence that is forced upon us through our encounters with illness and suffering to a position of hopeful prayer and praise.

The psalms of lament provide us with a language that allows us to tell it like it is but still continue to worship God in ways that make even our experience of suffering faithful. In articulating the reality of pain and suffering within the context of prayer, the psalms of lament enable faithful sadness and a healing catharsis that need not slip into selfish moaning.

By giving voice to the terrible reality of the situation of suffering and the fear of dying, the psalms of lament make the experience real, but within a context where God is also real, present, and assumed to be active.

The Psalms of Lament as the Language of Praise and the Language of Jesus

Although Luther did not explore this connection in his work, the psalms of lament are deeply intertwined with the theology of the cross. Indeed, the psalms of lament form the language of a practical theology of the cross. In his *Prayer Book of the Bible,* Dietrich Bonhoeffer explores the role of the psalms in the life of the Christian. He argues that prayer is not something people do naturally. Just as the disciples asked Jesus how to pray, so also must we be taught how to pray. Bonhoeffer suggests that the Lord's Prayer provides a template for the shape of prayer, and that the psalms provide us with godly content for praying. The psalms, Bonhoeffer argues, are the "prayer book of the Bible." Prayer is not simply a human-oriented pouring out of one's heart. Rather, it means "finding the way to and speaking with God, whether the heart is full or empty. No one can do that on one's own. For that one needs Jesus Christ."[38] True prayer, then, is prayer that is spoken with Jesus and to Jesus. Bonhoeffer draws out what he means by this in an illuminating way:

> It can become a great torment to want to speak with God and not be able to do it — having to be speechless before God, sensing that every cry remains enclosed within one's own self, that heart and mouth

38. Dietrich Bonhoeffer, *Life Together* and *Prayer Book of the Bible* (Minneapolis: Augsburg Fortress Press, 1996), p. 155.

> speak a perverse language which God does not want to hear. In such need we seek people who can help us, who know something about praying. If someone who can pray would just take us along in prayer, if we could pray along with that person's prayer, then we would be helped![39]

For Bonhoeffer, the person who will teach us to pray at all times and in all circumstances is Jesus. And Jesus desires to teach us the language of the psalms. In the psalms, "we pray along with Christ's prayer and therefore may be certain and glad that God hears us."[40] The psalms are the prayer book of the Bible.

Such a suggestion raises some important issues. If the Bible is God's word given to and for human beings, then why does it require a prayer book? If the psalms were written hundreds of years before Jesus was born, how could he speak the psalms? Bonhoeffer argues that in the psalms, Christ was working in, through, and with the psalmists, building up God's people and pointing toward the cross and the resurrection (Acts 2:30ff.):

> In the Psalms of David it is precisely the promised Christ who already speaks (Heb. 2:12; 10:5) or, as is sometimes said, the Holy Spirit (Heb. 3:7). The same words that David spoke, therefore, the future Messiah spoke in him. Christ prayed along with the prayers of David or, more accurately, it is none other than Christ who prayed them in Christ's own forerunner.[41]

Like David, we pray the psalms with Jesus and with the words of Jesus:

> It is the incarnate Son of God, who [on the cross] has borne all human weakness in his own flesh, who here pours out the heart of all humanity before God, and who stands in our place and prays for us. He has known torment and pain, guilt and death more deeply than we have. Therefore it is the prayer of the human nature assumed by Christ that comes before God here. It is really our prayer. But since the Son of God knows us better than we know ourselves, and was

39. Bonhoeffer, *Life Together* and *Prayer Book of the Bible,* p. 155.
40. Bonhoeffer, *Life Together* and *Prayer Book of the Bible,* p. 156.
41. Bonhoeffer, *Life Together* and *Prayer Book of the Bible,* p. 159.

> truly human for our sake, it is also really the Son's prayer. It can become our prayer only because it was his prayer.[42]

The Christ who comes alongside us in our pain and suffering and who seeks to redeem and reconnect us with the Father speaks to us and with us in the rich language of the psalms. When we pray the psalms, we are using the language of God himself! In the psalms of lament, Jesus speaks out from his position within human suffering and provides us with a language and a life-world that enable us to tell it like it is. But these are also words that spring from heaven itself. In enabling faithful sadness and honest praise, the psalms offer a deep and moving language of the cross, recognizing the glory of God even when it is hidden in the depths of human pain, suffering, and death. Learning to pray the psalms in times of sadness and joy is learning to speak with the language of Jesus.

It is perhaps because of this that almost all of the psalms of lament end in praise. They initiate and sustain a movement from the depths of despair to the possibility of a life that is re-oriented toward the glory of God even when that glory is revealed in ways that disappoint us or do not meet our expectations. Psalm 3 (NASB) provides an example:

> But You, O Lord, are a shield about me, my glory, and the One
> who lifts my head.
> I was crying to the Lord with my voice, and He answered me
> from His holy mountain. *Selah.*
> I lay down and slept; I awoke, for the Lord sustains me.

Learning to lament in times of serious illness may be a forgotten yet vital end-of-life practice which, in a culture that is profoundly death-denying and keen to avoid or medicalize suffering, holds much potential for facilitating ways of dying that are healthy and faithful.

Practicing the Theology of the Cross

Perhaps if Lisa had been given the opportunity to lament, she would have written some wonderful stories that would have allowed her life to

42. Bonhoeffer, *Life Together* and *Prayer Book of the Bible,* p. 160.

end in a very different way. Maybe if Dr. Rayson's worldview had been shaped by a theology of the cross rather than by medicine's theology of glory, his continuing regret over his experience with Lisa would have been an experience he didn't have to endure. But their experience is not wasted if we can use it to God's true glory. If their experience challenges us all to think differently and to work through what it might mean to put the cross at the center of our end-of-life practices, then God's glory will be revealed in the midst of both of their sufferings.

If what I have been saying about the psalms is correct, then we should prioritize praying the psalms as a vital aspect of our spiritual devotions and a crucial pre-emptive element of end-of-life care. I am, of course, not attempting to make praying the psalms a form of therapy! The point is not that "the psalms are good for your health." Our praying of the psalms, including the psalms of lament, is an act of worship that expresses our deep love for God and our trust that he is with us and for us in all things. As Thomas Merton puts it, "The Church loves the Psalms because in them she sings of her experience of God, of her union with the Incarnate Word, of her contemplation of God in the Mystery of Christ."[43]

There is no question that this practice will be restorative and health-bringing if we define health as being in right relationship with God at all times and in all things. It will also bring insights into suffering and pain that will benefit patients and clinicians in deep and profound ways. But ultimately the point of the practice of praying the psalms is to recognize who God is and where God is when we hurt.

The Psalms in Clinical Practice

But is there a role for the psalms in clinical practice? That is a difficult question to answer. The language of the psalms in general and of the psalms of lament in particular certainly stands in sharp tension with the technological and restorative language that tends to dominate the medical/clinical discourse. Language of God and forms of transformation that do not necessitate freedom from disease and suffering sound

43. Thomas Merton, *Praying the Psalms* (Collegeville, Minn.: Liturgical Press, 1986), p. 9.

more than a little odd in a clinical context. And yet, such dissonance needs to be held in tension with the experience of patients.

For many people it is precisely the language of lament that captures the essence of their experience. Of course, people want to be cured, but they also want to have the full extent of their pain acknowledged. They want doctors to tell it like it is, and for their situation to be seen for what it is. They want doctors to look at their suffering and not always to look through it. Arthur Kleinman expresses it this way:

> What do patients most appreciate in the medical care they receive? Arguably, it is the attention that care givers devote to the experience of menacing symptoms and grave loss as much as technical interventions that improve outcome.[44]

By using or facilitating the use of the psalms of lament within a clinical context, the clinician is provided with a language of faith, hope, and transformation that is not normally available. Combine this with modes of clinical practice that seek to take seriously the practical theological implications of the theology of the cross, and there emerges the real possibility of models of end-of-life care that hold in creative tension the hope of physical restoration with the centrality of spiritual sustenance and transformation.[45]

For end-of-life clinicians, the theology of the cross and the practice of lament are potentially vital tools in terms of their own mental health and spiritual life. How do clinicians and others deal with their constant exposure to suffering, pain, and death? Where do they find answers to their own question: "Where is God in the midst of this suffering?" What do they do when they are confronted with situations that force them to face their own anger and confusion over the horrors they witness? How do they sing the Lord's song in this strange world of medicine?

An answer to these questions lies in the practice of lament. Lament

44. Kleinman, in Mary-Jo DelVecchio Good et al., *Pain as Human Experience* (Berkeley and Los Angeles: University of California Press, 1994), p. 13.

45. Perhaps we should move our focus away from medicalizing research, which is fascinated by whether or not prayer can heal, and begin to explore the possibility that prayer as it is made manifest in the practice of lament might have much more clinical utility.

has the potential to allow health-care providers to begin to pray and praise even when that is the very last thing they want to do. Lament will allow them to become honest and faithful Christians who see suffering, pain, and death not as opportunities to show off the latest medical technologies, but as loci for divine encounters within which the God who has broad shoulders absorbs the pain and the anger of the moment and stands with them as they stand in solidarity with the suffering patient. Lament allows clinicians to recognize that God is with and for them even in the midst of the darkest of sorrows.

Reflection on the theology of the cross has enabled us to gain some deep theological and practical insights into the nature and goals of end-of-life care. It has enabled us to locate God in the midst of suffering and has provided us with a language that can bring healing and transformation despite the ravages of illness. Jesus is with us and for us in all things. Our task as human beings is to learn how to stay in touch with him, and even to praise him at all times. Lisa never got to write her stories, but her own story has moved us to begin to rethink what it means to care, to suffer, and to die with faithfulness and hope.

CHAPTER 7

Practicing Compassion for Dying Children

Tonya D. Armstrong

What does it mean to practice compassion faithfully? Answering this question is difficult because the notion of compassion is in great need of clarification in the political, medical, and social discourse of contemporary America. The difficulty of answering this question and the seriousness of the need for clarification become even more evident if we consider the condition of dying children[1] and their families. Despite the difficulty, there are important theological resources for answering this question, resources that deserve careful consideration.

In this chapter I will briefly examine child mortality trends in the United States, the unique experiences of the dying child, and familial challenges of caring for a dying child. I will describe contemporary attitudes toward suffering and note the concomitant crisis of compassion in which we currently find ourselves. I will draw attention to a theological (that is, Christological) form of practicing compassion, rooted in the life of Jesus of Nazareth. Through exploring some theological and pastoral insights drawn from the Christian tradition, I will posit that the church is equipped and poised to show leadership in and to the world in the embodiment of compassionate practices toward children and youth, particularly those at the end of life.

Our ability to exhibit leadership, however, is dependent upon our

1. Unless otherwise noted, the term *children* used throughout this chapter refers broadly to persons from infancy to twenty-one years of age.

Unless otherwise indicated, all of the quotations from Scripture in this chapter are taken from the New International Version of the Holy Bible.

holistic comprehension of the implications of God's compassion for our identity in Christ, our lives in community, and our practices of compassion. In speaking to the church, I am invoking both our identities as persons who engage in practices of worship with a particular body of Christian believers, and our identities as persons who are called in our respective vocations to serve the world. In other words, I am speaking to both formal caregivers (i.e., caring professionals such as health-care providers and chaplains) and informal caregivers (i.e., faith community volunteers).[2] I encourage readers to resist the tendency to dichotomize these identities. Building from the life of Jesus as the model of compassion, I will outline a spirituality of compassionate practice focused on the care of dying children which suggests new paths that current forms might take. In so doing, I hope to "re-member" (draw back together that which has been dismembered) a deeply significant way of practicing end-of-life care throughout the ages.

A Few Words about Context

I approach the task of writing about compassion for dying children as a clinical child and pediatric psychologist and a pastoral theologian. I have been trained to provide consultation, evaluation, and psychotherapeutic treatment for children and adolescents who suffer from psychiatric and medical disorders. As such, I intentionally place myself in clinical and research contexts where I am actively engaged with the cognitive/mental, affective/emotional, behavioral, and spiritual narratives of suffering children. Because of the ways that the stories of children in general, and suffering children in particular, are often marginalized, I seek to give voice to "the least of these."

Clinical work with children necessarily involves parents or legal guardians, and sometimes other family members. Because of this necessity, and because of my training in family systems theory and practice, I have become sensitized to the needs of families with a suffering child. Families are complex networks that are often maintained by inter-

2. Unless specified as "parental or family caregiver," the term *caregiver* in this chapter refers to biologically unrelated persons who provide formal or informal care to the dying or their families.

actional patterns, for better or for worse. Dealing with a chronic and/or life-threatening condition has significant and stressful repercussions for parental figures, siblings, and even extended family members, yet the responses of siblings in particular are often overlooked in our interventions. It is my conviction that any approach to practicing compassion must attend to the needs of the entire family, which ultimately requires some coordination of efforts between various caregivers.

Moreover, I arrive at this task with the lenses of a pastoral theologian. I probe the question of "Where is God in this suffering?" with children, families, clinicians, and faith communities alike. I frequently observe the spiritual proclivities of even the youngest patients, and help them struggle to make meaning of illness and suffering. Alongside family members, I wrestle with questions of good versus evil in light of their own theological understandings, now juxtaposed with the experience of serious childhood illness. With clinicians I engage in the translational work of interpreting the behaviors of suffering children as a mode of expressing their spiritual needs or desires. (For example, a child who appears to be noncompliant with medical procedures may in fact be holding a particular theological view of healing that needs to be engaged by the health-care provider and/or the chaplain.) Respectfully, yet perhaps prophetically, I remind faith communities of our long history of care for the suffering and of scriptural directives to actively attend both to children and to the sick.

Taken together, these perspectives from psychology, theology, clinical practice, and Christian ministry are, I hope, integrated in my work in a manner that appreciates the complexities of the suffering child/adolescent and family, respects the worth and capacity for wholeness of each person, and effectively responds (or facilitates an effective response by other caring persons) to the needs of each person. Because I recognize the inherent limitations of each discipline, I seek opportunities for dynamic interchanges between reflection and praxis across disciplines and life experiences.

Contemporary Forms of Compassion for Dying Children

Although children's mortality rates have improved dramatically in the past century, there are still approximately 55,000 children in the United

States who die each year[3] due to the top five causes of death: accidental injury, malignant neoplasms (i.e., cancer), congenital abnormalities, homicide, and heart disease. If we consider the top five causes of death for youth from the age of ten to the age of nineteen, we note that suicide emerges as a leading cause of death, even in early adolescence.[4] But whatever the cause, we tend to locate the death of any child squarely in the realm of the absurd.

In order to move toward a posture of compassion with dying children and their families, it is important to listen to their stories and understand the nature of their sufferings. Perhaps bearing some similarity to Job's narrative, the narrative of each dying child reveals suffering in several realms, including the physical, emotional, social, behavioral, spiritual, and cognitive realms. On the one hand, each child's diagnosis, disease progression, prognosis, familial configurations, and cultural considerations are unique factors that require interdisciplinary approaches (both within and beyond medical settings) to attend to these needs. On the other hand, dying children share a common experience not entirely unlike that of their much older counterparts. Anthropologist Myra Bluebond-Langner, in her groundbreaking work *The Private Worlds of Dying Children,* makes this candid observation:

> Children, in American society, are "in process," "not yet fully formed," as childhood is a period of formation, of becoming. Socialization is by definition forward-looking, . . . not a period of concluding or of summing up. Dying children, however, do not fit comfortably into such a view. Although, like other children, they are sensitive, intelligent, kind, willful, and young, they will not "become," they have no future. . . . Dying children are more like the elderly than their own healthy peers – without futures, worried, often passive, unhappy, burdened with responsibilities for others and their feelings. They even resemble old people – either bald or disheveled, emaciated or bloated, incapacitated, generally sickly, and most of all losing, failing with time. Their worth can only be mea-

3. Marilyn Field and Robert Behrman, *When Children Die: Improving Palliative and End-of-Life Care for Children and Their Families,* Committee on Palliative and End-of-Life Care for Children and Their Families, Board on Health Sciences Policy (Washington, D.C.: Institute of Medicine, National Academy Press, 2002), p. 41.

4. Field and Behrman, *When Children Die,* p. 41.

sured by what they do now, unlike other children, who have time to prove themselves.[5]

Although Bluebond-Langner uses elderly persons here as a reference group, there are stark contrasts between even the elderly and children with life-threatening illnesses. While both groups generally experience apprehension when it comes to thoughts of impending death, children are often more dependent on their families for broad-based support, having never established significant independence. Because they have fewer social networks and fewer psychological coping skills, children must rely on their families to provide assistance in these roles. Depending on their age, they may exhibit significantly less receptive and expressive language, demonstrate magical thinking, and require more concrete communication, thereby tolerating only brief discussions about the complexities of their illness and prognosis.

Moreover, children have fewer life experiences from which to develop a balanced perspective on their medical conditions. Positively, children are often more fun-centered and trusting of others and thus can be easier to engage by unfamiliar caregivers; at the same time, children likely have a greater capacity for disappointment when they perceive that this trust is repeatedly betrayed. Because many of these differences that characterize children's experiences with life-threatening illness are unexpressed or unrecognized, children often suffer silently in their fear, pain, and alienation.

Even with respect to similarly aged peers, dying children often differ from their well counterparts because they have a sense of a foreshortened future that isolates them in the present. By virtue of what they frequently experience as physical constraints, emotional turmoil, and long-term hospitalizations, dying children are often cut off from peer and community supports. Real or perceived experiences of rejection, embarrassment about physical appearance, and a distorted body image are other factors that create or further generate distance between dying children and their peers. Institutional restrictions on hospital visits from other children, while protective and well-intentioned, further contribute to experiences of isolation.

5. Myra Bluebond-Langner, *The Private Worlds of Dying Children* (Princeton: Princeton University Press, 1980), pp. 212-13.

Furthermore, dying children face considerable anxiety in confronting numerous painful, often invasive procedures that at the very least are perceived as threatening their bodily integrity. Perhaps most frightful is the prospect of death, and thus many children encounter anticipatory grief (their own and that of loved ones). Other emotions evoked include anger, worry, sadness, disappointment, and frustration. These emotions may be internalized, contributing to significant yet invisible distress, or externalized, yielding a range of behavioral concerns. Children's well-documented need for routine is significantly disrupted, while uncertainty regarding their futures progresses at an uncontrollable rate. Cognitive limitations in understanding the universality, causality, non-functionality, irreversibility, and non-corporeal continuation (i.e., afterlife) of death further exacerbate the ability of children to adjust to the chronic and terminal phases of life-threatening illness.[6]

Nevertheless, parents and caregivers are strongly ambivalent about approaching and addressing children's isolation. For exceedingly apparent reasons, the death of a child is difficult to accept for all kinds of caregivers. Family, friends, and health-care providers alike can be unconsciously complicit in contributing to the isolation that dying children experience. In her study, Bluebond-Langner noted that children's experiences with their caretakers included long absences from the room, brief interactions (presumably out of fear of excessive emotional displays), and avoidance of disease-related topics of conversation. Specifically, most adults tended to eschew discussions about the child's condition, medications, physical appearance, other children's deaths, future events and holidays, and future plans in general.[7] Sadly, many children are left to fend for themselves at times of greatest vulnerability.

As a result, children who have become disenchanted with the medical establishment, particularly through their own experiences of mistrust, may employ distancing strategies as protective mechanisms. These include refusing to talk, feigning sleep, continually lashing out or crying out, withdrawing, and/or engaging in practically inaudible or superficial

6. Mark W. Speece and Sandor B. Brent, "The Development of Children's Understanding of Death," in *Handbook of Childhood Death and Bereavement,* ed. Charles A. Corr and Donna M. Corr (New York: Springer Publishing Co., 1996), pp. 29-50.

7. Bluebond-Langner, *The Private Worlds of Dying Children,* pp. 201-2.

conversation.[8] Dying children may reason that they can exert control over their interactions, if over nothing else that is happening to them. Their sense of control may sometimes be expressed as noncompliance with medical procedures and/or medication regimens. Thus, the needs of children at the end of life are commonly intense and multifaceted.

Lest we adopt a myopic viewpoint that only narrowly regards the child's concerns, we must briefly acknowledge the needs of the family facing the death of a child. Qualitative data on the influence of spirituality in families coping with childhood chronic illness provide some insight into their complex challenges.[9] Content analyses from in-depth interviews with five families dealing with pediatric nephrotic syndrome[10] revealed a number of recurrent stressors, including the impact of dealing with treatment challenges, frequent clinic visits, and travel of nearly fifty miles on average (each way) for diagnostic evaluations, medical procedures, surgeries, follow-up visits, and/or dialysis treatments.

Additionally, families also reported significant financial burdens associated with medical treatments, including the direct costs of visits, procedures, long-term hospitalizations, and the like, and the indirect costs of time away from work, transportation, lodging, and meals. Strained relationships were also reported as a significant stressor, particularly among family members, as one parent often traveled for medical care with the ill child, leaving behind other family members, including minors, to support themselves. Indeed, a number of parents expressed concern over possible neglect of well siblings over time. Patterns of negative attention-seeking behaviors among siblings appeared to be prevalent among these families, and some siblings acknowledged feelings of resentment or jealousy toward the ill child. Perhaps due to

8. Bluebond-Langner, *The Private Worlds of Dying Children,* p. 207.

9. Tonya Armstrong, "The Impact of Spirituality on the Coping Processes of Families Dealing with Childhood Chronic Illness," Ph.D. dissertation, University of North Carolina, 1998, pp. 121-22.

10. Pediatric nephrotic syndrome is a life-threatening illness typically characterized by renal failure and subsequent dialysis treatment. Many children with this illness eventually require renal transplantation to survive. Even following transplantation, a number of children and families in this study experienced significant challenges in their quality of life. While death was not imminent for most, the constant threat to life was ever-present and alienating. In fact, the chronicity of this illness, often extending over a period of years, may have exacerbated their alienation.

the disruptive nature of dialysis treatments, academic difficulty among ill children was common.

With respect to the role of spirituality in their lives, families tended to view God as the ultimate source of healing and the basis of family togetherness in the face of overwhelming odds. While two families seemed to view their spirituality primarily through church involvement and "trying to live right," the remaining families expressed an enduring connection with a Higher Being regardless of whether they were in close proximity to their communities of faith. In terms of the role of spirituality in explaining the disease, some families generally appeared to focus less on understanding the "why" and more on expressing gratitude for life itself and relying on God's ability to change their circumstances.

With regard to identifying concrete supports, families often coped with illness by striving for family togetherness. Family time was often combined with church attendance to gain the emotional resources needed to make it through the week. Also, while most families agreed that community and extended family support for the illness was often short-lived, many agreed that the Ronald McDonald House had been a tremendous source of support.[11] Additionally, families viewed their physician and supporting medical staff as providing significant medical as well as emotional support. Specific coping strategies ranged from denial and suppression of competing activities to positive reinterpretation, acceptance, and adopting a sense of humor.

Regarding experiences of personal well-being, a number of families expressed some weariness in dealing with pediatric nephrotic syndrome over time. While most were hopeful about the possibility of successful transplants or improvements in functioning for their children, they also acknowledged their own eventual vulnerabilities as caregivers and shared concerns about how their children would fare without them. These concerns were particularly significant for the families in which the ill child also had cognitive impairments. Nearly all families expressed faith that God would provide a greater quality of life in the

11. The Ronald McDonald House program began in 1974 as a way to provide a "home away from home" for families of seriously ill children receiving treatment at nearby hospitals. To find out more about this program, visit http://www.rmhc.org/rmhc/index/about.html.

future, but few individuals seemed capable of articulating their dreams of how life would look in the future.

What was striking from both the quantitative and the qualitative data collected in this study was the serious dearth of church or faith-community support for these families, even those who identified themselves as faithful Christians and had demonstrated a high degree of involvement in religious communities before illness struck. Overall, they perceived that their greatest sense of community was derived from hospital staff. While many patients and their families would not hesitate to agree that the love of Christ was displayed in these settings, the intentional, ongoing witness of the Christian community was less clear. Indeed, compassionate practices of the church were largely absent in the lived experiences of these families.

What Are Our Contemporary Attitudes toward Suffering?

If the experiences of these few families are generalizable to a broader population of families dealing with a child's life-threatening illness (and I fear that they are), this state of affairs is a powerful indictment of the church's abandonment of one of its primary missions. So what has allowed us to "abandon ship"? From my perspective, this abandonment has much to do with our contemporary attitudes toward suffering.

Within the broader context of our dialogue about Christian practices at the end of life, I believe that compassion is a particular manifestation of God's love to the suffering and, through God's transformation, *our* love for them. Simply put, compassion is the recognition of and internalization of the suffering of another. It is conceptually related to notions of pity, empathy, and mercy, but reveals important distinctions. Compassion reflects pity in that we demonstrate an emotional response to another's suffering. Compassion is similar to empathy in that we enter into, directly identify with (typically through our own previous experiences), and indirectly experience the suffering of another. Compassion also shares with mercy the sense of being moved to act on behalf of another. However, compassion surpasses mercy in that the latter has more juridical connotations that do not necessarily indicate the sharing of suffering. Further, compassion transcends empathy and pity in that we are compelled to share suffering and exhibit a tangible response to suffering. Rather than demonstrating mere civility or sentimentality, compassion reveals a deep commitment to bearing and responding to the suffering of another.

Often when we reflect on suffering, we think of pain or distress resulting from a physical condition. Nevertheless, suffering is commonly associated with mental anguish, emotional misery, spiritual anomie, and financial disintegration. A person's need for compassion is especially acute when distress emerges simultaneously from multiple sources.

This is perhaps why Job's narrative of suffering and redemption is so compelling. Job suffered intense physical pain, familial devastation and betrayal, financial ruin, and unsolicited social critique. Given his multifaceted suffering, each of us may find a place of common experience with Job. Perhaps because we are reminded of our own sufferings, we are often eager to rush through the story of Job, moving quickly beyond the long suffering of Job and his companions to arrive at the "happy ending," the place where the righteous man gets his just rewards. It is an outcome that we deem as much more consistent with our postmodern sensibilities than the first forty-one chapters of the book.

Our contemporary attitudes toward suffering are also shaped to a significant degree by our experiences with technology. How are we poised to suffer with another of God's creatures when the technological advances of our time have lulled us into the erroneous belief that we have transcended suffering? Traditional and alternative therapies are widely available to the masses, we reason, and science is just on the cusp of delivering us from all contingencies. Suffering, after all, is not just an occasional reckoning with the painful forces of life that we have yet to control, nor is it a mere inconvenience of contemporary life; on the contrary, it impedes our pursuit of the "good life"; it places us behind schedule in our best-laid, would-be well-executed plans; it creates awkward literal and symbolic distance between us and "the Joneses"; and ultimately, it represents the embarrassment we suffer from not having conquered it already.

As difficult as we find it to comprehend other forms of suffering, we struggle particularly with the notion of children at the end of life. How do we make sense of the sufferings of dying children? From a theological perspective, we are often met with what theologian and bereaved parent Nicholas Wolterstorff calls "the biblical silence of God."[12] He suggests that some of our questions to God are misguided questions, given the divine speech that God has already shared.[13] Consistent with God's intent that we live until we are "full of years" and that we flourish on earth in the community of persons during those years, redemptive suffering serves our flourishing. But Wolterstorff calls into question the soul-making theodicy first propagated by Irenaeus, a prominent bishop of the early church, since it speaks only of the benefits of suffering to those who survive, and not of the benefits of suffering to those who die. Neither can we blindly accept the notion that there are clear distinctions between God's creating and maintaining intent and God's desires and commands. Wolterstorff rejects the notion that God uses one person, particularly the suffering of that person, for the good of another.

In the absence of self-satisfying answers to our queries, Wolterstorff suggests particular ways that we can live in the silence of God. These ways of living, both passive and active, reveal patient, hopeful responses to the mystery of death. He encourages holding on to God by maintaining practices of devotion, keeping alive the protest against early death and unredemptive suffering, and taking advantage of opportunities to own our own suffering redemptively. Speaking out of the experience of his own son's sudden death, Wolterstorff offers insights that provide relevant implications for those of us who would enter into the particular sufferings of dying children and their families.

A Crisis of Compassion

By what means, then, do we enter such suffering? Does Jesus' obvious compassion for children through healings and blessings demonstrated in the Gospels exercise no influence in the contemporary church? Some may argue that the Pauline metaphor of the body of Christ pro-

12. Nicholas Wolterstorff, "The Silence of the God Who Speaks," in *Divine Hiddenness: New Essays,* ed. Daniel Howard-Snyder and Paul K. Moser (Cambridge: Cambridge University Press, 2002), p. 215.

13. Wolterstorff, "The Silence of the God Who Speaks," p. 216.

vides evidence that practices of compassion are primarily the domain of those so gifted to edify the body in this way. "There are different kinds of gifts, but the same Spirit. There are different kinds of service, but the same Lord. There are different kinds of working, but the same God works all of them in all men. Now to each one the manifestation of the Spirit is given for the common good" (1 Cor. 12:4-7). Is compassionate caregiving a spiritual gift, only manifested in a few, or is it a virtue that can be cultivated by all who claim the name of Christ? Theologian Oliver Davies, author of *A Theology of Compassion,* posits,

> The defining content of virtue is an other-centered intentionality which manifests in cognition, affectivity, and will. Compassion, then, rather like "love," is not itself a virtue (such as almsgiving or forgiveness), but is rather a kenotic or agapic state of mind which precipitates in virtuous acts. It is a clearly identifiable structure which forms the common ground of those actions in the world in which the self shows itself ready to put itself concretely at risk for the sake of the other.[14]

It is possible, then, that the state of mind steeped in agape is generally accessible across persons of different spiritual gifts, yet requires deeper cultivation in our contemporary culture. Only kenosis (i.e., the emptying of the self) permits the conscious placing of the self at risk. While Davies' primary point of phenomenological experience pertains to the self-dispossessive acts of Etty Hillesum and Edith Stein in sharing the fate of Jewish victims of the Shoah, it can be extended to apply to the discussion here, because there is a very real, albeit psychological, risk in the compassionate care of dying children and their families. In the context of life-threatening illnesses, compassionate acts eventually culminate in the death of the child and a reconfiguration of the caregiver's attachment to the child, even as she bears the role of assisting in the family's meaning-making and bereavement care.

Even after we have acknowledged the phenomenological experience of suffering, the task of compassionate caregiving still remains elusive because we may draw needless distinctions between our own suffering and that of others. From a detached, sympathetic stance, we

14. Oliver Davies, *A Theology of Compassion* (Grand Rapids: William B. Eerdmans, 2001), p. 18.

may be motivated to ensure our obedience to Jesus' commands in Matthew 25 without getting "sullied" in the process. Do we strive to nourish the hungry and thirsty, entertain the stranger, clothe the naked, look after the sick, and visit the imprisoned, all while avoiding chances to bear the pain of their sufferings? Perhaps we want to remain sufficiently occupied (preoccupied?) in caregiving such that we become distracted from our own sufferings, or reject suffering's implications for our lives altogether.

Given the current state of our alienation from one another, I assert that we as the church have reached a crisis via our impoverished reflection and praxis around compassionate ministry. The reasons for this are threefold. First, to the degree that we have become complicit with, even influential in, the alluring trends of postmodern society (e.g., individualism, narcissism, consumerism), we have relegated the commands of Jesus to a low priority. Second, our current cultural arrangements create problems in the institutions of family, church, and community. It is increasingly difficult to swim against the tide that has significantly eroded these institutions since the Enlightenment. Third, in light of these contextual challenges, the church struggles to rightly appropriate ecclesial and liturgical resources that form disciples of Christ for the righteous life lived in God's image. In the midst of this crisis, however, I argue for the recovery of the source of compassion that makes compassionate ministry intelligible: the life and ministry of Jesus the Christ.

Jesus as the Model of Divine Compassion

The Judeo-Christian tradition is replete with revelations of divine compassion. God is described as "a gracious and compassionate God, slow to anger and abounding in love, a God who relents from sending calamity" (Jonah 4:2). God manifests God's compassion through saving acts, most notably the liberation of the Israelites from slavery in Egypt. Davies observes that the compassion of God is "intimately linked with the action of God for his people, with his own self-naming and with the life of the saints who follow God's ways."[15] The prophets of the Old

15. Davies, *A Theology of Compassion,* p. 240.

Testament portrayed God as standing in solidarity with the alien and the oppressed. Furthermore, God continually instructed God's people to carry out justice in concrete ways: "Is not this the kind of fasting I have chosen: to loose the chains of injustice and untie the cords of the yoke, to set the oppressed free and break every yoke? Is it not to share your food with the hungry and to provide the poor wanderer with shelter — when you see the naked, to clothe him, and not to turn away from your own flesh and blood?" (Isa. 58:6-7).

Even before the birth of Jesus of Nazareth, Zechariah prophetically declared in his song that Jesus is the compassion of God (Luke 1:78). Our hope lies in the "transformation of humanity by the supremely compassionate act of God in the incarnation."[16] The Incarnation exhibits compassion precisely because of the kenosis freely chosen by Christ in his embrace of humanity in its vulnerability, oppression, and suffering. Simultaneously, in the emptied and humbled Christ, we become acquainted with God's true divinity, according to *Compassion,* a book authored by Henri Nouwen, Donald McNeill, and Douglas Morrison.[17] Further, at the outset of his ministry, Jesus describes himself as being on the side of those crushed by various forms of oppression (Luke 4:18-19). Consistent with this declaration, Jesus becomes well-known for his compassionate acts of healing.[18] These acts of healing are extended to children as well as adults, to the oppressed as well as the affluent. Jesus heals not only the son of a royal official and the daughter of an established synagogue ruler, but also the daughter of an alien, the Syro-Phoenician woman. However, authors Nouwen, McNeill, and Morrison draw our attention beyond Jesus' numerous miraculous acts of healing to the compassion that moved Jesus to perform these acts. While our compassion will ultimately be manifested in concrete practices, Nouwen and his colleagues persuade us of the importance of a compassionate way of life.

How are we so formed for a compassionate way of life, especially in light of the self-obsessed tendencies of our contemporary culture? In his book titled *Compassionate Ministry,* Bryan Stone suggests that we are

16. Davies, *A Theology of Compassion,* pp. 248-49.

17. Henri Nouwen, Donald McNeill, and Douglas Morrison, *Compassion: A Reflection on the Christian Life* (New York: Doubleday, 1982), p. 26.

18. Nouwen, McNeill, and Morrison, *Compassion,* p. 14.

created in God's image for freedom, community, and creativity.[19] While these three things permeate the breadth of our different forms of service to Christ, they are particularly relevant for the praxis of compassionate ministry to dying children. First, God's gift of freedom situates us to engage in compassionate ministry in God's kingdom, which certainly includes the bedside of the dying child. Stone describes the gift and its meaning this way:

> Here then is the central proclamation of the kingdom which Jesus announces. Freedom from ourselves – from apathy, fear, anxiety, and self-reliance – is freedom for creatively loving others, understood as the historical project of the kingdom of God.[20]

Freedom, then, is a gift in that it liberates us for servanthood. The fear of joining the suffering of another and thus becoming vulnerable ourselves is replaced by the joy of self-denial as the suffering child and family receive comfort. Our freedom, however, is always in tension with our obligation to use our liberation to unfetter rather than to enslave others.

The relational nature of God the Father and Mother, demonstrated through active engagement with the Son and the Holy Spirit, the other persons of the Godhead, carries tremendous implications for our development for and through the community of believers. Our corporate life together is enabled by God's care and sustenance, by Eucharistic fellowship, and by daily, concrete practices of love. Out of fellowship, we are alienated, blind to our brokenness, and numb to the pain of another. Whereas individualism dehumanizes us, compassionate ministry (first practiced in devotional and corporate life, then shared with the world) re-humanizes us.[21]

God's endowment of creativity affords us endless opportunities for imagining and embodying new ways of practicing compassion with those who have traditionally fallen outside the purview of the church's ministries, such as children at the end of life and their families. In this way, we view dying children and their families as the recipients of compassionate ministry. The same creativity also permits us to integrate

19. Bryan Stone, *Compassionate Ministry: Theological Foundations* (Maryknoll, N.Y.: Orbis Books, 1996), p. 18.

20. Stone, *Compassionate Ministry*, p. 75.

21. Stone, *Compassionate Ministry*, pp. 84-96.

new voices, such as those of the dying and bereaved, into imaginative dialogue about what experientially characterizes the practices of compassionate ministry. Through the encouragement of their voices, dying children and their families become the expert architects of compassionate ministry done effectively.

Given the deeply compassionate nature of God, how does the *imago Dei* figure into our understanding of our formation for compassionate care? Because God is compassionate, we, too, are called to be compassionate. Stone distinguishes between knowing about God and knowing God; the latter implies intimacy:

> All personal knowledge entails implications for more objective knowledge, that is, for the way we understand the world. . . . The kind and quality of our personal relations are bound in some degree to influence the way that we understand and experience the world in which we live. . . . It is inevitable therefore that our personal knowledge of Jesus Christ will have profound implications for our knowledge and understanding of the world, of which, according to faith, he is the centre.[22]

Knowing God is undoubtedly a function of the degree to which we embrace the spiritual disciplines practiced by the Christian community for centuries. Yet we often underestimate the degree to which knowing God reflects the process of yielding our lives to God's mysterious unfolding, particularly when our circumstances do not correspond to our finite expectations. Intimacy with God intensifies as we begin to grasp our identity as new creations in Christ. As such, we draw close to others in new ways:

> In compassion the self experiences the other primordially, not as "second subject" whose experiences are to be exploited for our own pleasures ("sharing another's joys") but as another who suffers and whose sufferings – against any perceivable self-interest or motivation of the self – become not our own, since they are always recognized as being the suffering of another, but become the cause of our action as if they were our own.[23]

22. Stone, *Compassionate Ministry,* p. 228.

23. Davies, *A Theology of Compassion,* p. xix.

The experience of sharing suffering is not about a distorted sense of self-sacrifice or legalism. For Nouwen and his colleagues, it is about listening for God, accepting God's invitation into compassionate ministry, and obeying God's leading. We are sustained by God's care in the midst of suffering, and we trust God that compassionate ministry does not end in suffering itself, but in the glory that we share with Christ. I believe that this glory is not solely limited to an eschatological hope realized in the return of Christ; God also graciously allows us to experience this glory daily through freedom, community, and creativity. God's graciousness to us lays bare the heart of compassion:

> Here we see what compassion means. It is not a bending toward the underprivileged from a privileged position; it is not a reaching out from on high to those who are less fortunate below; it is not a gesture of sympathy or pity for those who fail to make it in the upward pull. On the contrary, compassion means going directly to those people and places where suffering is most acute and building a home there.[24]

Not only are we sustained by God's care in the midst of suffering, but we are sustained by each other as members of Christ's body. Restorative practices of faith communities have been so implicit in compassionate ministry that they seem on the verge of extinction. Restoration, as an explicit mutual practice, reveals an important means for God's remembering of the community. In Nouwen's conception, compassion is not so much about specific gestures as it is a way of living together.[25] Without that, compassion cannot flourish:

> Without a sense of being sent by a caring community, a compassionate life cannot last long and quickly degenerates into a life marked by numbness and anger. This is not simply a psychological observation, but a theological truth, because apart from a vital relationship with a caring community a vital relationship with Christ is not possible.[26]

Although some of our care will take the form of individual exchanges with dying children, we should not understand this work as separate

24. Nouwen, McNeill, and Morrison, *Compassion,* p. 25.
25. Nouwen, McNeill, and Morrison, *Compassion,* p. 47.
26. Nouwen, McNeill, and Morrison, *Compassion,* p. 59.

from broader practices of compassionate ministry that require our ongoing engagement in, reflection on, and intercession for each other's lives.

In reflecting on the nature of compassion, theologian Oliver Davies references philosopher Martha Nussbaum's analysis of compassion. She defines compassion as cognitive in our awareness of another's distress, affective in how we are moved by that distress, and volitional in that we actively seek to remedy it.[27] In fact, Nussbaum describes compassion as the "basic social emotion."[28] Davies further contributes an ontological dimension to compassion, asserting that compassion is always about the relation of the self to the other:

> I shall argue that compassion assumes the self-possession and self-knowing of the subject, without which the subject cannot put itself at risk for another but can only be put at risk by forces alien to itself. If compassion is knowingly to put oneself at risk for the sake of the other, then self-dispossessive virtue is predicated upon a prior state of self-possession. Within this "knowingly," then, we can begin to discern the possibility of a language of being, which can enable the self performatively to articulate its own sense of existing, precisely as a subject who comes to itself in and through the other.[29]

Here, Davies promotes the primacy of the developed self (i.e., the self that possesses and knows itself) in the capacity for demonstrating compassion. He also speaks of the intentionality of compassionate practice. The risk of entering into the suffering of another must be freely chosen. Moreover, compassionate practice depends on the suffering other in the formation of the self. Davies is not suggesting a symbiotic masochism; rather, he is invoking the metaphor of the interdependent body of Christ.

Related to Davies's concept of the developed self, Nouwen introduces the notion of voluntary displacement to describe the process by which we move away from the "ordinary and proper places" toward a deep recognition of our own brokenness and thereby the enhanced capacity to connect with the brokenness of other persons. While physical

27. Davies, *A Theology of Compassion,* p. 18.
28. Davies, *A Theology of Compassion,* p. 239.
29. Davies, *A Theology of Compassion,* p. xx.

(i.e., geographical) displacement has characterized the lives of many saints, Nouwen acknowledges that ". . . for many people [voluntary displacement] does not even mean physical movement, but a new attitude toward their factual displacement and a faithful perseverance in their unspectacular lives."[30]

Rather than choosing the terms of our displacement (even when voluntary), we are drawn to discern what displacement God is already unfolding in our lives, and thus to discern to which compassionate practice(s) God may be drawing us. To revisit Wolterstorff's notion of God's silence, we may be called to interpret God's silence not necessarily as an invitation to develop new program initiatives for dying children, for example, but rather as an occasion upon which to reflect on ways that we have chosen against becoming intimately familiar with the broken lives of dying children we already know in our families, institutions of work, and faith communities.

Compassion as Spiritual Practice

It is the compassionate way of life that naturally leads to compassionate practices. The apostle Paul suggests in his Second Epistle to the Church at Corinth that the very nature of the God who created and called us has implications for the nature of our service to our brothers and sisters:

> Praise be to the God and Father of our Lord Jesus Christ, the Father of compassion and the God of all comfort, who comforts us in all our troubles, so that we can comfort those in any trouble with the comfort we ourselves have received from God. For just as the sufferings of Christ flow over into our lives, so also through Christ our comfort overflows. (2 Cor. 1:3-5)

More specifically, close examination of the quality of the comfort we have received from God will result in the quality of compassion and comfort that we express to the body of Christ, as well as to those "in any trouble." Rather than becoming bankrupt in the character of our

30. Nouwen, in Nouwen, McNeill, and Morrison, *Compassion,* p. 65.

service, we discover a rich reservoir out of which flows the infinite compassion of God, by God's people, for God's people. However, this fluid process is not automatic; on the contrary, it requires intentionality, commitment, and the disciplined life.

Given that we are made in the image of God, I suggest that practicing the art of compassion is a grace, a privilege of being God's creatures. Certainly, compassionate practices are enhanced through our Christian formation, but the building blocks of our capacity for compassion are a part of our givenness. What, then, does it look like to practice compassion in contemporary life? First, I assert that loving God, loving our neighbors, and loving ourselves are symbiotic processes. Nonetheless, an argument for loving ourselves may seem to many a radical proposal. But it does indeed apply. In the interplay between person and community there is a need for a focus on what Richard Foster terms the "inward disciplines," those spiritual practices that are developed as we are alone with God. Graceful practice of the inward disciplines of meditation, prayer, fasting, and study supports the expression of the outward and corporate disciplines, including compassionate presence.

Compassionate practices are particularly needed in palliative and end-of-life care, where the amelioration or relief of suffering is a primary goal. Hospitalized children fare best when medical and other care settings adapt the physical environment, routines, and programs to age-appropriate standards, while promoting opportunities for play, education, and other typical activities of childhood.[31] With regard to child patients whose lives and environments appear dominated by health-care professionals, persons primarily in the role of faith-community representatives often wonder whether they can share any particular or unique contribution. Inasmuch as informal caregivers are able to embrace their own alienation in these systems, their internalization of children's suffering deepens. For all types of caregivers, I offer hospitality, presence, and listening as three compassionate practices that serve dying children and their families in tangible ways.

31. Field and Behrman, *When Children Die,* p. 67.

Tangible Practices of Compassion: Hospitality, Presence, and Listening

Practicing the art of compassion necessarily suggests the extension of hospitality to the suffering. In ancient times, hospitality was extended to the stranger or alien in need of food, lodging, clothing, protection, and inclusion in religious celebrations.[32] I have suggested earlier that dying children suffer from alienation at several levels, reveal multiple needs, and often desire inclusion. It follows, then, that dying children are in desperate need of hospitality. Much like Christ, who is indeed its source, vital hospitality meets the alien at his point of need. The story of the Good Samaritan (Luke 10:25-37) exemplifies the provision of multiple needs, including bodily care, transportation, lodging, and the arrangement for continuing care. Surely it was the synergistic interactions of all of these gifts that promoted the healing of the suffering victim.

In addition to these concrete gifts of hospitality, the provision of presence is perhaps a less tangible but still profoundly meaningful element of compassionate practice. Presence is a giving of both time and space. Time, that most precious commodity, is perceived as perhaps one of the greatest sacrifices in our presence with those who suffer. The very act of being fully present radically subverts the consumerist ordering of our activities toward productivity, efficiency, and acquisition. By choosing to share space with children experiencing pain and suffering, we are rejecting the potential for other more immediate, tangible rewards. Our presence reminds the suffering that they are indeed made in the image of God, validates their worth, enhances their sense of dignity, and militates against the alienation experienced all too often by the suffering and others at the margins of our human existence.

Given overloaded schedules and overwhelming institutional demands, health-care providers in particular may be judged, rightly or wrongly, to demonstrate a diminished capacity for presence. However, genuine presence can begin with gestures as simple as greeting other persons in the patient's room with eye contact and verbal acknowledgment. Beyond this initial joining with the child and family, health-care

32. Walter A. Elwell, entry for "Hospitality," in *Evangelical Dictionary of Theology*, ed. Walter A. Elwell (Grand Rapids: Baker Publishing Group, 1996).

providers can faithfully express presence through an engaged and attentive attitude toward the whole experience of the patient and family.

Perhaps the most important by-product of our presence with suffering children is learning to suspend our results-oriented strategies. To be sure, there are a number of results that we prefer to accomplish with a wide range of suffering children: effective medical procedures; the remission of life-threatening illness; enhanced pain and symptom management (e.g., the effectiveness of opioid analgesics); the healing of family rifts; and the redress of the socio-economic conditions that may have contributed to the suffering at its inception. In fact, Nicholas Wolterstorff posits that part of our divine inheritance dictates that "whenever and wherever we spot an opening, we shall join the divine battle against all that goes awry with reference to God's intent [that we live full of years, and that during those years we flourish]. We shall join God in doing battle against all that causes early death and all that leads to unredemptive suffering: disease, injustice, warfare, torture, enmity."[33]

That is precisely why thoroughgoing practices of compassionate care require our presence at the depths of our being. Perhaps it is not sufficiently healing to merely be present in body. Our souls can be quite perceptive of when another is truly engaged and invested in us. Psychological absence can often be more meaningful and more painful than physical absence. Thus practices of compassion require both physical and psychological presence. To risk overstating the obvious, we are most present when we are focused in the present. Rather than tending to personal or environmental distractions, we can offer our self-decentered attention to suffering children and their family members, which allows the provision of a third practice of compassion: listening.

While effective communication with dying children and their families is a crucial aspect of coordinating and implementing the most compassionate care, it is in fact a challenging task, particularly in medical settings where the sheer number of interactions between patients, loved ones, and caring professionals can complicate attempts at dialogue. Even where systems of communication have been carefully developed, health-care providers often emphasize the presentation of information to consumers. This style of communication can provide a false sense of complacency because it masks two erroneous assumptions.

33. Wolterstorff, "The Silence of the God Who Speaks," pp. 227-28.

The first erroneous assumption is that helping children and their families to access and examine more information about their conditions is equal to, or even superior to, knowing those persons who provide care. Just as knowing about God is not the same as knowing God, knowing about one's illness is not the same as knowing those to whom one has entrusted one's life. The second erroneous assumption is that the flow of communication is unidirectional, from the caregiver to the patient, particularly among young patients. But the opposite is true. Verbal as well as nonverbal communication flows in both directions.

Listening is challenging precisely because of the extent of self-dispossession that it requires. Listening draws our attention to another's concrete experience of brokenness, challenges us to confront our own places of brokenness, validates the dignity of the other, and permits us to embody the compassion of God as we absorb the suffering of the other. We are paying attention to the content of the conversation, but we are also attending to the process of the conversation. For example, we notice the presence or absence of religious or spiritual language. We listen for repetition, and we listen for that which remains unspoken. Nouwen observes, "The simple experience of being valuable and important to someone else has a tremendous recreative power."[34] It is a relief for a dying child to learn (again) that she is precious to a member of the human family; it is a gift for that child to learn that she is precious to God.

Dying children are but one group of persons needing compassionate care. Their parents, siblings, and extended families will likely benefit greatly from bereavement support, sometimes for a significant period of months or even years after the children's death. Children with chronic illnesses and children whose emotional suffering puts them at higher risk for early death are others awaiting attention from family members, health-care providers — and yes, the church. As hospitable, present, and listening persons, we invite reflection rather than deliver glib reassurances. Beyond the bedside, compassionate care occurs in the pew, at the table, on the playground, and in virtually all other places of human activity. Bereaved family members and friends deeply desire opportunities to keep alive the memories of their deceased loved ones.

34. Nouwen, in Nouwen, McNeill, and Morrison, *Compassion,* p. 80.

As the church, it is crucial that our ecclesial, administrative, and academic leaders acknowledge these barriers to care, reflect on the manifestation of these barriers in their specific locales, and give direction to clergy and laypersons alike in these practices. Bryan Stone observes that compassion is not only recognizing and sharing suffering, but also working toward liberation from that suffering.[35]

Compassionate ministry can and should at times take the form of one-to-one care, yet it finds its fullness in the role of advocacy – what Stone terms the "liberation community." Rather than simply gathering information, we empower dying children and their families to voice their lament, and in so doing to participate more actively in their own forms of healing. Stone's concept includes notions of mutuality and participation in the life of Christ, as well as dimensions of social, political, and spiritual transformation.[36]

In end-of-life care for children and their troubled families, compassionate ministry involves for the caregiver an explicit awareness of God's image in every creature, self-dispossession, voluntary displacement, steady movement toward the disciplined life, and a willingness to tangibly practice hospitality, presence, and listening. These are the signposts on the journey toward God's freedom, community, and creativity for God's creatures. Best of all, they show us the path to love.

35. Stone, *Compassionate Ministry,* p. 59.

36. Stone, *Compassionate Ministry,* p. 83.

PRACTICES OF HEALING AND HOPE

CHAPTER 8

Healing in the Midst of Dying: A Collaborative Approach to End-of-Life Care

Abigail Rian Evans

> *It is not only that death means the loss of relationships as we have known them, or that death threatens the meaning of life itself for many dying people. But such distress is magnified when care of those facing death takes place in medical settings where the sorrow and meaning of parting receives secondary attention, where the demands of technology and even bureaucracy are priorities. Care for the human spirit is still too often an afterthought in the medical environment.*[1]

These words ring true for many people's experience of dying in America. We have lost the art of dying well because we have allowed our deaths to be orchestrated by the medical profession. Even the advent of advance directives, which were to return control to the patient, have further exacerbated the medicalization of death by adding a series of treatment choices.

Forms such as the "Five Wishes" have introduced values and palliative-care options to living wills that have at least broadened the conversation about choices. Hospice care has also helped to humanize the dying process with pain management, spiritual care, an aesthetically pleasing environment, and caring staff. For hospice, the goal is quality of life, not length of life.

1. David McCurdy, "A Sweeter Sorrow," *Park Ridge Center Bulletin*, May-June 2001.

Unless otherwise indicated, all of the quotations from Scripture in this chapter are taken from the New Revised Standard Version of the Holy Bible.

The medicalization of death was not always the case. Historically, death was overseen by clergy, not doctors, as the early doctors were priests. Faith communities founded and sponsored hospitals, and nursing and medicine were perceived as religious callings. During the Renaissance and Reformation, with the split of science and religion, medicine and theology went their separate ways.[2] With the founding of Clinical Pastoral Education (CPE) by A. T. Boisin in the 1940s and its expansion under S. Hiltner, there developed a subspecialty of hospital chaplains who had clinical training.

Chaplains provide clinically oriented pastoral care in the medical center, integrating particular theory and techniques regarding the place of religion in health care with a commitment to the spiritual well-being of patients, their families, and staff. In many settings this has provided clergy a place on the modern medical-care team. However, this has resulted in parish pastors and rabbis relegating the care of the dying to these professionals.

According to a recent assessment by the American Medical Association's Institute for Ethics, clergy are not much better prepared than any other Americans to support the chronically or acutely ill through death and dying. The 1997 Gallup survey "Spiritual Beliefs and the Dying Process" illustrated American dissatisfaction with dying in America. What people want is to die at home among close family and friends, with recognition of the deeper spiritual dimensions of dying and assurance that their families will not be overburdened with their care or neglected in their loss. The survey findings suggest that people do not trust professional caregivers with spiritual care and support in their dying days. Only 36 percent of respondents saw the clergy providing broad spiritual support in their own dying days. Fewer than 30 percent would look to physicians for spiritual comfort; 21 percent would desire this from nurses.

Renewed Interest in Spirituality and Church Life

In spite of the dissatisfaction with clergy, people may be turning to God and the church in these uncertain times, looking for a sense of

2. Edwin R. DuBose, "Preparing for Death," *Park Ridge Center Bulletin,* May-June 2001, pp. 3-4.

meaning and purpose. The church is more than a place of religious rites; it tries to address those eternal questions that go to the core of our being. In uncertain times we turn to religious symbols that will give us hope and inspiration to carry on – a place to struggle with the theodicy questions of suffering and a God of love. We want a community that witnesses to the power of God's love even in the midst of hardship and suffering. In recent years the church has been a rallying place during crises such as 9/11, the southeast Asia tsunami, and Hurricane Katrina. The church has provided not only comfort but also concrete help.

Even those who do not participate in a faith community look to spiritual resources to face their own dying and that of their loved ones. For the last fifteen years, research has increased on the potential effects of religion and spirituality in treatment interventions and outcomes, including the effects of spirituality on end-of-life care. David Larson, Dale Matthews, Harold Koenig, Keith Meador, and others have led this movement. Strengthening this interest have been the palliative care movement – with its stress on physical, emotional, social, and spiritual support during dying – and the Joint Commission on Accreditation of Healthcare Organizations, with its standard on a patient's right to spiritual care.[3]

However, the type of spiritual care offered in a pluralistic, multicultural setting is often watered down to the lowest common denominator. Severed from religion, it is often devoid of content. There is a danger in routinized spiritual care, where we seem to "domesticate the spirit" or make spirituality an instrumental value that would put us in touch with the transcendent. We need ways to assess spiritual needs and even spiritual illness. In addition, legitimate questions are raised about standards for spiritual care. What are the best practices? Should spiritual caregivers be credentialed? Can we assume that general theological education and ordination are sufficient? What type of spiritual care is wanted and needed? How can we begin care before the last days of a person's life?

If we turn to spiritual care as the answer to the medicalization of death, we need rigor and clarity as to its content and use. I believe the answer lies not in generally introducing spiritual care into end-of-life

3. DuBose, "Preparing for Death," pp. 3-4.

treatment, but in developing and implementing a collaborative model of end-of-life care, where all health-care professionals plus the patient/person are involved. The following is an exposition of this model.

The Collaboration of Healers

We need a new collaborative model for health-care professionals in the care of the sick or sorrowing patient and her family. In particular, their complementary responsibilities are important, and their mutual interest is in the patient/person's well-being. True cooperation among religion, medicine, and nursing depends upon mutual respect. It also requires recognition that caring and curing are both parts of a response to the patient, who should be an active participant in her own care and decisions about it. Specific roles for each person are important as well as where and how they can collaborate in end-of-life care.

Since we turn to many persons as we face dying and our own death, it is desirable to incorporate the roles of the pastor, the physician, and the nurse as co-equals and collaborators. Since the 1980s, the new subspecialty of parish nursing has provided innovative models of cooperation among these healers. Historically, cooperation between the pastor and the physician was often inhibited by the pastor's belief that sickness originated from sin and the doctor's fear of what this belief would do to the patient. Furthermore, when the sacrament of healing became extreme unction after the eighth or ninth century, the very appearance of the priest might appear to hasten death, since the patient anticipated the last rites. (Since Vatican II, there has been a return to the sacrament's original nomenclature: the sacrament of healing.) This was compounded by the heresy that God sends disease, so it is a cross to be borne. This erroneous doctrine of vicarious suffering, as Evelyn Frost names it, is the wolf in sheep's clothing. So the sufferer is pointed to the pains of the cross instead of the joys of the resurrection.[4] The Incarnation, not the cross, should form the essential character of Christian life.

Recently we have physicians such as Edmund Pellegrino who acknowledge that religion enriches medicine by more fully recovering the sources of medicine's morality and by enhancing medicine's healing re-

4. Evelyn Frost, *Christian Healing* (London: Mowbray, 1954), p. 187.

lationship with those it seeks to serve.[5] Especially in the area of medical ethics, religion provides its grounding in three ways: (1) it provides an ultimate justification for morality; (2) it provides an integral humanism that is the benchmark for judging competing moral concepts; and (3) it provides a call to sublime sacrifice that surpasses what philosophers would think "reasonable."[6]

Religion is a needed source of healing if medicine is to mobilize every resource on the patient's behalf. Using the religious resources of healing is crucial to the physician's covenant to help the patient become "whole" again. These resources are especially needed in the case of serious illness, where, Pellegrino says, "we must reassemble our whole life and repair our whole humanity." These needs can be partially met by medication, surgery, compassion, and caring. Pellegrino observes, "Acknowledgment of God as the source of healing is a needed antidote to the hubris that is so seductive to contemporary medicine."[7] And he adds, "There is in every serious illness an encounter with the question of God."[8] Besides assisting the physician, religion may offer the believer the only satisfactory meaning for his illness, suffering, and death. Religion, of course, is embodied by the pastor/priest as medicine is by the doctor. The roles and relationships of physicians and clergy are important to examine. (The nurse, of course, is key, but there is not space to develop this relationship here.)

Both physicians and ministers, starting from different ends of the spectrum, confront wounded humanity. Physicians start with the anatomical, physiological, and diagnostic. Ministers begin with the need for reconciliation, the need to deal with guilt, the meaning of illness, and the person's spiritual destiny. Pastors are involved in the healing of spirit, soul, and psyche. "The minister," says Pellegrino, "is the indispensable mediator with the transcendent power outside man, with whom reconciliation must be effected."[9] The physician works with ma-

5. Edmund Pellegrino, "Religion and Sources of Medical Morality and Healing," *New York State Journal of Medicine,* December 1981, p. 1859.

6. Pellegrino, "Religion and Sources of Medical Morality and Healing," p. 1862.

7. Pellegrino, "Religion and Sources of Medical Morality and Healing," p. 1863.

8. Edmund Pellegrino, "Beyond Bioethics: The Christian Obligations of Christian Physicians," lecture presented at Marquette University, Milwaukee, Wisconsin, March 1981, p. 6.

9. Pellegrino, "Religion and Sources of Medical Morality and Healing."

nipulation, drugs, or reassurance; the minister works with prayer, sacraments, pastoral care, and the preaching of the Word. Both use touch, words of reassurance, and their own presence summoned by the patient's need. Their functions may overlap in the personal, social, and psychological areas of the patient's life. The physician and the pastor may contact the patient at the same point.

Often the pastor's initial visit is in response to a physical problem that may have spiritual dimensions. In some pastoral visits, "spiritual" questions are never discussed. Of course, in the daily work of a pastor there may be endless visits where no disease is present, but a need for reconciliation or forgiveness is the occasion for the call. However, the sick person's physical condition summons both pastor and physician to his presence.

The basis for cooperation between pastor and physician is that both are agents of God, who is the source of all healing. Their respective disciplines both provide health and healing. Until quite recently, a faith/science dichotomy and a mind/body dualism marked our age, which made physician/pastor cooperation difficult. Now, however, physicians live in a post-Newtonian era, accepting a more integrated approach to health care, and pastors are learning how to translate spiritual resources into meaningful language and hard data.

The common meeting ground of medicine and theology is the service and love of humankind. To love means to conform one's actions to the concrete needs of one's neighbor. More specifically, the aim of both medicine and theology is to understand more clearly the reason for human suffering and to seek ways to relieve it. As medicine is called upon to sustain life, theology can assist in exploring the meaning of life as well as avenues for spiritual healing. Physicians can give the diagnosis, which pastors are not equipped to do. Pastors can give the support of a caring community to sustain and to help in healing. Especially when no cure is possible, pastors can reduce suffering, relieve anxiety, and give inner peace during times of stress.

When the physician can do no more to heal the ill person, the task of caring for the patient is not over. The patient constantly struggles to adapt. She must not only bear life, but also grow in the face of personal problems. When confronting suffering, the pastor and the physician acutely need each other's support. They are dealing not with a disembodied illness, but a suffering person. Both the doctor, who is faced with an incurable illness despite all efforts at healing, and the pastor, who earnestly prays for healing, are equally in need of God's grace.

In the moments of crisis and failure, the pastor may have a special responsibility to sustain the physician. These occasions may range from frequently affirming the importance of the doctor's calling to wrestling over an ethical dilemma (for example, when a doctor's colleague performs an incorrect procedure in the operating room, does she report him if he will subsequently lose his license?). They may include assisting doctors in their constant confrontation with old age, disease, and death, or comforting the doctor whose patient died when his knowledge was insufficient or he had not done everything possible to save the patient. The pastor needs an enlightened and sensitive concern for these various issues facing the physician. Of course, caring may also be a concern of the physician.

Like other adversities such as war, injustice, and poverty, disease confronts the individual and the community with a call from God to respond to it. It is precisely at the point of crisis and human suffering that the pastor and the physician intersect in responding to the patient's needs. Together these professionals should help the patient to be involved in his own health care. The pastor may lay open the needs of the patient and provide the impetus for him to seek medical treatment, or the physician may be alerted to spiritual questions that are best handled by the pastor. Practically speaking, this entails consultation between the professionals, probably at the initiative of the pastor.

In the relationship between the physician and the pastor, one has a choice between assigning each a separate sphere of healing or developing a collaborative model. In the former model, the pastor would deal with the spiritual and mental problems – the soul, not the body. The physician would care for the body and the mind as it affected the body. In this paradigm the intersection of the clergy and the doctor would be in the area of mental health and counseling. This model perpetuates a division between mind/body/spirit and forces doctors to be body mechanics. If the overlap between these professionals is only at the center, as Pellegrino expressed it, then what happens at the fringes? Pastors are not simply to sustain patients in the midst of illness or provide a comforting exit from life, but also to help them to return to health.

Pastor and Parish-Nurse Collaboration

Historically the nurse has often been the health-care professional who bridged the gap between the physician and the pastor through her holistic care and intense interaction with the patient. (Of course, this has shifted as nurses have taken on more administrative tasks, and "nurse extenders" provide more of the bedside care.) The parish nurse has provided a new model for bridge-building between the pastor/priest and the physician – between religion and medicine.

A parish nurse is a registered or licensed nurse who generally works on the staff of a local church or a hospital relating to a congregation. It is one of the fastest-growing nursing specialties, and now provides a model for pastor/nurse collaboration. It is crucial for a parish nurse (or faith community nurse, as it is now called) to be part of the church staff in order to give her credibility with the congregation. Committees may come and go, but a staff member is regarded more seriously. A parish nurse knows she's being taken seriously when her name is listed under the names of the pastor and the deacons in the church bulletin and on the church letterhead.

In some instances a parish nurse meets with the pastor on a weekly basis, especially to discuss whom they have visited, and attends staff meetings and retreats. Together they decide on the course of action, working as a team to try to bring a person to a healthier place in life, both spiritually and physically. If the parish nurse sees a patient she thinks is in need of deeper spiritual direction than she is equipped to provide, she alerts the pastor; if after a home visit the pastor is concerned that a person is not receiving proper care or has a physical ailment, the pastor can call the situation to the attention of the parish nurse.

The pastor can offer the parish nurse perspective on what it means to heal, curbing the nurse's desire to cure and helping her negotiate thorny theodicy questions. When the physician can do no more to heal the ill, the task of caring for patients is not over. As patients struggle to adapt to their limitations and pain, the parish nurse and the pastor are there to assist in that adaptation. In the face of suffering, all healers need one another's support. The doctor who pronounces the illness to be incurable, the patient who must adjust to the news, the parish nurse who cares, and the pastor who prays for healing work together for the patient's good.

The key element that separates the parish nurse from other public health or community health educators may be her freedom within the religious community to emphasize and enhance the spiritual dimensions of health. At this point the cooperation between the parish nurse and the pastor is most fruitful. However, one problem of the parish nurse movement is that even after almost twenty years, most parish nurses work as volunteers. So the question is whether this subspecialty will continue to grow and flourish since the establishment of standards of practice by the American Nurses Association (ANA) in 1998.

The Role of the Patient as Healer

Having made a few preliminary remarks about the collaborative approach to healing, I want to focus now on two healers – the patient and the pastor. Perhaps, in the face of death, the role of the patient as healer may seem odd, but I would argue that it is still very important.

The focus on the patient as person, to borrow a phrase from Paul Ramsey, should always be central. The physician is to enhance the agency, knowledge, and comfort of the patient, assisted by the nurse, pastors, family, friends, and other healers. Of course, this is not always the case. There are two possible responses by a physician to the patient's weakened state: (1) to take control of decision-making for the patient; and (2) to abdicate any responsibility, pretending that the patient is the same as a well person. Neither option is appropriate.

Knowledge alone cannot bridge the basic inequality between the physician and the patient. This inequality stems primarily from the patient's dependency that, for physician Eric Cassell, is a necessary state of illness. This dependency creates a willingness to receive what is important for the patient/physician relationship. While the patient is needy, the physician appears omnipotent. Of course, some patients prefer this type of relationship, but it should be their choice and not assumed.

In spite of this reality, I would argue that there exists a threefold theological basis for the patient as healer: (1) the dignity and worth of each person as a locus of value that illness cannot alter; (2) the responsibility of each person to be a steward of creation, including oneself; and (3) the reality that healing is more than physical cure so that the patient may participate in bringing spiritual and emotional healing even in the midst of dying.

The centrality of the patient as healer is not arbitrarily asserted, but theologically grounded in the dignity and equality of all persons. This worth depends not upon the degree of knowledge or expertise of the individual, but upon her inherent value as a child of God. Furthermore, the patient should be viewed as a moral agent with ethical responsibilities. Truth-telling and confidentiality are not injunctions only to the doctor.

Although one must readily acknowledge that illness may create a partial impotence to exercise the functions of personhood, it does not necessarily create an impotence to be a person. An individual's value is not contingent upon health even in the last stages of dying. "Hence it seems to be a fundamental demand of the ethics of the sickbed that the sick person should not cease to let himself be addressed and to address himself, in terms of health, and the will which it requires rather than sickness, and above all to see to it that he is in an environment of health."[10]

First, viewing the patient not as broken or diseased, but as a precious individual, mandates contesting disease and fighting sickness as the intrusion of death into the stream of life.[11] Furthermore, this view recognizes that a person is not just a body, but has a spiritual side to his or her nature.

Second, this theological view reinforces the involvement of the patient as possible in all levels of decision-making. How would this model function with the incompetent, the seriously ill, or the comatose patient? It is precisely in interpreting the patient's wishes that this becomes the guide for surrogate decision-makers, not my wishes but the patient's wishes. Advance directives enable the patient, while able, to express his or her desires. Patients may choose to hand their responsibility back to the health-care professionals, to family, or to friends, but by doing so are still exercising their agency.

It is evident that an individual patient's ability to be a healer is determined to a large degree by the kind of person she is. A person who has faced other crises courageously may react more optimistically to cancer than someone who has failed repeatedly in other challenges. Ear-

10. Karl Barth, *Church Dogmatics: The Doctrine of Creation, III/4* (London: T&T Clark, 1961), p. 358.

11. Barth, *Church Dogmatics: The Doctrine of Creation, III/4*, pp. 363, 367.

lier success, however, does not guarantee victory. When illness no longer permits one to perform the past roles of mother or corporate president, a special kind of suffering results from the loss of personal identity. This suffering may produce a sense of hopelessness. It is precisely at this point that vibrant faith in God may sustain hope, whether it be of immediate cure or ultimate victory in eternity, and that the nurse, chaplain, family, and friends may become the symbols of hope and healing.

The sick role can be rejected or embraced. For example, Miriam Siegler and Humphry Osmond describe the case of a middle-aged doctor who had an acute coronary heart attack and would not acknowledge his condition and stop working; hence he died twenty hours later. On the other hand, a seventeen-year-old with a brain tumor thought if he was "good" and followed all the doctor's instructions, he would be healed; he also died.[12] Acknowledging the sick role may be important for entering treatment, but it may also raise false expectations regarding recovery or encourage a degree of passivity.

The human spirit may help a patient develop the will to be well — an important step toward healing. On the other hand, if someone is starved for attention, illness may be the best vehicle for obtaining it. Then again, there may be some sickness that is the person's fault. Medically speaking, if a person has a wound, he has to admit he has a wound; then the doctor has to open it up and remove all foreign particles so that it can heal. This same principle is at work in mental and spiritual healing, which may need to precede physical healing.

Faith, of course, can affect a patient in a variety of ways. Choices in treatment will be influenced by one's value system, and recovery may be linked to one's personal faith. Studies at Johns Hopkins Medical Center illustrate that the faith factor is significant in a patient's recovery from a wide variety of illnesses.[13] It appears that the faith itself rather than the object of the faith is of primary importance.

The first element of faith is expectancy. The use of placebos with patients has shown that expectancy of improvement may actually produce improvement. Suggestion is another powerful force. Personality

12. Miriam Siegler and Humphry Osmond, *Models of Madness, Models of Medicine* (New York: Macmillan, 1974), p. 23.

13. Edgar Jackson, *The Role of Faith in the Process of Healing* (London: SCM Press, 1981), p. 23.

type is also a factor. Usually the religious person has a mood of expectancy, is more open to suggestion, is hopeful, and is able to relate himself to others in a life-modifying relationship.[14]

Cultivating a sense of hope about oneself and the course of one's illness is central to recovery. Hopelessness creates a sense of futility. Regaining hope is central in a patient's becoming a healer – it involves a balance between giving the person emotional support to prevent self-destruction and encouraging the person to accept responsibility for his situation. Hope becomes grounded in a realistic appraisal of life. However, being hopeful is no guarantee of physical recovery.

Coupled with this perspective is the patient's teaching responsibility to the doctor. Edmund Pellegrino and Eric Cassell discuss this responsibility in relation to selecting and evaluating proper treatment for a patient. The doctor does not give one well-being/well-working; one needs to achieve it as a result of active responsibility.

Indeed, Cassell clearly delineates that the course of an illness is influenced by its host, so diagnosis and treatment are tied to knowledge of and from the patient. The patient is a teacher in that he assists other healers by giving clear and accurate information. The subjective data from the patient about his illness are as important as the scientific information about the patient's disease.[15] Michael Balint underscores this point in his landmark book *The Doctor, the Patient, and Illness,* a work that for decades was the basic text for British medical students. Here he substantiates, by a study of various cases analyzed by a group of doctors, the importance of the patient's assistance in arriving at an accurate diagnosis. As he expresses it, the physician should "release the doctor that is within the patient."[16] This is not just about the patient's recital of symptoms and an accurate case history, but includes both the importance of sharing perceptions about the course of one's disease and one's responsibility in enabling healing.

The active role of the patient is an important factor in explaining why healing occurs in some cases and not in others, but it certainly is not the only factor. As the patient teaches, she also becomes a healer.

14. Jackson, *The Role of Faith in the Process of Healing,* p. 29.

15. Eric Cassell, *The Healer's Art* (New York: Penguin Books, 1979).

16. Michael Balint, *The Doctor, the Patient, and Illness* (London: International University Press, 1957).

These two roles of teacher and healer merge when a patient participates in decisions about her treatment.

The patient is also a healer even in the midst of dying when recognizing the importance of spiritual and emotional healing. The patient may work to this end even as the body is wasting away, as Paul explains in 2 Corinthians 4:16: "So we do not lose heart. Even though our outer nature is wasting away, our inner nature is being renewed day by day."

In conclusion, the patient is the central but not the primary healer. The patient is central because she initiates the relationship and enlists other healers. However, once involved in a relationship with professional healers, the patient does not serve as the primary healer. She relies on the expertise and knowledge of the professionals. Hence the role of the patient as healer is fluid, but the patient should be actively involved as long as possible. Hopefully, this framework assures that the patient's best interests are being served and grounds the centrality of the patient.

The Role of the Pastor/Chaplain

Grave illness separates us from all that is familiar and draws us closer to the God who calls us into being and back to God's full presence at the end of our lives. Words of God's continual love and care for us in the midst of dying need to be declared. Outlining some specific roles and forms of ministry of the pastor/chaplain in end-of-life care may help to differentiate this role from that of other health-care professionals. We might even refer to these as the healing means available to clergy as medicine and surgery are available to the physician. As the pastor uses these forms of ministry to the sick and dying, healing will be enhanced in the fullest sense of the word.

Be a Caring Presence

The pastor's caring presence is based on mutuality. Compassion moves us toward companionship, which is another type of assistance. The root of companionship is the recognition of our mutual need. We are bound together by our mutual brokenness, our common need. Companionship springs from fraternalism, not paternalism.

Paul defined interrelatedness in Galatians 6:2: "Bear one another's burdens, and in this way you will fulfill the law of Christ." This passage has a twofold thrust: we must bear one another's burdens, and carry our own loads. So we are responsible for others' problems and health – that is, the weight of their difficulties – but we are also accountable for our own actions. Our companionship is rooted in this twofold injunction: each person has a personal responsibility – an individual accountability – that cannot be shifted over to someone else, but that person can also rely on community concern.

We are interconnected precisely because of our need and shortcomings. Companionship is thus a reflection of how we care. Companionship involves a one-on-one relationship, a covenanting between two people, a presence with, an availability.

Carry the Symbols of Hope and Healing

The pastor conveys the symbols of health and healing, relating to people as persons, not as patients. (One must admit that pastors sometimes label people as sinners to be judged rather than individuals to be helped.) As people face sickness and struggle to regain some wholeness, they are challenged to accept and overcome the undeniable fact of their fragility. Symbols of healing may involve sustenance in the face of pain and suffering – assisting people to live in the midst of their brokenness. The questions emerge: What is the ultimate concern? Where does one stand amid the ambiguities of suffering? What does one believe about health and disease?

There are three possible answers. One is that the ultimate truth lies in despair and disintegration, and all attempts to use positive healing resources are against our basic nature. From this perspective, there is no sense in struggling against disease because treatment is wrong and to be avoided. This may sound stark, but it is the logical outcome of promoting only the negative side of life. One sees it sometimes in patients who refuse therapy.

On the opposite side is the view that although disease is real, the ultimate truth about the relationship between human nature and disease is that one must struggle against it. This is seen in the natural attempts of the human body to reject disease by its development of antibodies, and in the care and concern of the medical, nursing, and allied health professionals. The final possibility is a middle-of-the-road, noncommittal path. Here disease and healing are equally important or unimportant. An attitude of indifference prevails.[17]

Finally, the pastor may help the patient to identify with the symbols of healing, to interpret the symbols, and to cooperate with the physician and the hospital. The fact is that despite our fragility, despite our being severely compromised in the face of illness, in spite of our brokenness, there is hope. Hope has been scientifically proven to contribute significantly to the healing of people not only from mental or spiritual illness, but also from physical illness. This is not a hope built on ephemeral things; it is a hope that is grounded in the living God, a God who is Lord and Creator and Savior.

Incorporate the Patient into a Faith Community

Faith communities are strong places of support and advocacy for those who are dying. The pastor can put the patient in touch with those resources. Congregations can respond effectively to health needs that touch the most sensitive part of people's lives; meeting them constitutes a fundamental part of a congregation's ministry.

Concern, support, and the presence of others are very important in the healing process. The images of the Christian church in 1 Corinthians 12, Romans 12, and Ephesians 4 describe the *ecclesia* in terms of a body with many members, a ministry with many callings, a unified spirit with many gifts. The community both strengthens us and defines us; the pastor is called to make those connections. A person in isolation can languish in loneliness and guilt. The church provides a resource for liberating people from "exaggerated individualism" and the isolation of contemporary life. The church functions as a community of acceptance and reconciliation. It can testify to the love and healing of God, which is available at all times, not just in moments of crisis.

17. Melvyn Thompson, *Cancer and the God of Love* (London: SCM Press, 1976).

The power of forgiveness, communication, and companionship can often prevent, arrest, and alleviate disease.

Certain illnesses and diseases may be labeled as unacceptable or beyond our area of concern. Those struggling with AIDS, drug addiction, mental illness, or certain types of disabilities often are shunned by society. These people, marginalized by virtue of their illness or medical condition, might not receive the top medical treatment – might not, in fact, receive any health care; tragically, they are often ostracized by the church as well. But the church can become the voice for such powerless people as well as provide concrete assistance. Assuring a decent and fair minimum of care for all persons, especially for the underserved and poor, is a crucial need in our society, where there are millions of medically uninsured (45.8 million in 2004)[18] who are put in medical warehouses to die.

Provide Sacramental/Liturgical Resources

Traditionally, one of the most recognized roles of the pastor is as a worship leader and presider over the sacraments. This role is perhaps one of the most powerful ones as a source of healing. Corporate worship often provides the context for the pastor's use of sacraments – liturgical resources for healing. In the words of Paul Tillich, worship happens when people touch the ground of their being. The danger is when we make the transcendent into the commonplace, thereby stripping worship of its most important element – awe. Our response completes the act of worship, and its complete meaning entails relating people to their call to ministry in the world. "Thus, liturgy not only has consequences for life. Life has consequences for the liturgy. Christians move always from prayer and praise in the church to life and work in the world. The two activities, properly understood, flow into each other, and reinforce each other to the greater glory of God. When the connection is broken both worship and witness suffer."[19]

18. U.S. Census Bureau Health Insurance Data, Highlight, Health Insurance Data 2004, http://www.census.gov/hhes/www/hlthins/hlthin04/hlth04asc.html.

19. Charles P. Price and Louis Weil, *Liturgy for Living* (New York: Morehouse Publishing, 2000), p. 61.

Understanding the interconnectedness between worship and pastoral care is important as we reflect on healing services and prayers for seriously ill persons and their families. Leslie Weatherhead refers to the healing service conducted by the pastor as a liturgy for service. It is not often that we think of that dimension. When the pastor conducts a healing service, whether it is at a bedside or in the context of a public worship service, it is to equip the patient for service. How can we interpret that? What form of service would this be for the patient? In addition, the response by the participants in the service is part of what brings healing. Jesus often gave instructions to the persons he was healing (e.g., go to the pool and wash, take up your bed and walk, go to the temple). Our response to these healing services and to worship in general should be one of service.

When we refer to the pastor's use of sacraments with ill persons, we usually think of the sacrament/rite of healing. The power of the rite of healing, like the power of the Eucharist, rests in the corporate nature of these rites — we are joined with one another as well as with Christ.

Rituals should be an integral part of the pastoral ministry to the dying and should reflect the symbols of life and hope in the midst of death and dying. Often rituals related to death contain three phases as "rites of passage" — separation, transition, and re-incorporation. Rituals can help people enter the mainstream of life as well as enter into their dying, notes William Willimon.[20] Rituals ideally arise from within the context of a broader and more comprehensive lived experience of the persons involved, a context that extends far beyond the fragile boundaries of the ritual itself.

In his foreword to *A Manual for Ministry to the Sick,* Martin Dudley writes, "Christians are called to serve Christ in their neighbors. When we stand by a sickbed or attend the dying, we are to be there with the respect and the tenderness which is appropriate to being in the presence of Christ. There should be no room for any kind of exploitation of a person's vulnerability at such moments, but rather a note of gentleness and attention."[21]

20. William Willimon, *Worship as Pastoral Care* (Nashville: Abingdon Press, 1982).

21. *A Manual for Ministry to the Sick,* ed. Martin Dudley (London: SPCK, 1997).

Pray and Read Scripture

There has always been a strong expectation that clergy pray and read Scripture at the bedside of ill persons. People need the deep resources of inspiration and sustenance that prayer provides at all times, but especially when they are gravely ill. As William James said, "We should always be open to a great deep where the tides rise." In the midst of crisis, people feel up against something that is overwhelming and need inner strength and resources that may be absent. Many people believe that if they work hard enough or will something singlemindedly enough, it will come to pass, but eventually that doesn't work, and the gravely ill can only say, "Spirit of God, descend upon my heart."

The Bible has no lack of clarity as to when we should pray – always. The key passage is in 1 Thessalonians 5:17: "Pray without ceasing." So clergy should always have prayer on their lips. Prayer is a deep, interior attitude, not just saying prayers but making prayer a habitual and constant foreground and background of daily living. Pastors need to be constantly sending up prayers to God so that they are hearing the voice of God and not merely tuning in to their own inner voices.

Before a pastor visits the dying, she should be saturating herself in prayer. When praying for the sick, one of the issues is how specific prayer should be, especially in light of a specific illness and diagnosis. There is nothing wrong with asking God to respond to a particular need. In fact, the writer of James seems to urge this. "Are any among you suffering? They should pray" (James 5:13). First Kings 17 and 18 recount the story of Elijah and his specific prayers. For example, he prayed that Israel would stop worshiping Baal and return to the true God, and asked God to work a miracle through the rain and the fire so that this might happen.

It may be easiest to pray in desperate circumstances, but too often a feeling of desperation may block the energy that can be released in prayer. Paul gives us an important reminder in Philippians 4:6: "Do not worry about anything, but in everything by prayer and supplication with thanksgiving let your requests be made known to God." Even when prayers are answered, clergy need to remind others to give God thanksgiving and praise.

The prayer tradition of Jesus and Paul was continued in the early church. The elders came not simply to visit but to pray for healing, and to encourage others to do the same. Thus the visiting pastor should be accompanied by the elders whenever possible. "Therefore confess your sins to one another, and pray for one another, so that you may be healed. The prayer of the righteous is powerful and effective" (James 5:16). Indeed, the knowledge that a group is praying for an ill person's recovery can have tremendous power.

Teaching people how to pray is also an important part of the pastor's role. Prayer is intended to bring one into accord with God's will, not to be used to bribe God or beg for favors. We should not bargain with God – "If you heal me, I'll believe" – but trust and obey God. Prayer is no magic rite, but it often equips one to face problems. It provides no substitute for penicillin or physical therapy, but it can bring a change of heart, which medicine alone cannot do. Medicine eliminates the physical barriers inhibiting the body's own healing process, while prayer unclogs the pores of the soul, opening one to God's grace. Medicine differs from prayer in that medicine can be administered without acknowledging God's power.

For the dying person and his family, the results of prayer are utmost on their minds. There are several reasons why prayer is so neglected in the twenty-first century, but perhaps one of the biggest reasons is confusion over the meaning of answered prayer. One of the most important results of praying for others is giving them an openness to God and an acceptance of life's challenges with the knowledge that God is in control. "What then are we to say about these things? If God is for us, who is against us?" (Romans 8:31). The answers we look for are not always the ones that God gives; we must trust in God while realizing that we live in a broken world. Often the answers may involve not physical healing but the healing of broken relationships or reconciliation with a loved one before the person dies.

Provide Spiritual Assessment and Care

The pastor's last form of ministry to the dying is to provide spiritual assessment and care. We often refer to spiritual care, but it cannot be adequately given without spiritual assessment. "Spiritual care" is a term much bandied about of late, but it is fast becoming a term devoid of meaning. It should include recognition of spiritual needs and a range of conditions from spiritual distress to spiritual disintegration. The pastor counsels individuals in order to reveal spiritual roadblocks to healing, to put people in touch with their inner resources for healing, to open them up to God's power of healing, and to integrate them into a community that will provide support and service – that is, the church.

The spiritual dimension contributes to self-esteem, a sense of purpose, and a set of goals and objectives in life. These can provide the necessary power and energy to bring change to a person's life, a matter of interest to us specifically in the areas of treatment, recovery, and long-term health. As a member of the healing team, the pastor/chaplain has special responsibilities for undertaking spiritual assessment as a prelude to spiritual care.

The spiritual history is the foundational element of the spiritual assessment. In most cases, the chaplain will need to ask specific questions of a spiritual nature, respectfully listening to the patient's description of his or her spiritual experiences; the chaplain will then assess the developmental, psychodynamic, and therapeutic implications of the presented history. This approach is similar to the clinician's careful, nuanced listening for psychodynamic and relational problems in a patient's life. Including the spiritual elements of a patient's earlier life is part of the larger goal of understanding the current role that spiritual factors may play in the onset, and possible amelioration, of the patient's problems.

This in-depth spiritual/religious assessment should include the role of religion during the patient's developmental years; the patient's involvement in a religious community (in the past and the present); the patient's concept of God and the role of prayer and meditation in his or her life; specific values and beliefs held by the patient; and rituals specific to the patient's religious/spiritual tradition. Of course, if this assessment has not been done before and the person is too sick to talk, the chaplain will need to depend on family members to provide this information.

The chaplain should determine who was instrumental in teaching the patient about spirituality, and the nature of the patient's relationship with these individuals; the chaplain should also find out whether the patient currently sees himself or herself as religious/spiritual. This approach can help determine whether religion during the developmental years was helpful, harmful, or neutral. If religious practices are part of the picture, then it is important to determine if the patient is currently receiving support from a religious community and whether there have been changes in his or her relationship to it.

One of the fundamental questions regarding belief is, "Do you believe in God, and how would you describe God and your relationship to God?" For the committed religious person, information gained from this line of inquiry may be as relevant as the person's views regarding his or her parents. An assessment of the role of prayer and devotional practices is also pertinent. For the religious person, a more extensive conversation about his or her beliefs is important, because each tradition has values and beliefs seen as essential by adherents. The meaning of illness and suffering, the conception of the moral and virtuous life, the idea of what constitutes a healthy family, and the sources of spiritual authority – for example, scriptures, religious teachings, and tenets – may all be relevant for assessment. Such core beliefs can powerfully determine an individual's behavior, and if the pastor/chaplain does not inquire about them, an entire treatment process may be undermined.

The patient's beliefs may mean that certain rituals and spiritual practices are important to him or her. These may be part of childhood practices continued into adulthood, or more recently acquired aspects of the person's life. The chaplain should take note of differences between parents and children, and between spouses, regarding the importance of certain aspects of belief as well as participation in religious rituals.

Proclaiming God's Universal Truth in Particular Situations

Having discussed spiritual care, it is important to note that it may include a theological dimension. The pastor is a healer as she proclaims universal truths in particular situations. These truths include the following: that each person has infinite worth; that illness is not necessarily a sign of sin; that when sin does cause illness, forgiveness is available; and that death, though an enemy, has been conquered and need no longer be feared. The pastor can provide a prophetic function, calling on spiritual resources and theological truths about health, healing, and healers. Pointing to God's love as reflected in all healing is crucial and may include showing how even medical diagnosis, prognosis, and therapy may have Christological dimensions.[22]

Since the pastor, unlike the physician, does not usually deal in categories of sickness, she is more free to clarify the individual nature of the person's illness. According to medical statistics, only one in ninety-nine persons is disabled by illness, but that is little comfort to those among the one percent. The pastor is oriented toward restoration rather than diagnosis, so she can move away from a statistical approach to illness. She is concerned with affirming the person's sense of worth in the face of the limitations and sufferings of illness. This task involves listening as well as speaking. She proclaims the universal truths mentioned above and then applies them in this particular situation.

The prophetic function of the pastor – calling people to remembrance – is very important. Throughout the Hebrew scriptures the role of the prophets was sometimes to pronounce judgment, but it was always to call to remembrance.

The pastor as healer may assist the patient in making health-care decisions. She should interpret the tradition of the religious community that she represents. Here she functions as a moral expert on the tradition. In this role the pastor can support the patient as decision-maker in the midst of all his doubts and anxieties. Many times one's personal views and the church's teachings may conflict; hence the pastor assumes a counseling role to help the person struggle through his choices. She must help the patient to clarify his values and be a moral guide without being judgmental. Confidentiality is the hallmark of this relationship.

Knowing when and to whom to refer people with needs beyond a pastor's expertise is especially important. Referrals – whether to a psychiatrist, a psychologist, or a thanatologist – are often part of helping people to make decisions. I would strongly advise pastors not to provide counseling for more than three sessions unless they have advanced training in pastoral counseling. Pastors can do more harm than good if they are ill-equipped to make the proper assessment.

This pastoral role of assisting in decision-making may be a new and very important role for the church as bio-ethical quandaries in-

22. Robert A. Lambourne, "The Healing Ministry of the Church," notes from a lecture presented at the University of Birmingham, Birmingham, England, n.d., p. 1.

crease. Another important aspect of decision-making is to see the long-term consequences of a decision, particularly as complexities grow.

In summary, we have examined a model of care at the end of life where all healers work in collaboration to provide the best care, comfort, and empowerment in the patient's final days. The patient is returned to the central place of our concern and is involved as long as possible in choosing how to live while dying. For the Christian, the passage from life to physical death is but the prelude to life eternal in God's presence, where every tear will be wiped away.

CHAPTER 9

Compassion: A Critical Component of Caring and Healing

Christina M. Puchalski

When people are overwhelmed by illness, we must give them physical relief, but it is equally important to encourage the spirit through a constant show of love and compassion. It is shameful how often we fail to see that what people desperately require is human affection. Deprived of human warmth and a sense of value, other forms of treatment prove less effective. Real care of the sick does not begin with costly procedures, but with the simple gifts of affection, love, and concern.

His Holiness The Dalai Lama[1]

Compassion is critical to the care of patients and their families. According to Webster's, *compassion* comes from two Latin words: *cum,* which means "with," and *pati,* which means "to suffer." Thus the act of compassion is to suffer with another. The Dalai Lama talks of compassion as "defined in terms of a state of mind that is nonviolent, non-harming, and non-aggressive. It is a mental attitude based on the wish for others to be free of their suffering and is associated with a sense of commitment, responsibility, and respect towards the other."[2] Compassion is an attitude, a way of approaching the needs of others and of

1. His Holiness The Dalai Lama, quoted in *Time for Listening and Caring: Spirituality and the Care of the Chronically Ill and Dying,* ed. Christina M. Puchalski (New York: Oxford University Press, 2006).

2. His Holiness The Dalai Lama and H. Cutler, *The Art of Happiness* (New York: Riverhead Books, 1998), p. 114.

helping others with their suffering. But it is also a way of being, a way of service to others, a spiritual practice, and an act of love.

Suffering

Suffering is inevitable in life. It starts with the birth process and proceeds through life toward aging and eventual dying. Suffering can result from individuals feeling alienated from themselves, others, God, or from their ultimate source of meaning. People suffer from loss of relationships, shattered dreams, stress, and illness. Suffering can also result from persistent worry, anxiety, and loneliness. Suffering has been associated with conflict, loss, powerlessness, isolation, and the stress of competing obligations and responsibilities.[3]

Suffering may arise from the basic insecurities all people feel – a lack of self-worth, an overactive sense of guilt, a need to control things that can't be controlled, or a struggle with knowing the difference between where one can take action and make changes and where one can't effect change. In this way, suffering is linked to a feeling of powerlessness.[4] Suffering has been identified as a factor that can diminish autonomy and threaten one's inherent dignity. Indeed, Eric Cassell writes of suffering as a threat to our personhood.[5] People suffer until that threat is removed, or until they can accept it and deal with it.

The clinical encounter may be the first place where patients reckon with suffering. The language they use may be disease- or illness-centered, but underlying their descriptions may be profound suffering of a deeper kind. People may not be in touch with this suffering or easily find words to describe it. Thus, what we hear in the health-care setting are descriptions of symptoms or frustrations.

3. See K. Doka, C. H. Rushton, and T. A. Thorstenson, "Caregiver Distress: If It Is So Ethical, Why Does It Feel So Bad?" *AACN Clinical Issues* 5, no. 3 (1994): 346-52. See also D. Kahn and R. H. Steeves, "The Experience of Suffering: Conceptual Clarification and Theoretical Definition," *Journal of Advanced Nursing* 11 (1986): 623-31.

4. C. H. Rushton, "Care-Giver Suffering in Critical Care Nursing," *Heart and Lung* 21, no. 3 (1992): 303-6.

5. Eric Cassell, "The Nature of Suffering and the Goals of Medicine," *New England Journal of Medicine* 2 (1982): 639.

Illness and disease can cause suffering in many dimensions — the physical, the emotional, the social, and the spiritual. Thus, suffering can be manifested as physical pain, depression or anxiety, social isolation, and spiritual or existential distress. A patient can manifest or even express spiritual distress as physical pain. Spiritual or existential distress can also exacerbate the presentation of other symptoms such as agitation, anxiety, and depression. Some studies suggest that existential and spiritual issues may be of greater concern to patients than pain and physical symptoms.[6]

When patients talk of pain, they may be referring to pain in one of any of these four dimensions but using clinical words to address it. This situation can be exacerbated by health-care professionals, who are trained in a discipline-specific model and use language that they are familiar with. The questions that physicians ask, for example, center on a disease model of care. Only recently have there been educational changes, which focus more on a patient-centered model of care. Inherent in nursing education is the model of caring presence, but technological advances and a focus on a model of care based on scientific evidence have also influenced nursing education. While these advances have helped prolong life and often improve the quality of life, they have de-emphasized the importance of a spiritual or compassion-centered care model where a patient's suffering — including psychosocial, spiritual, or existential suffering — can be attended.

Healing and Compassionate Care

Often healing is associated with cure, but it is much broader than a cure or a fix. Healing has to do with a spiritual process or life journey. Healing may involve reconciling with God, friends, or family, or finding a deeper sense of meaning and purpose in life. In one study of consolation, the authors found that in the midst of compassion, the sufferer was able to shift his perspective and experience meaning in the

6. See W. Breitbart, B. Rosenfeld, and S. Passik, "Interest in Physician-Assisted Suicide among Ambulatory HIV-Infected Patients," *American Journal of Psychiatry* 153 (1996): 238-42; and M. J. Field and C. K. Cassel, *Approaching Death: Improving Care at the End of Life* (Washington, D.C.: Institute of Medicine, National Academy Press, 1997).

midst of suffering.[7] Healing for loved ones may also mean being able to let go and allow a relative to die and be at peace with that dying.

One of my patients, Sarah, had gone to an orthopedist for back pain. An MRI revealed pathologic vertebral fractures; a subsequent PET-CT scan showed widespread metastatic disease. Sarah had no prior diagnosis of cancer and was doing quite well apart from the backache. When I told her and her daughter of her likely diagnosis and the suggested next steps, Sarah exclaimed, "I do not want tests, nor chemo nor anything. . . . Just let me go — it's my time." Both her daughter and I encouraged some minimal testing so that we could get a diagnosis and have more information upon which to make an informed decision. During a subsequent hospitalization, the diagnosis ended up being metastatic adenocarcinoma of the lung with a poor prognosis.

Prior to her hospital stay, Sarah had mentioned to her daughter and to me that if she died soon, that was God's will, and she was very much at peace with that. Her daughter and I were not at the same place. On the fifth day of her hospitalization, Sarah went into a coma. Tests did not reveal any specific etiology. All of us were perturbed – we all wanted an answer. Sarah had aspiration pneumonia; maybe she was septic even though the blood cultures were negative. There were long discussions with the family about trying to "fix" what was going on. Family members prayed for healing, most meaning a cure. One morning on the way to the clinic, I decided to visit Sarah early rather than during my usual midday hospital rounds. When I saw her, she was apneic, breathing slowly with long pauses. She was actively dying.

I called the family, got Sarah a private room, and called for the chaplain. I stayed with the family for a while and then saw them periodically throughout the day. What I witnessed was a letting go. Prayers for healing turned to gratitude to God for sparing their mother and sister undue suffering. There was a letting go — both by the family and by me. We were all being healed; we were all accepting Sarah's dying and also celebrating her life. The medical personnel learned to accept Sarah's dying without having a scientific reason for it. Instead of talking about vital signs on our rounds, we talked about mystery and acknowledging our inability to control life or death. In her dying, Sarah inspired healing for many.

7. A. Norberg, M. Bergsten, and B. Lundman, "A Model of Consolation," *Nursing Ethics* 6 (November 2001): 544-53.

Healing takes time, it takes support, and it cannot happen on anyone's schedule. But it can happen in the context of compassionate care. My journey with Sarah and her family could not have happened as it did if we – the doctors, nurses, social workers, and chaplains – did not really listen and become fully present to Sarah and her family. We needed to open up fully to Sarah, to her family, and to the whole process to be aware of all that was happening. Taking lab tests and interpreting them did not give us the information to transition from diagnostic care to palliative care. Knowing when and how to have Sarah's family change her code status from "full code" to "do not resuscitate" took time, sensitivity, and intuition.

Compassion results in good quality of care, in appropriate course of action, and, ultimately, in healing. Good diagnosis and treatment are contingent on the powers of observation. Clinicians look at the patient's body, examine test results, and review scans. But there is another level of observation, one Edith Stein calls the "super-individual observation."[8] Compassion allows one to be empathic; it allows one to utilize intuition to understand a situation or a person on a deeper, perhaps spiritual level. But unlike pure empathy, which is the action of vicariously understanding or being sensitive to another's situation, compassion moves us to a conscious and spiritual experience of the other's suffering with a desire to support her through her suffering and alleviate it if possible. We perceive things about the patient and family that stem from a nonphysical level, one that cannot be measured or even studied. Compassion opens us up to that level of super-individual observation. It then calls us to take what we have observed and serve others with love – to help alleviate their suffering and support them through that suffering.

Compassion requires that the health-care professional or caregiver open up to something unknown. Feelings may arise, tears may flow, and grief may ensue. It takes a certain amount of vulnerability to become open, to be fully compassionate. Compassionate care does not allow for distancing. In being fully present and loving to another, one's own pain and suffering may emerge. It takes skill to be able to handle that appropriately.

8. Edith Stein, *Philosophy of Psychology and the Humanities,* trans. M. Baseheart and M. Sawicki (Washington, D.C.: ICS Publications, 2000), p. 148.

In being compassionate with others, we love them unselfishly and without demand, expectation, or an agenda. People suffer deeply and often feel unloved or alone. As health-care professionals, we should not turn away from the deep suffering of others, even though it may cause us discomfort or sadness. St. John of the Cross, a sixteenth-century mystic, wrote, "One ought to have deep compassion for the soul God puts in this tempestuous and frightful night. . . . The soul is deserving of great pity because of the immense tribulation and the suffering of extreme uncertainty about a remedy."[9]

With Sarah there was angst and suffering because of her illness and dying, but in large part because of the uncertainty of the course of her dying. In order to be compassionate with others in the midst of uncertainty, health-care professionals have to be able to be comfortable with not knowing. They have to know how to interweave their professional roles of certitude and expertise with their human roles of mystery and insecurity. Cure may be in the realm of science and knowing, but healing is often in the realm of mystery.

Compassionate care calls the health-care professional to hold the patient or the person who is suffering in a love that eventually allows that individual to heal. People can become open to healing the spiritual woundedness that they feel by finding some hope in the midst of despair.[10] Compassionate care calls the health-care professional to love his or her patients and to serve them altruistically. As William Osler wrote, "To serve the art of medicine as it should be served, one must love his fellow man."[11]

Theoretical and Ethical Frameworks for Including Compassion in Care

In 1998 the Association of American Medical Colleges (AAMC), responding to concerns by the medical professional community that young doctors lacked these humanitarian skills, undertook a major

9. St. John of the Cross, *The Collected Works of St. John of the Cross,* trans. K. Kavanaugh and O. Rodriguez (Washington, D.C.: ICS Publications, 1991), p. 407.

10. E. O'Donnell, editorial, *Spiritual Life* 1 (2003): 49.

11. William Osler, "The Evolution of Internal Medicine," in *Modern Medicine: Its Theory and Its Practice* (Philadelphia: Lea Brothers, 1907), p. 34.

initiative – The Medical School Objectives Project (MSOP) – to assist medical schools in their efforts to address these concerns. The report notes that "Physicians must be compassionate and empathetic in caring for patients. . . . They must act with integrity, honesty, respect for patients' privacy, and respect for the dignity of patients as persons. In all of their interactions with patients they must seek to understand the meaning of the patients' stories in the context of the patients' and family and cultural values."[12] The American College of Physicians convened an end-of-life consensus panel, which concluded that physicians should extend their care for those with serious medical illness by being attentive to psychosocial, existential, or spiritual suffering.[13] In its Code of Medical Ethics, the American Medical Association states, "The physician shall be dedicated to providing competent medical care with compassion and respect for human dignity and rights."[14]

Nurses have always been called to care for those who are sick and highly vulnerable.[15] Nursing theories include aspects of compassion as part of patient care.[16] In addition, one of six essential features of professional nursing practice is the establishment of a caring relationship to facilitate health and healing.[17] Social workers are trained to be a compassionate presence – to listen with empathy, assess a person's psychosocial network, and help draw in appropriate resources to help the patient do as well as possible.[18] All pastoral and spiritual care has a fundamental role: to attempt to help others – through words, actions,

12. Association of American Medical Colleges, *Contemporary Issues in Medicine: Communication in Medicine,* Report 1 (Washington, D.C.: Association of American Medical Colleges, 1998), p. 27.

13. B. Lo, T. Quill, and J. Tulsky, "Discussing Palliative Care with Patients," ACP-ASIM End-of-Life Care Consensus Panel, *Annals of Internal Medicine* 130 (1999): 744-49.

14. American Medical Association, *Principles of Medical Ethics* (Chicago: American Medical Association, 2004).

15. M. Simons, "The Cycle of Caring," *Nursing Adminstration Quarterly* 28, no. 4 (2004): 280-84.

16. J. Watson, "Becoming Aware: Knowing Yourself to Care for Others," *Home Healthcare Nurse* 17 (1999): 317-22.

17. American Nurses Association, *Nursing's Social Policy Statement,* 2d ed. (Silver Spring, Md.: American Nurses Association, 2003).

18. National Association of Social Workers, *Code of Ethics,* 1996; revised 1999. See http://www.socialworkers.org/pubs/code/code.asp.

and relationship – to experience the reality of God's presence and love in their lives. The chaplain seeks only to engage sufferers and to reframe their perspective on suffering in the context of life's incongruities. The chaplain listens to the voices of the suffering as they tell their stories. The chaplain serves as a witness to their stories and intentionally mirrors unconditional love.[19]

The Clinical Practice of Compassion

It is clear from the patients' stories, from the concepts about healing, and from the theoretical and ethical framework of medicine, nursing, social work, and chaplaincy that compassion is an essential element of clinical care. There is also data which suggests that patients judge their physicians by how compassionate they are and that patients want to have more compassionate physicians treating them. According to a 2004 survey sponsored by the Kaiser Family Foundation and the Harvard School of Public Health, 55 percent of Americans are "currently dissatisfied with the quality of care in this country." Many patients believe that what is lacking is compassion.[20] To enhance end-of-life care in one community hospital system, a survey is used to provide patients' feedback to the hospital. Physician compassion is included on this survey and is rated as important by patients.[21]

Interestingly, another group of investigators hypothesized that one way religiosity may result in positively influencing health is through encouraging compassionate attitudes and behaviors toward others.[22] In this study, college students participated in a survey assessing their religiosity, psychological well-being, compassionate attitude and behavior, social support, depressive symptoms, and stress. The research-

19. C. M. Puchalski, B. K. Lunsford, M. H. Harris, and R. T. Miller, "Interdisciplinary Spiritual Care," *Journal of Palliative Medicine* (August 2006).

20. D. M. Sanghavi, "What Makes for a Compassionate Patient-Caregiver Relationship?" *Journal on Quality and Patient Safety* 32, no. 5 (May 2006): 283-91.

21. M. Hodges, M. R. London, and J. Lundstedt, "Family-Driven Quality Improvement in Inpatient End-of-Life Care," *Journal of Healthcare Quality* 28, no. 2 (March-April 2006): 20-26, 31.

22. P. Steffen and K. Masters, "Does Compassion Mediate the Intrinsic Religion-Health Relationship?" *Annals of Behavioral Medicine* 30, no. 3 (2005): 217-24.

ers found that a compassionate attitude is related to positive psychosocial outcomes, including reduced depressive symptoms and reduced perceived stress.

This has an interesting potential application to health-care professionals. There have been a number of anecdotal reports from physicians, nurses, and other health-care professionals that being compassionate enables them to find more meaning in their work and experience less stress.[23] One of the reasons for this could be that most clinicians are called to a work of service and compassion. The stress could result from work environments that inhibit their expressions of compassion.

In the clinical setting, compassionate care involves being fully present to the patient and family. The language of presence reflects that this type of care is spiritual care and that it is fundamentally relational.[24] Presence refers to the behaviors, attitudes, and values that the health-care professional brings to the encounter. By being present, the health-care professional has the intentionality to be open, to connect to others, and to honor mystery and the unknown. The latter in particular implies humility as the health-care professional and patient and family walk a journey together that may have many unplanned and unexpected turns. This reframes the focus from solutions in care to a partnership and relationship of care.

One becomes present with a patient by emptying oneself of distractions, including agendas. Instead of focusing on getting the list of medications that the patient takes and the patient's past medical history, for example, the health-care professional lets go of that agenda and focuses on the patient and what the patient needs and feels. Presence does not require words or even actions. The spiritual aspects of presence imply a reciprocal giving and receiving. Both parties enter into a relationship of presence.

Gabriel Marcel describes the relationship of presence as always risky, potentially painful, but allowing those who practice it to be en-

23. C. M. Puchalski, S. McSkimming, and S. Cleary, "Creating Healing Environments," *Health Progress,* May-June 2006, pp. 30-35.

24. K. Meert, C. Thurston, and S. Briller, "The Spiritual Needs of Parents at the Time of Their Child's Death in the Pediatric Intensive Care Unit and During Bereavement: A Qualitative Study," *Pediatric Critical Care Medicine Journal* 6 (2005): 420-27.

riched. Inherent in being fully present to another is a profoundly deep respect for the other.[25]

In a review of questionnaires and transcripts of a study done by the Kenneth B. Schwartz Center in fifty-four hospitals in twenty-one states, responses to the question of what makes for a compassionate patient-caregiver relationship fell into three main categories: communication, common ground, and respect for individuality.[26] Communication involved a caring style and clear, honest content, especially around difficult issues. Caregivers can exhibit compassion through thoughtful listening and by acknowledging that there are no answers to suffering and to the huge number of questions surrounding dying. Sitting in silence with the patient or family, or holding a hand or giving a hug, may be the best mode of communication at times.

The style of communication described in the above study included attention to the body language and nonverbal cues of the patient as well as being kind and caring. As stated above, compassion enables one to observe on a deeper level – to perceive or sense a feeling, motive, desire, fear, or hope that is not being expressed verbally. In the study, compassionate care depended on showing empathy for a patient's experience of illness. Study participants noted that caregivers could choose to care deeply for patients as part of compassionate care.

Part of common ground is sharing personal information with patients appropriately, admitting error, and being comfortable with uncertainty. It is critical to treat patients with dignity, as individuals and not as statistics. So much of medicine involves prognostication based on evidence-based data. But each person is a unique being and, as one of my patients stated, "a statistic of one."[27] Each person's beliefs, values, history, and personality enter into how that person understands his or her illness or situation. Compassionate care allows the caregiver to foster and support a more unified and integrated sense of the pa-

25. Gabriel Marcel, in P. O'Connor, "A Clinical Paradigm for Exploring Spiritual Concerns," in *Death and Spirituality,* ed. K. Doka and J. P. Morgan (Amityville, N.Y.: Baywood Publishing Co., 1993), p. 139.

26. Sanghavi, "What Makes for a Compassionate Patient-Caregiver Relationship?" 283-91.

27. R. Oziel and D. Oziel, "Rhonda – Patient as Teacher," in *Time for Listening and Caring,* ed. Puchalski, pp. 353-59.

tient's life and experience of illness. To do this, the caregiver must enter into a relationship with the patient as an individual — as unique and whole, not broken. Rachel Naomi Remen writes, "Helping, fixing, and serving represent three different ways of seeing life. When you help, you see life as weak. When you fix, you see life as broken. When you serve, you see life as whole. Fixing and helping may be the work of the ego; service is the work of the soul."[28]

Seeing the patient as whole enables the health-care professional to see many dimensions of that person's life and being that transcend the illness and, in doing so, to help the patient reframe his or her experience and integrate it into his or her whole life. Thus, compassionate care is based on respect for the individual. To truly respect a person, one needs to be humble and in awe of the other person. Compassionate care calls the health-care professional to sit with a patient in a sacred space held together by love and a call to serve.

Compassionate care is grounded in a service model of care. Furthermore, it stems from the spiritual values of love, respect for others, and unselfish service to others. In this way, compassionate care forms the basis of spiritual care. Love — what many call the highest of spiritual values — is the root of compassionate care. Love is invisible. It is implicit in all relationships and is a concept that is found in all cultures and societies. Patients who suffer often need love and caring, and thus the support of compassionate care. Erik Erikson writes, "If we intend to define love, we may say that love is the divine or the humanity in human beings."[29] So in compassionate care, the divine or the humanity within the health-care professional connects with the divine or the humanity within the patient and family. With the love of caregivers, people can experience profound healing, as manifested through personal and spiritual transformation.

Jackie is a patient of mine who has end-stage adenocarcinoma of the lung. Jackie has dealt with an enormous amount of suffering in her life: a failed marriage, conflicts at work — many losses, both personal and financial. She learned to survive by being a loner and by focusing

28. Rachel Naomi Remen, *Kitchen Table Wisdom: Stories That Heal* (New York: Riverhead Books, 1997).

29. Erikson, quoted in M. Arman and A. Rehnsfeldt, "The Presence of Love in Ethical Caring," *Nursing Forum* 41, no. 1 (January-March 2006): 8.

all her attention on God. Daily mass, prayer, and the rosary helped Jackie cope with life's difficulties.

When I first met Jackie as my patient, I found her difficult to reach. She looked away from me as I tried to connect and establish rapport. She sat slouched, as if the weight of an enormous burden rested on her shoulders. I sensed a deep pain and suffering, but I couldn't penetrate the barrier of protection she had placed between her and me – probably between herself and the rest of the world.

After the usual medical-history questions and social chitchat, I turned to the spiritual history. Jackie's whole persona changed. She sat upright and looked straight into my eyes as she proclaimed her "love for the Lord." Sensing my openness to the discussion, she shared details of her faith and how that faith helped her conquer much of her pain. She pulled out a book of poetry by Pope John Paul II and explained how he was an example of Christian love and passion for her. She saw him as someone who walked Jesus' path and explained that that was her goal for herself – to see Jesus in everyone.

On her next visit, Jackie brought a plate for me depicting Pope John Paul to help guide me in my work of "compassionate service to others," as she put it. Over the years we developed a wonderful professional friendship. As she shared her life and herself with me, she began to open up and to trust. Being compassionate toward her enabled me to have the gift of her presence and wisdom as well as the fulfillment of deep meaning in service to others.

Nine years later, I diagnosed Jackie with lung cancer. She proceeded with chemotherapy and did well for two years. But then she had a recurrence, and additional therapy failed to slow the growth of the tumor. Jackie entered home-hospice care. At this point her own spiritual journey deepened. During our talks and visits, her wisdom opened my own eyes and soul to profound experiences of even deeper compassion and care for another.

Within two months Jackie began to fail and had difficulty living alone. Financial considerations were great, and thus the only options for her were moving into a nursing home or moving in with relatives who weren't in the area. The hospice nurse, Valerie, and I debated about the next course of action. Jackie didn't want to move in with her son and his family. But she also was fearful of nursing homes.

Valerie made a connection with Joseph's House, a nonprofit community in Washington, D.C., that provides a home for people dying of AIDS and cancer. Jackie was accepted and currently resides in Joseph's House, journeying toward her death. I visited her there and stayed for the community dinner. Jackie was radiant as she basked in the love and compassion that the staff and other patients showed her. Later that evening she told me that she finally had what she had always wanted: a community of people who cared. She explained that she saw Jesus in everyone in a way she never had before. It was a profound spiritual experience for her. Jackie told me that she had been so fearful of dying but that that fear was no longer there. Her experience of Jesus in others enabled her to experience his closeness to her and gave her the assurance that death would be a true union with him. The compassion that all of us showed Jackie — our commitment to be with her in the midst of her suffering — enabled her to heal. Her healing was manifested as a sense of peace and acceptance. It also opened all of our hearts to an even greater love and knowledge of what ultimately is meaningful in our lives.

Many authors, clinicians, and others have written about the profound transformation that a person undergoes in the experience of dying and in the experience of love. This transformation influences the person's view of life, personality, and choices and priorities.[30] In Jackie's case, it was as if she was existentially awakened in her experience of love and compassion. For people like Jackie, their experiences of compassion may open them to new possibilities — may help them reframe their suffering and find meaning and purpose in their lives, in their suffering or in their dying. And, as seen in Jackie's case, the act of being compassionate can also transform the clinician and the other people who express compassion to the sufferer.

A study on "witnessing as an ethical basis of caring" has demonstrated how caregivers are transformed by acts of kindness and compassion toward others.[31] My own sense of what is of value in my life has been deepened in my encounters with Jackie. In her expression of seeing God in others, she has deepened my own sense of God's presence in others and transformed my experience of God to a more contemplative and profound sense of who God is in others and in my own life. Jackie

30. M. Arman and A. Rehnsfeldt, "The Hidden Suffering among Breast Cancer Patients — A Qualitative Metasynthesis," *Qualitative Health Research* 13, no. 4 (2003): 510-27.

31. Arman and Rehnsfeldt, "The Presence of Love in Ethical Caring," pp. 4-12.

has also helped me reframe my own sense of woundedness as a purpose and foundation for a profession of service and love. This experience, like all of my experiences with patients, deepens my commitment to clinical care. It energizes me and helps me feel whole and integrated in a profession that I find sacred and holy.

As illustrated by Jackie's story, compassion is not a one-way street. It is born out of relationships. In these relationships neither party can hide behind professionalism or other guises. There is no possibility of detachment or distancing. Both parties are vulnerable and open to new feelings and experiences. This is why one of the barriers to good compassionate care may be the fear of exposing oneself, of being hurt and experiencing unwanted feelings, which could uncover old wounds or unresolved issues. Thus, a prerequisite for compassionate care is reflective, insight-oriented work on the part of health-care professionals so that they can be in touch with issues that could arise in their interactions with patients. It is also recommended that health-care professionals have some venue for processing issues as they come up in their clinical encounters with patients — either in therapy, spiritual direction, counseling, or peer-support groups such as Balint groups.

Training in Compassion

Professional education conveys not just knowledge and skills but also attitudes, values, and behaviors. Training more humane physicians has been a focus of medical education for the last two decades.[32] This is important, because it has been documented that medical students and residents grow more cynical and less compassionate over the course of their education.[33]

32. Subcommittee on Evaluation of Humanistic Qualities in the Internist, American Board of Internal Medicine, "Evaluation of Humanistic Qualities in the Internist," *Annual Internist Medicine* 99 (1983): 720-24.

33. See D. J. Self, D. E. Schrader, D. C. Baldwin Jr., and F. D. Wolinsky, "The Moral Development of Medical Students: A Pilot Study of the Possible Influence of Medical Education," *Medical Education* 27 (1993): 26-43. See also C. Feudtner, D. A. Christakis, and N. A. Christakis, "Do Clinical Clerks Suffer Ethical Erosion? Students' Perceptions of Their Ethical Environment and Personal Development," *Academic Medicine* 69 (1994): 670-79.

Compassion and respect are considered positive patient-directed attitudes.[34] There has been an increased effort in medical education to teach these attributes through courses on spirituality and health;[35] through preclinical courses to increase moral sensitivity and empathy via literature, film, and experiential media;[36] and through other student activities such as the White Coat Ceremony and memorial services for the body donors of the anatomy lab.

There are also ethics-of-caring courses in some medical schools. These courses emphasize moral decisions and face-to-face contacts. The courses refocus on the doctor's responsibility for the individual patient.[37] The ethics of caring assumes that connection to others is central to what it means to be human. It focuses on the relationship aspect of care and how relationship (rather than alienation) gives meaning to people's existence. The ethics of caring is based on being responsive to and for others and becoming a caring person. Studies have shown that students want to be receptive to caring, to spirituality, and to compassion.[38] Yet doctors lose that interest and inclination in their training.[39]

How can the receptivity to care and compassion be retained in medical training? Some of the courses, such as those in spirituality and medicine as well as humanities and the ethics of caring, have provided

34. M. Lipkin, "Integrity, Compassion, and Respect," *Journal of General Internal Medicine* 1 (1986): 65-67.

35. C. Puchalski, "Spirituality and Medicine: Curricula in Medical Education," *Journal of Cancer Education* 21, no. 1 (2006): 14-18.

36. S. H. Miles, Lane L. Weiss, J. Bickel, R. M. Walker, and C. K. Cassel, "Medical Ethics Education: Coming of Age," *Academic Medicine* 64 (1989): 705-14. See also L. A. Deloney and C. J. Graham, "Wit: Using Drama to Teach First-Year Medical Students about Empathy and Compassion," *Teaching and Learning in Medicine* 15, no. 4 (Fall 2003): 247-51.

37. W. T. Branch, "The Ethics of Caring and Medical Education," *Academic Medicine* 75, no. 2 (2000): 127-32.

38. W. T. Branch, "Professional and Moral Development in Medical Students: The Ethics of Caring for Patients," *Trans-American Clinical and Climatological Association* 109 (1998): 218-30. See also C. Puchalski and S. Cleary, "An Evaluation of Spirituality and Medicine Integrated Three-Year Curriculum," 2006.

39. F. Inglefinger, "Arrogance," *New England Journal of Medicine* 303 (1980): 1507-11. See also R. S. Ort, A. B. Ford, and R. E. Liske, "The Doctor-Patient Relationship as Described by Physicians and Medical Students," *Journal of Health and Human Behavior* 5 (1964): 25-34.

students with the opportunities to reflect on the meaning and purpose of their work, on what it means to be a compassionate healer. Other courses use standardized patients to provide feedback to students about compassionate and respectful behavior. Usually, however, these courses occur in the first two years, or the preclinical years, of medical school. In the clinical years, the impact of the mentors and attending physicians is much greater. Most teaching occurs in clinical venues and with a multitude of different role models. These role models have the potential to reinforce or discourage certain behaviors and attributes.

One study showed that attending physicians rarely corrected behaviors that were undesirable, such as lack of respect, rudeness, or uncaring attitudes toward patients. Reasons cited included lack of opportunity to observe interactions fully, sympathy for learners' stress, and the unpleasantness, perceived ineffectiveness, and lack of professional reward for giving negative feedback.[40] This indicates how important it is that role modeling extend to personal characteristics and attributes such as compassion and respect. This could be the most powerful way to teach compassionate care.

In addition, courses on spirituality and health as well as humanities and medicine have offered seminars and small-group discussions where students can reflect on and process the issues that come up in their interactions with patients and families. The sharing of patient stories as well as the stories of the medical students is critical to the process of understanding what compassionate care is all about and how to practice it well. Physicians who are role models and other health-care professionals can also impart their wisdom about compassionate care by demonstrating their ability to be caring and compassionate not only with patients but also with students.

Medicine as a Spiritual Practice

As we have seen, compassionate care stems from deep spiritual values of love, altruism, and service. Courses in humanities and medicine and in spirituality and medicine are grounded in these values. The courses

40. J. Burack, D. Irby, J. Carline, R. Root, and E. Larson, "Teaching Compassion and Respect," *Journal of General Internal Medicine* 14 (1999): 49.

are based on the ethical obligation that physicians have to attend to all dimensions of a patient's suffering. Thus compassion is central to what is taught in these courses. M. R. McVay writes that a course in medicine and spirituality is "a simple path to restore compassion in medicine."[41] The health-care system will improve if health-care practitioners are attentive to patients' spiritual beliefs and values; focus on all dimensions of care, including the spiritual; and recognize the importance of love and compassion in care.

Practicing medicine and health care then becomes more than a job. It becomes a profession and a calling similar to the priesthood. Because of the intimate nature of what health-care professionals do and the commitment to be present to the patient and to be altruistic in all that is done, the practice of medicine is a spiritual one. When medicine is practiced from that perspective, the suffering of patients and families is attended to fully. They are treated with respect and dignity. Out of the sacred, compassionate relationship formed between the health-care professional and the patient, the fruits of healing may be born.

41. M. R. McVay, "Medicine and Spirituality: A Simple Path to Restore Compassion in Medicine," *South Dakota Journal of Medicine* 55, no. 11 (2002): 487-91.

CHAPTER 10

Hope in the Face of Terminal Illness

Richard Payne

. . . He looks on the bright side of everything,
Including me. He thinks I'll be all right
With doctoring. But it's not medicine —
Lowe is the only doctor's dared to say so —
It's rest I want — there, I have said it out —
From cooking meals for hungry hired men
And washing dishes after them — from doing
Things over and over that just won't stay done.
By good rights I ought not to have so much
Put on me, but there seems no other way.
Len says one steady pull more ought to do it.
He says the best way out is always through.
And I agree to that, or in so far
As that I can see no way out but through . . .

Robert Frost, "A Servant to Servants"

The administration of a placebo, a harmless, pharmacologically inert preparation, can nonetheless exert powerful physiological and medicinal effects.[1] Holding onto hope — the expectation of good in the future

1. H. K. Beecher, "The Powerful Placebo," *JAMA* 159 (1955): 1602-6.

Unless otherwise indicated, all of the quotations from Scripture in this chapter are taken from the New Revised Standard Version of the Bible.

— can likewise be potent in its effects. Exploring notions of hopefulness can be critical to the concerns of health-care professionals and spiritual leaders in the care of seriously ill and dying individuals.

But individuals rendered vulnerable by disease and suffering can embrace false expectation if they are not given candid information. Dying patients and their families deserve honest and truthful information about their medical prognosis. A major supposition of this discussion is that even when terminally ill patients get bad news about their prognosis, we can help them find ways to remain hopeful. Physicians can maintain honest and truthful relationships with their dying patients and can fulfill the requirements of the Hippocratic Oath to "do no harm" if they engage patients in a professional manner and utilize skills of empathic engagement to assist terminally ill patients in reframing hope and meaning in their lives. The following cases provide a real-world context for further discussions of concepts of hope, truth-telling, and the goals of medicine to heal the suffering.

Case Studies in Palliative Medicine

Patient Narrative #1: Hopelessness and Loss of Meaning in Life

The patient was a seventy-year-old Russian woman, a first-generation immigrant to the U.S. She was admitted to the hospital for evaluation and treatment of severe abdominal and back pain and for re-assessment of treatments for widely metastatic colon cancer. Intravenous opioid analgesics were administered, and CT scans of her abdomen and pelvis were done. Within forty-eight hours of the woman's admission to the hospital, her physical pain was well-controlled, and a diagnosis of progressive stage IV colon cancer was established through a joint effort with the palliative care and medical oncology teams.

The patient's husband had died several years prior to her colon cancer diagnosis, and she now lived alone. She had friends and neighbors, and belonged to a faith community. She had few visitors, and she did not request communication with anyone other than her sons. She and her late husband successfully raised two sons, both of whom lived many miles away with their wives and children, and did not visit frequently.

On the same day that this patient was given information about her medical condition and prognosis, she asked me to "stop beating around the bush" and turn up the intravenous morphine infusion so that she could die. Her request for assisted suicide was not granted; rather, intense palliative-care interventions ensued, which involved counseling by physicians, nurses, and social workers on the palliative care team, psychiatric consultation, and the involvement of hospital chaplains. The patient was discharged from the hospital approximately one week later and referred to a community-based hospice program. Her physical pain remained well-controlled, but she still had thoughts of meaninglessness, hopelessness, and being a burden on her family. These emotions persisted until her death several months later.

Patient Narrative #2: Guilt, Anger, and Lost Hope

This patient was a thirty-eight-year-old Latino woman with HIV-AIDS and metastatic endometrial cancer, seen in an oncology clinic in a community hospital in Harlem, New York. She had several opportunistic infections complicating her HIV-AIDS, and severe physical pain relating to bone and nerve involvement of the endometrial cancer. She was admitted to the medical service of the hospital, and the palliative care team was consulted. The palliative care interventions included pain management and assessments and interventions by a social worker and a chaplain. She was treated with antiretroviral medications and oral opioid analgesics and adjuvant anticonvulsant analgesics to manage neuropathic pain. Medical reassessment revealed advanced HIV-AIDS and cancer, with a grim prognosis for surviving either disease.

The patient was a single mother with three children (all minors). She was poor and required public assistance. Her children, siblings, and friends were unaware of her HIV-AIDS diagnosis, but were aware that she had cancer, although they did not know the extent of her disease. She was mentally depressed and spiritually distressed, expressing anger and open hostility to God. She was on occasion angry and confrontational with the medical staff.

Palliative interventions included multiple family meetings, pastoral counseling, and legal advice regarding the custody of her children. She died after several weeks in the hospital. She was able to reconcile her guilt and shame regarding her AIDS diagnosis with some family members, but not others. She died with an enduring sense of guilt and anger, and a sense of unfairness and lost hope regarding her death at so young an age.

These patient stories illustrate several dimensions of the issues surrounding hope and hopefulness in the context of terminal illness. The immediate outcome of frank and truthful discussions with these patients appears to have been lost hope on their part, with requests for assisted dying and profound spiritual distress being the consequences. Of course, this is the great fear of many physicians – that honest, truthful discussions could lead to a loss of hope in patients. Therefore, to avoid doing harm (as required by the Hippocratic Oath), physicians often avoid having truthful discussions that involve bad news.

Although the major goal of the interventions of the palliative care teams – attending to and relieving suffering – were only partially successful in these two cases, they remain illustrative of my larger point. In this chapter I will discuss the role of the physician as healer in the care of patients with terminal illness, in the context of the practice of palliative care. This healing art requires practicing medicine at the highest degree of professionalism, including utilizing the skills of empathic communication and mastering skills that facilitate the means for patients to reframe notions of hope and meaning in their lives despite a bleak medical prognosis.

The Palliative Care Physician as "Healer" in Cases of Incurable Illness

There has been much recent criticism of the quality of end-of-life care.[2] This criticism has focused on the fragmented nature of care, the overutilization of intensive care units and mechanical ventilation of cardiac resuscitation in dying patients, the poor quality of pain and symptom assessment and management, and the generally inadequate training of physicians to care for dying patients.[3]

2. M. J. Field and C. K. Cassel, *Approaching Death: Improving Care at the End of Life* (Washington, D.C.: Institute of Medicine, National Academy Press, 1997).

3. See "A Controlled Trial to Improve Care for Seriously Ill Hospitalized Patients:

Those who have described the shortcomings in this area of medical care have called for a greater emphasis on the practice of palliative medicine as the most effective strategy for improved outcomes of care both for patients with advanced life-limiting illness and for their families, who experience sickness with them. A reasonable working definition of palliative care is as follows: "an approach [to medical care] that improves the quality of life of patients and their families facing the problems associated with life-threatening illness, through the prevention and relief of suffering by means of early identification and impeccable assessment and treatment of pain and other problems, physical, psychosocial, and spiritual."[4]

The physician usually leads a multidisciplinary palliative-care team of health-care professionals who (1) promote effective communication, (2) coordinate patient care that is continuous (i.e., 24 hours a day, 7 days a week), and (3) anticipate and guide patients and families through routine care and crises, providing expertise in pain and symptom management, and attending to their concomitant medical, psychosocial, and spiritual concerns (see below). To be competent in palliative medicine, physicians must practice the highest form of professionalism, defined succinctly as the ability to keep the best interests and well-being of the patient as the supreme goals or concerns. This requires, first and foremost, a set of fundamental competencies, including a thorough grounding in the scientific knowledge and natural history of disease.[5] Interviewing and counseling skills are critical, as is the ability to communicate in an empathic manner (see below). These are fundamental competencies in palliative medicine because they provide the physician with the means to understand the needs of patients and their relationships with their families and loved ones.

Hospice represents both a philosophy of interdisciplinary compassionate care for the dying and a delivery system for this care. It is a subset of palliative care, applied to individuals who are dying. In the United States, most palliative care teams are hospital-based and care for individuals with advanced chronic illness, many of whom may not

---

The Study to Understand Prognoses and Preferences for Outcomes and Risks of Treatment (SUPPORT)," *JAMA* 274 (1995): 1591-98.

4. World Health Organization, *Cancer Pain Relief and Palliative Care* (Geneva: World Health Organization, 1990), pp. 11-122.

5. L. L. Blank, C. K. Cassel, and K. M. Foley, "American Board of Internal Medicine (ABIM) End-of-Life Patient Care Project," 1996.

be facing imminent death. Hospice programs are usually free-standing and community-based, providing care in the home to dying patients. Hospice care is also a covered government benefit or entitlement under the federal Medicare payment system, and many private health-care insurers, as well as Medicaid, also pay for these services. The best practices to meet the needs of persons living with advanced illness emphasize the seamless bridging of hospital-based palliative care into hospice services offered in the community if patients are likely to die within six months of discharge.

Surveys and opinion polls taken of the public about end-of-life care, and interviews of individuals facing end-of-life medical decisions, have identified very specific needs of patients and families at life's end. For example, a recent AARP-North Carolina hospice-center survey of elderly North Carolinians indicated that a sizable majority of respondents agreed that the following things were "very important" when facing end-of-life decisions:

- being at peace spiritually
- not being a burden
- knowing what medications and treatments are available
- getting honest answers from doctors
- having things settled with family
- having physical comfort
- understanding treatment options
- being free from pain
- having finances in order
- receiving visits from friends and family
- knowing how to say good-bye to loved ones[6]

These goals and desires describe both medical and "non-medical" needs, and generally match the goals that palliative care seeks to achieve. They are also consistent with a summary of desirable outcomes reported by the National Hospice Work Group (NHWG), a network of twenty-three of the largest hospices in the United States. The NHWG has summarized the outcomes that define high-quality end-of-

6. G. Straw and R. Cummins, "AARP North Carolina End-of-Life Care Survey" (Washington, D.C.: Knowledge Management, 2003).

life care as (1) safe and comfortable dying, (2) self-determined life closure, and (3) effective grieving.[7] The third outcome was not stated explicitly in the AARP-North Carolina survey, although the concepts of "having things settled with family," "not being a burden," and "knowing how to say good-bye" are critical to the healthy grief and bereavement of family members following the death of the patient.

Spiritual Issues at Life's End and the Role of the Physician

Spiritual matters are often at the forefront of patients' thoughts as they struggle with the knowledge that their life may end soon from disease.[8] The survey responses from the AARP-North Carolina survey are consistent with this, with the desire to "be at peace spiritually" being chosen as one of the highest priorities at life's end. Other factors such as "not being a burden" and "knowing how to say good-bye" also fall within the realm of spiritual needs at the end of life and should be objects of pastoral and spiritual care. Other profound spiritual issues for many dying patients include the fear of not being remembered, guilt and/or shame over past behaviors (which may have led directly or indirectly to their illness), anger at God, and a sense of abandonment by God and others.

The physician and the health-care team are expected to acknowledge and validate the spiritual concerns of patients. Attending to these spiritual concerns is an important role of palliative care, and is usually accomplished in several ways.[9] If one defines religion as "a search for significance in terms of the sacred,"[10] then the particularities of one's

7. T. Ryndes et al., "Report on the Alpha and Beta Pilots of End-Result Outcome Measures." This report was constructed by the Outcomes Forum, a joint effort of the National Hospice and Palliative Care Organization and the National Hospice Work Group. See http://host1.bondware.com/\nhwg/news.ez?viewLink=49&Form.sess_id =2089739&Form.sess_key=1211807749.

8. B. Lo, D. Ruston, L. W. Kates, R. M. Arnold, C. B. Cohen, et al., "Discussing Religious and Spiritual Issues at the End of Life: A Practical Guide for Physicians," *JAMA* 287 (2002): 749-54.

9. B. Lo, L. W. Kates, D. Ruston, et al., "Responding to Requests for Prayer and Religious Ceremonies by Patients Near the End of Life and Their Families," *Journal of Palliative Medicine* 6, no. 3 (2003): 409-15.

10. K. I. Pargament, *The Psychology of Religion and Coping* (New York: Guilford, 1997).

religious convictions are crucial in making meaning out of stressful and desperate health circumstances.[11]

In the Christian context, a powerful New Testament text asserts, "Do not be conformed to this world, but be transformed by the renewing of your minds, so that you may discern what is the will of God — what is good and acceptable and perfect" (Rom. 12:2). The "renewing of the mind" is, in essence, making meaning of one's existence and one's relationship with God. For the faithful, this can be powerful, hope-preserving "medicine."

For health-care professionals, a critical aspect of caring is to be present and to utilize empathic communication skills to support the spiritual and emotional needs of their dreadfully ill patients. This requires that they listen to patients and explore with them their hopes, fears, distress, desires, dreams, and sufferings (physical, spiritual, and emotional). Often physicians need to take detailed spiritual histories or spiritual inventories of their patients to assist them in articulating and defining the existential issues most important to them.[12] Two models of spiritual assessment appear in the table on page 213. A comprehensive spiritual assessment informs the palliative care team about how to incorporate the patient's spiritual (or religious) practices and preferences such as prayer and other sacred rituals (e.g., the use of incense, candles, singing and chanting, etc.) into their overall care plan, even within a hospital setting. The spiritual assessment also highlights the need to engage and prioritize the importance of the patient's faith leader or the medical chaplain as part of the care team.

As illustrated in the cases of the two patients described above, the spiritual concerns of persons with terminal illness typically revolve around issues such as the need to see the meaning of their lives in the present context; the need to have the value of their lives recognized; the need for companionship (not to be abandoned); the need to die in a way that is determined by their cultural and spiritual preferences; and, in some sense, the need to be given "hope" in the face of hopeless illness. But hope for what?

11. C. L. Park, "Religion as a Meaning-Making Framework in Coping with Life Stress," *Journal of Social Issues* 61 (2005): 707-29.

12. See Abigail Rian Evans' chapter in this volume.

Table 1. Two Models of Spiritual Assessment

HOPE Model

The HOPE model provides four domains that cover basic areas of inquiry for conducting a spiritual assessment:

H: Sources of hope, meaning, comfort, strength, peace, love, and connection
O: Organized religion
P: Personal spirituality and practices
E: Effects on medical care and end-of-life issues

In this model, the physician presents a series of questions to the patient from each of the domains. The purpose is to determine the patient's spiritual support systems, religious affiliations, and personal spiritual practices, as well as ways in which the physician's understanding of the patient's spirituality can improve care.

Source: G. Anandarajah and E. Hight, "Spirituality and Medical Practice: Using the Hope Questions as a Practical Tool for Spiritual Assessment," *American Family Physician* 63 (2001): 81-89.

FICA Model

Similar to the HOPE model is the FICA model, which focuses on the following four areas:

F: Faith or beliefs
I: Importance and influence
C: Community
A: Address

These areas provide useful questions for determining the role of religion or spirituality in an individual's life:

- What is your faith or belief?
- Is your faith important in your life?
- Are you a part of a spiritual or religious community?
- How would you like me to address these issues in your care?

Source: C. Puchalski and A. Romer, "Taking a Spiritual History Allows Clinicians to Understand Patients More Fully," *Journal of Palliative Medicine* 3, no. 1 (2000): 129-37.

Honesty, Truth-Telling, and Empathy — and Their Impact on Hope

> If we were as good at listening to our patients as we are at telling them things, we would learn that hope is not automatically equated with survival. Hope means different things to different people; and hope means different things to the same person as he moves through different stages of his illness and his emotional reaction to it . . .
>
> Howard Brody, "Hope," *JAMA*, 1981

According to the AARP-North Carolina survey, one of the needs endorsed by a majority of people was receiving "honest answers from doctors" about end-of-life care. I suspect most individuals were defining *honesty* as "not deceptive or fraudulent; genuine," and as that which is "characterized by truth; not false; sincere; frank." (Interestingly, another definition of *honesty* is "without affectation; plain," which I suspect is not what most individuals would want if they were patients; see below.) These definitions and concepts of honesty require that the doctor "tell the truth." But do dying patients and their families really want to know the "truth"? Are patients harmed by knowing "the truth," and, if so, are physicians nonetheless still morally obliged always to tell the truth? Does knowing the truth about a poor medical prognosis take away hope?

The ancient philosopher Plato argued that medicine may be the only profession that should be exempt from the necessity to always tell the truth.[13] The Hippocratic Oath is, in fact, silent on the issue of truth-telling. The major rationalization for these positions is perhaps best summarized by the physician B. C. Meyer, who said, "Ours is a profession which traditionally has been guided by a precept that transcends the virtue of uttering truth for truth's sake, and that, so far as possible, does no harm."[14] Even the great Shakespeare once quipped, "The miserable have no other medicine, but only hope."[15] Many others

13. S. Bok, *Lying: Moral Choice in Public and Private Life* (New York: Vintage Books, 1978), p. 222.

14. B. C. Meyer, "Truth and the Physician," *Bulletin of the New York Academy of Medicine* 45, no. 1 (1969): 59-71.

15. William Shakespeare, *Measure for Measure,* act 3, sc. 1.

also support this notion and add that given the inevitable degree of medical uncertainty in any clinical encounter, we in fact risk deceiving patients by asserting that we know "the truth."

However, we should not confuse "truth" with "truthfulness." In fact, much empirical evidence supports the conclusion that patients and families want honest and truthful relationships with physicians and other health-care providers, and can understand the nuances and differences associated with "truth" as an absolute certainty, and "truthfulness" as a mode of communication, respect, and honesty.[16]

The countervailing and more ethically appropriate position is to always tell the truth. In fact, Sigmund Freud made this declaration: "Since we demand strict truthfulness from our patients, we jeopardize our whole authority if we let ourselves be caught by them in a departure from the truth."[17] The requirement to tell the truth underpins medical professionalism. Physicians are authentic professionals because they can command a sense of trustworthiness that is founded on a basic honesty in their relationships with patients. R. Rhodes and colleagues define medicine in terms of a "socially constructed" profession, and they assign two fundamental principles to medical ethics and professionalism. The first is a fiduciary responsibility for physicians to act for the good of their patients and society, especially since medicine deals with people made vulnerable through illness. The second principle says that physicians must be trustworthy and must be seen to be deserving of this trust. This analysis holds that these two fundamental principles directly lead to critical "corollary" values of professionalism, which are professional competency, caring, confidentiality, nonjudgmental and nonsexual regard of patients, and respect for patients' values. For example, professional competency is valued because "physicians with skills and competency are worthy of trust," and caring is valued because "patients are inclined to trust physicians who genuinely care about their well-being and because caring doctors are likely to fulfill their obligations [to patients] in the face of conflicting desires."[18]

There is much evidence that truthful discussions with patients do

16. J. McIntosh, "Patients' Awareness and Desire for Information about Diagnosed but Undisclosed Malignant Disease," *Lancet* 2 (1976): 330-33.

17. Sigmund Freud, *Collected Papers,* II (1953).

18. R. Rhodes, D. Cohen, E. Friedman, and D. Muller, "Professionalism in Medical Education," *American Journal of Bioethics* 4, no. 2 (Spring 2004): 20-22.

not produce enduring harm. Though the two patient narratives provided earlier highlight some of the consequences of delivering bad news to patients, one can assert that the patients were more likely to "come to terms" with their circumstances and make healthier choices and have more productive conversations with friends, family, and caretakers in light of really knowing the truth about their medical condition.

Also, there are no empirical data supporting higher rates of suicide, or even higher rates of requests for assistance in dying, after honest "bad news" discussions between patients and their doctors.[19] In fact, Dame Cicely Saunders, the founder of the modern hospice movement, taught that most patients find their own sources of strength and resiliency if they are given enough time and direction.[20]

Yet the long tradition of the Hippocratic Oath emphasizes, rightly, the requirement to "First, do no harm." If one accepts that all people – no matter how open-minded or faithful to beliefs in an afterlife in communion with God – will experience some psychological distress when their doctor confirms that they are dying, the question then becomes: How does one maintain honesty, tell the truth, and yet not risk the patient's losing hope? The answer lies in the relationship between the truth-teller – the doctor – and the receiver – the patient. The key issue is how the truth is told; it centers on the concept of clinical empathy.

Truth-Telling, Empathy, and Sympathy

Empathic communication focuses on going beyond the facts and naming the affect associated with the circumstances or hard "truths." When it is done skillfully by experienced clinicians, there is much to suggest that the truth is comforting if it comes with empathy.[21] Recall my earlier description of two of my patients. When the first patient asked me to "turn up the morphine," my empathetic response was, "Your loneliness and sense of being a burden must be a terrible weight. Is that why you

19. K. Foley and H. Hendin, *The Case against Assisted Suicide: For the Right to End-of-Life Care* (Baltimore: Johns Hopkins University Press, 2002).

20. Cecily Saunders, "Telling Patients," in *Ethics in Medicine,* ed. S. Reiser, W. Dyck, and W. Curran (Cambridge: MIT Press, 1977), pp. 238-40.

21. Jodi Halpern, *From Detached Concern to Empathy: Humanizing Medical Practice* (Oxford: Oxford University Press, 2001).

want to die now?" Similarly, when the second patient had an emotional outburst, my empathetic response was, "This all seems so unfair. You have a right to be angry and frightened." These responses started conversations that provided a basis for deeper honest discourse in which we explored their fears, their anxiety, and their existential concerns.

It is ironic that patients and families often complain that medical personnel (particularly physicians) often come across as "cold" and unempathetic in their communication styles or bedside manner. Most people choose to go into the field of medicine because they are inspired to help people; the identification with and understanding of another's situation, feelings, and motives — the very definition of empathy — would seem to go hand in hand with this helping motivation. In fact, many physician-philosophers argue that physicians' emotions can help them "attune to . . . and understand patients' emotions" and that therefore doctors should strike an "appropriate balance between clinical distance and sympathy."[22]

However, the traditional medical posture is to teach and practice the value of emotional detachment of physicians from patients. This has been justified along several lines, including the need to remain "objective" and "impartial" in treating patients. Some degree of emotional detachment is critical to the physical performance of surgery and other medical interventions and procedures. (Perhaps medical students first encounter detachment during the dissection of cadavers in gross anatomy class.) In addition, emotional involvement with patients has been presumed to be a cause of psychological burnout among physicians. However, all of these premises can be challenged on empirical grounds — the possible exception being the performance of surgery and other highly technical medical procedures. In fact, contemporary clinical teaching re-emphasizes the skills of empathic communication[23] and is supported by many studies and observations that "emotional communication in the patient-physician relationship positively influences healing."[24]

Medical educators have made the distinction between empathy and

22. Halpern, *From Detached Concern to Empathy,* p. 15.

23. W. Buckman, *How to Break Bad News: A Guide for Health-Care Professionals* (Baltimore: Johns Hopkins University Press, 1992).

24. Halpern, *From Detached Concern to Empathy,* p. 67.

sympathy.[25] The critical distinction here is that physicians should never "put themselves in the patient's shoes" (which is a definition of sympathy); an "appreciation of another's feelings and problems is quite different from joining in them, and in so doing, complicating them beyond resolving."[26] C. Airing and others have argued for the use of empathy, which does not require emotional "interactions" with patients, but rather involves a more "intellectual" engagement to infer what patients are thinking, to avoid the pitfalls of entering into sympathetic physician-patient relationships that risk errors in clinical judgment related to over-identification and projection.[27] As Airing notes, the subtle distinction between "appreciation" of another's feelings and problems and actually "joining" in them is the critical and clinically significant difference between empathy and sympathy.

Empathic behaviors can be seen in primates and even rodent species, and are certainly evident by two years of age in humans.[28] It is now possible to identify specific areas of the brain (the amygdalae) that are activated when subjects are emoting empathetic thoughts.[29] This suggests that hominoids are, by virtue of evolutionary mechanisms with putative survival benefits, "hardwired" to express empathy. If we are "hardwired" for this trait as a result of natural selection and evolution, then why isn't empathy always exhibited in medical encounters? It would seem that empathic behaviors and modes of communication are sometimes "professionalized away"! As the famous Boston physician Oliver Wendell Holmes once said, "The face of the physician, like that of a diplomatist, should be impenetrable. . . . Some shrewd old doctors have a few phrases always on hand for patients that will insist on knowing the pathology of their complaints without the slightest capacity of understanding the scientific explanation."[30] The paternalistic tone of

25. Halpern, *From Detached Concern to Empathy,* p. 149.

26. C. Airing, "Sympathy and Empathy," *JAMA* 167, no. 4 (1958): 448-52.

27. See Halpern, *From Detached Concern to Empathy,* pp. 67-68.

28. F. de Waal, "Homo homini lupus? Morality, the Social Instincts, and Our Fellow Primates," in *Neurobiology of Human Values,* ed. J. P. Cangeux, A. R. Damasio, W. Singer, and Y. Chisten (Berlin: Springer-Verlag, 2005), pp. 17-36.

29. L. Carr, M. Iacoboni, M. C. Dubeau, J. C. Mazziotta, and G. L. Lenzi, "Neural Mechanisms of Empathy in Humans: A Relay from Neural Systems for Imitation to Limbic Areas," *Proceedings of the National Academy of Sciences* 100 (2003): 5497-5502.

30. Oliver Wendell Holmes, *Medical Essays, 1842-1882,* Chapter 5: "Scholastic and Bed-

this comment, in addition to the reasons cited above, give ample support for rejecting this "old school" teaching.

Empathetic communication provides a vehicle for honest and less destructive truth-telling that does not need to be hope-destroying. Again, the use of language and the clarity of definitions are important. In the most common usage of the term *hope,* we usually mean what we would like to happen. In encounters with terminally ill patients and their families, all parties have feelings about what they want – namely, a return to health and the staving off of death. Therefore, if there is a sense that this desire is not realistic, usually patients will not ask about their prognosis, and physicians will not volunteer the "bad news" unless it is unavoidable. In this regard, the first of the two patients I described earlier was exceptional. To make matters worse, when physicians are in the (unavoidable) position of being compelled to give the bad news, they often deliver it in a very factual, un-empathetic manner in an unwise attempt to be as "objective" as possible. Given such circumstances, empathy can be seen as an essential clinical tool that is critical for truthful, less wounding communication and constructive emotional engagement with patients.

In addition, if one approaches hope from a different definitional paradigm – not equating "hope" with "optimism" (see below) – then there are real possibilities to tell the truth, to provide honest answers, and to "do no harm" to the patient in the process. This is mindful of Norman Cousins' admonition that the problem here lies more with the "art of medicine" than with the ethics of medicine.[31]

Reframing Hope in the Face of Terminal Illness

> . . . in your hearts, sanctify Christ as Lord. Always be ready to make a defense to anyone who demands from you an accounting of the hope that is in you; yet do it with gentleness and reverence.
>
> 1 Peter 3:15-16

side Teaching." See http://www.gutenberg.org/catalog/world/readfile?fk_files=103003&pageno=1.•

31. Norman Cousins, "A Layman Looks at Truth-Tellling in Medicine," *JAMA* 244 (1980): 1929-30.

This passage of Scripture may be interpreted in many ways. As taught by St. Thomas Aquinas in his *Summa Theologica,* hope is not only a virtue — a thing having a good or meritorius quality — but, most importantly, a theological virtue — a thing having a specific moral quality. Hope is a virtue because "the virtue of a thing is that which makes its subject good, and its work good likewise. . . . Wherefore, insofar as we hope for anything as being possible to us by means of the Divine assistance, our hope attains God Himself, on Whose help it leans. It is therefore evident that hope is a virtue because it causes a human act to be good." Hope is a theological virtue because, as Aquinas writes, "God is the principal object of hope. . . . A virtue is said to be theological from having God for the object to which it adheres. . . . Charity makes us adhere to God for His own sake, uniting our minds to God by the emotion of love. . . . Hope makes us adhere to God, as the source whence we derive perfect goodness, i.e., insofar as, by hope, we trust to the Divine assistance for obtaining happiness." Therefore, the "hope that is in you" must surely be the presence of God and the ability to be present with the sick and dying as an instrument of God's work.[32]

Aquinas goes on to reflect on four qualities of hope. He says that hope should "seek the good," thereby fundamentally differentiating it from fear. Hope should also seek the good that is "in the future," thereby distinguishing hope from joy. In addition, hope should seek a "possible but difficult kind of good," thereby distinguishing it from unconditional desire or simply wishing. In other words, hope should seek a difficult good "that is possible to attain," thereby distinguishing it from despair.

Aquinas distinguishes the theological virtue of hope from unbridled optimism and acknowledges that some hopes may be "unobtainable through human powers alone, but [only] with divine help" (*Summa Theologica,* 2.7). Therefore, it is necessary to discriminate between the hope that comes from petitions to man (i.e., physicians) and the hope that can only be obtained by prayerful communication with God.

What are the implications of this theological teaching in light of contemporary medicine and the hopelessly ill? For example, patients who avoid decision-making in hopes of a miracle "cure" of their widely

32. St. Thomas Aquinas, "On Hope, Considered in Itself," in *Summa Theologica* (New York: Benziger Bros., 1947).

metastatic cancer may, on the one hand, be seen as hoping for a "difficult good." Yet, on the other hand, there are biological laws (also created by God) which render that hope of immortality impossible to achieve.

Perhaps this dilemma is resolved by reflecting on the theological significance of miracles. Theologically speaking, what we ask for from God is related to an individual's life of faith and the continuing development of the individual's relationship with God, and does not simply flow from a consensus on what may or may not be good for the health of the individual. In a religious sense, healing is never an end in and of itself. It is always intended to lead individuals to a position where they can be reconnected with God and find right relationship with God, self, and others. In other words, the point of religious healing is theological, not medical. From this perspective, the hope for healing petitioned for through prayers to God can be distinguished from simple wishing or despair.

Playwright and former Czechoslovakian president Václav Havel provides a basis for reframing hope in terminally ill patients. "Hope is definitely not the same thing as optimism. It is not the conviction that something will turn out well, but the certainty that something makes sense, no matter how it turns out."[33] For Christians, the "hope that is in us" is rooted in the ability to be present and to make a commitment to non-abandonment, caring, and love. The hope that is within patients may be expressed on a superficial level as the wish for a way out of their circumstances, by heroic medical rescues through scientifically based, technologically sophisticated medical means or through divine intervention. But in a more profound way, as expressed by Robert Frost in the poem that opens this chapter, it is really a hope that is captured by envisioning "a way through" for the vulnerable and the suffering.

The best way for us to help patients realize this hope is to nurture their spiritual lives and assist them in reframing their thinking about life's goals and meaning – to define and redefine the goals of care with patients and their families as the "hope" for a cure diminishes in the face of progressive disease. Howard Brody's comment quoted earlier in this chapter bears repeating here: "If we were as good at listening to our patients as we are at telling them things, we would learn that hope is

33. Václav Havel, *Disturbing the Peace* (New York: Alfred A. Knopf, 1990).

not automatically equated with survival. Hope means different things to different people; and hope means different things to the same person as he moves through different stages of his illness and his emotional reaction to it."[34] Beyond dispensing medications and performing procedures, the major focus of the work of the palliative care teams is to listen empathetically, maintain a compassionate presence, and help patients reframe their concepts of hope.

In this regard, Viktor Frankl's work has been enormously influential. Frankl, a survivor of the Nazi concentration camps of World War II, formulated a field of psychotherapy that he termed "logotherapy," which focuses on the critical nature of recognizing meaning in one's life as a foundation for maintaining hope, especially in the face of tragedy. Frankl wrote, "Life has meaning and never ceases to have meaning even up to its last moments. Meaning may change, but it never ceases to exist." He went on to say, "What matters, therefore, is not the meaning of life in general, but rather the specific meaning of a person's life at a given moment."[35] In this context we have an avenue for providing or helping to maintain hope, even for patients facing imminent death.

Frankl emphasized that the sources of meaning in life revolve around three major factors: one's work and deeds dedicated to causes (what he called "creativity"); one's life experiences involving relationships and roles; and, most importantly, one's attitudes toward suffering and existential problems. The great and what he called the "inevitable" existential problems in life involve attitudes about suffering, death, and guilt over the gap between one's goals in life and one's actual accomplishments. But, as Frankl noted, "We have the freedom to find meaning in existence and to choose our attitude toward suffering."[36] In W. Breitbart's "meaning-centered" psychotherapy trials, Frankl's work has formed the basis for structuring specific psychosocial interventions to reshape attitudes and find meaning in life despite the diagnosis of advanced cancer.[37]

34. Howard Brody, "Hope," *JAMA* 246, no. 13 (1981): 1411-12.

35. Viktor Frankl, *Man's Search for Meaning* (New York: Simon & Schuster, 1959), p. 171.

36. Frankl, *Man's Search for Meaning.*

37. W. Breitbart, "Spirituality and Meaning in Supportive Care: Spirituality- and Meaning-Centered Group Psychotherapy Interventions in Advanced Cancer," *Supportive Care in Cancer* 10, no. 4 (2002): 272-80.

In a discussion of hope and hopelessness at the end of life, M. D. Sullivan writes, "Hope at the end of life can come in various forms: for cure, for survival, for comfort, for dignity, for intimacy, or for salvation. Hopelessness at the end of life is therefore not simply the absence of hope, but attachment to the form of hope that is lost. . . ."[38] There are a number of general interventions utilized by palliative care teams to assist patients in finding meaning and new hope in their lives, even in the face of imminent death (i.e., helping them attach to the hope that is still present and possible).

As noted above, an absolute commitment to non-abandonment and to be present with the patients and families through the trajectory of illness is critical. This provides opportunity for reflective, ongoing supportive and empathic listening and communication with patients and families, especially in the face of crises or even at the actual moment of death. Asking a patient to participate in activities such as doing a life review, making a life journal or a scrapbook of their lives, recording an audiotape or videotape for their children or grandchildren – these are examples of exercises that can focus the individual on moments that have given life great meaning in the past, and can often shape notions of how life can be meaningful in the present.[39] Table 2 on page 224 gives a more wide-ranging list of clinical interventions that can support hope.

Partnering between the physician and/or medical team and the patient's spiritual and faith leader is also quite important. Effective partnering requires a degree of what Deborah van Deusen Hunsinger refers to as "bilingual" competency in medical and spiritual care. Hunsinger suggests that those who are serious about religion, theology, and spirituality should become bilingual – they should learn the language of both medicine and theology. Becoming bilingual means developing a degree of competency in a common language between theologians, pastors, and physicians, and recognizing the subtle but important distinctions between roles of caregivers who are attending to suffering and maintaining hope and meaning in the face of death.[40]

38. M. D. Sullivan, "Hope and Hopelessness at the End of Life," *American Journal of Geriatric Psychiatry* 11, no. 4 (2003): 393-405.

39. P. Rousseau, "Spirituality and the Dying Patient," *Journal of Clinical Oncology* 18, no. 9 (2000): 2000-2002.

40. Deborah van Deusen Hunsinger, *Theology and Pastoral Counseling: A New Interdisciplinary Approach* (Grand Rapids: William B. Eerdmans, 1995).

Table 2. Common Clinical Interventions That Support Hope

- Controlling physical symptoms such as pain, dyspnea, and fatigue
- Fostering interpersonal connectedness with family and loved ones
- Exploring spiritual beliefs
- Supporting personal goals and helping the individual make peace with decisions
- Affirming the worth and personhood of the individual
- Doing life reviews
- Getting care providers to commit to non-abandonment and to being present

Source: Adapted from P. Rousseau, "Hope in the Terminally Ill," *Western Journal of Medicine* 173 (2000): 117-18.

The "bilingual" physician would be in a good position to respond to the awkward and complex theological questions that emerge from the clinical encounter with patients and other (non-bilingual) physicians. Examples include responses to questions such as "Doctor, will you pray with me?" A bilingual doctor would not become defensive, mute, or flustered in the face of this question, but would approach it in a way that acknowledges both strands of the question. On one level, it might indicate the patient's distress and concern about a diagnosis or the progression of the illness. On another level, it might indicate that the patient also wants prayer for healing, consolation, or hope. The bilingual physician sees the importance of prayer for the patient and does not seek to gauge it solely as a request for God to respond mechanically to a petition for cure. Rather, the physician appreciates the uniqueness and power of the prayerful engagement between the patient and God, which may itself have healing power and offer hope. The physician does not need to pray with the patient, unless the patient has requested this and the doctor is comfortable doing so. The physician need only stand in silent respect with the patient and family while prayer is being said – this is all that is usually expected and required.

Another comment sometimes heard by physicians is "Doctor, I'm putting this in God's hands – miracles can happen." Theological reflection by a bilingually competent physician-healer might indicate a response to this question that recognizes an important distinction between divine healing and the typical notions of curing in a medical sense. It encompasses an understanding that ultimately the healing comes for that particular patient in reconciliation with God. We typically mischaracterize and misunderstand the hope of medical cure expressed by our patients by seeing it solely as a motive involving the restoration of health without reference to any necessary existential correlations. The two are not exclusive, but the distinction is important, and we can suggest this to our patients and recommend that they seek guidance from their faith leaders or spiritual counselors in conversation with health-care providers.

Conclusion

My goal of care for the two patients I described at the start of this chapter was to provide the best environment for them to "die well." In his book titled *The Four Things That Matter Most,* Ira Byock has emphasized that establishing this supportive environment ultimately allows the "healing" to occur in the face of terminal illness so that the patients can get to a place where they are encouraged and hopeful and can say four critical things to themselves and to their loved ones: "Good-bye," "I love you," "I forgive you," and "Please forgive me."[41] This requires that patients find meaning in their lives despite their imminent deaths while also looking anew at hope. The new hope should be the hope not to die alone; the hope not to suffer or experience undue physical pain; the hope not to be a burden to others; and the hope to leave a legacy and to be remembered by friends and families. It is the hope of finding not necessarily a way out but a way "through" the journey, often with human intervention and divine inspiration. Physicians practicing the art of palliative medicine must make these journeys through illness with their patients, and in so doing can fulfill their mission as true healers.

41. Ira Byock, *The Four Things That Matter Most: A Book about Living* (New York: Free Press, 2004).

CHAPTER 11

More than Sparrows, Less than the Angels: The Christian Meaning of Death with Dignity

Daniel P. Sulmasy

Any important question in the ethics of caring for the dying is bound to be so basic that it becomes a foundational question in general moral theology. This thesis is abundantly true regarding dignity. The breadth of implications that follow upon the Christian notion of dignity amply demonstrates that it is indeed a deeply foundational concept.

Because the concept is so foundational, I will take care to explicate it adequately before examining its role in the care of the dying. Accordingly, this chapter will be divided into seven parts. First, I will outline the historical roots of the theology of dignity, establishing that the contemporary notion of dignity in Christian theology is a very late development and reflects the influence of Kant, centuries after his death. Second, I will set forth three uses of the word *dignity*: the attributed, the intrinsic, and the inflorescent. Third, I will argue for the centrality of the intrinsic meaning of dignity as the foundational notion for ethics. Fourth, I will discuss several of the moral norms that follow from a duty to respect intrinsic dignity. Fifth, I will show how the notion of intrinsic dignity provides a conceptual explanation for the regard that Jesus shows for other human beings in the Scriptures and how intrinsic dignity can be understood as a robustly Christian theological claim. Sixth, I will explore the concept of "alien dignity," arguing that this theological understanding of dignity differs from what I have called intrinsic dignity only in the shades of emphasis, but that both notions of dignity index the same concept. Finally, I will delineate what a Christian understanding of respect for intrinsic dignity means concretely, both for dying persons and for those who care for them.

A Brief Theological History of Dignity

The word *dignity* has an interesting history in Western thought. I have developed this history at greater length elsewhere,[1] but a brief outline is needed here for the purposes of understanding the themes I will address in this chapter.

While it is often argued that the idea of dignity is essentially religious, it is hard to make this case from Scripture.[2] *Gedula,* the Hebrew word translated as *dignity,* occurs rarely in the Hebrew Scriptures and means something more like "nobility of character" or "personal standing in the community." The Greek word most accurately translated as *dignity, αξιοπρέπεια (axioprepia),* is not used in the New Testament. The phrase *το αξίομα (to axioma),* which is closer to "worthiness," is also not found, although the related word, *axios* — meaning "worth or desert" (as in "the worker is worth his wage") – is frequent. Another Greek word, *σεμνοτης (semnotes),* is sometimes translated as "dignity"; it occurs only three times in the Christian Scriptures, and is best translated as "seriousness."

Aquinas uses *dignitas* and its cognates 185 times in the *Summa Theologiae,* and it tends to mean the value something has proper to its place in the great chain of being. For example, plants have more dignity than rocks; angels have more dignity than human beings. In a nutshell, while Christians may have always had some concept of human dignity, philological studies suggest that until very recently "it had not been developed into either a clearly defined literary form or an internally consistent set of ideas."[3]

Likewise, Aristotle does not use the word *axioprepia.* He uses *semnotes* only three times, and not at all in the *Nichomachean Ethics.* In the *Eudemian Ethics* he defines *dignity (semnotes)* as a virtue, "the mean between servility and unaccommodatingness."[4] This hardly seems the way we use the word *dignity* today.

1. Daniel P. Sulmasy, OFM, "Death with Dignity: What Does It Mean?" *Josephinum Journal of Theology* 4 (1997): 13-23.

2. Sulmasy, "Death with Dignity: What Does It Mean?"

3. Charles Trinkaus, "The Renaissance Idea of the Dignity of Man," in *Dictionary of the History of Ideas,* vol. 4, ed. Philip P. Weiner (New York: Charles Scribner's Sons, 1973), pp. 136-47.

4. Aristotle, *Eudemian Ethics,* 2d ed., trans. Michael Woods (New York: Oxford University Press, 1991), 1221a.8, 17.

Roman Stoics, particularly Cicero and Seneca, made copious use of the word. Recent translators note that for the Romans, this Latin word literally meant "worthiness," and that in its common political meaning, it meant a person's "reputation or standing."[5]

Renaissance writer Pico della Mirandola is credited with being the first to make a connection between human freedom and human dignity.[6] In his oration "On the Dignity of Man," he argues that human dignity consists in the capacity to choose to become what one wants to be.

By contrast, Hobbes ties dignity to power. He writes, "The value or worth of a man, is as of all other things, his Price; that is to say, so much as he would be given for the use of his power." In turn, Hobbes offers this definition of *dignity:* "The publique worth of a man, which is the value set on him by the Commonwealth, is that which men commonly call DIGNITY."[7]

Although he never cites him, Kant's notion of dignity seems to be a response to Hobbes. Kant writes, "The respect I bear others or which another can claim from me *(osservantia aliis praestanda)* is the acknowledgment of the dignity *(dignitas)* of another man, i.e., a worth which has no price, no equivalent for which the object of valuation *(aestimii)* could be exchanged."[8] Kant connects this to human freedom – as the capacity for moral agency that is intrinsic to the nature of human beings.[9] He insists elsewhere that "Humanity itself is a dignity."[10]

The Kantian notion has a familiar ring. In another very long story, I have traced how this Kantian idea of dignity was married to the notion of human beings having been created in the image and likeness of God by a Kantian theologian named Antonio Rosmini, and how this subsequently made its way into Catholic theology, and was first explic-

5. M. T. Griffin and E. M. Atkins, "Notes on Translation," in *Cicero: On Duties* (New York: Cambridge University Press, 1991), pp. xlvi-xlvii.

6. Giovanni Pico della Mirandola, "Oration on the Dignity of Man," in *The Renaissance Philosophy of Man,* trans. Elizabeth L. Forbes, ed. Ernst Cassirer (Chicago: University of Chicago Press, 1948), pp. 224-25.

7. Thomas Hobbes, *Leviathan,* X, ed. Richard Tuck (Cambridge: Cambridge University Press, 1991), pp. 63-64.

8. Immanuel Kant, "The Metaphysics of Morals, Part II: The Metaphysical Principles of Virtue," Ak462, in *Ethical Philosophy,* trans. James W. Ellington (Indianapolis: Hackett, 1983), p. 127.

9. Kant, "The Metaphysics of Morals, Part II," Ak419-420, pp. 80-81.

10. Kant, "The Metaphysics of Morals, Part II," Ak462, p. 127.

itly used in the social encyclical *Rerum Novarum,* in which Pope Leo XIII defended the dignity of workers in the late nineteenth century.[11] Thus, it is by the retroactive baptism of a Kantian idea that *dignity* became an important word in Catholic theology.

Three Uses of the Word *Dignity*

Given the history I have outlined, it is clear that, historically, many people have used the word *dignity* to mean different things. I suggest that one convenient way to classify these uses is to distinguish between attributed, intrinsic, and inflorescent conceptions of human dignity.[12]

By attributed dignity, I mean that worth or value one confers upon others by acts of attribution. The act of conferring this worth or value may be accomplished individually or communally, but it always involves a choice. Attributed dignity is, in a sense, created. It constitutes a conventional form of value. Thus, we attribute worth or value to those we consider to be dignitaries, those we admire, those who carry themselves in a particular way, or those who have certain talents, skills, or powers. We can even attribute worth or value to ourselves by using this word. The Hobbesian notion of dignity is attributed.

By intrinsic dignity, I mean that worth or value that people have simply because they are human, not by virtue of any social standing, any ability to evoke admiration, or any particular set of talents, skills, or powers. Intrinsic value is the value something has by virtue of being the kind of thing that it is. Intrinsic dignity is the value that human beings have by virtue of the fact that they are human beings. This value is thus not conferred or created by human choices, individual or collective, but is prior to human attribution. Kant's notion of dignity is intrinsic.

11. Sulmasy, "Death with Dignity: What Does It Mean?" See also Juan R. Franck, *From the Nature of the Mind to Personal Dignity: The Significance of Rosmini's Philosophy* (Washington, D.C.: Catholic University of America Press, 2006), p. 179; and Leo XIII, *Rerum Novarum,* § 40. See http://www.vatican.va/holy_father/leo_xiii/encyclicals/documents/hf_l-xiii_enc_15051891_rerum-novarum_en.html.

12. Daniel P. Sulmasy, "Dignity and Bioethics: History, Theory, and Selected Applications," in *Human Dignity and Bioethics,* ed. E. D. Pellegrino (Washington, D.C.: The President's Council on Bioethics, 2007).

By inflorescent dignity, I mean the way that people use the word to describe the value of a process that is conducive to human excellence or the value of a state of affairs by which an individual expresses human excellence. In other words, inflorescent dignity is used to refer to individuals who are flourishing as human beings – living lives that are consistent with and expressive of the intrinsic dignity of the human. Thus, dignity is sometimes used to refer to a virtue – a state of affairs in which a human being habitually acts in a way that expresses the intrinsic value of the human.

The inflorescent use of the word is not merely attributed, since it depends upon some objective conception of the human and the value of the human. Nonetheless, the value itself to which this use of the word refers is not intrinsic, since it derives from the intrinsic value of the human. Aristotle's use of the word is inflorescent, as are some of the Stoic usages.

These conceptions of human dignity are by no means mutually exclusive. Attributed, intrinsic, and inflorescent conceptions of dignity are often at play in the same situation. But it is extremely valuable to be able to understand the various ways the word is used in order to understand ethical arguments invoking *dignity*.

The Primacy of Intrinsic Dignity

I want to argue that the notion of intrinsic dignity is foundational. From any perspective, but particularly from a Christian perspective, the intrinsic notion of dignity is the central notion.

The first reason that "intrinsic dignity" is the primary meaning of *dignity* is that it is necessary to postulate intrinsic dignity in order to make sense of the notions of attributed and inflorescent dignity. A human being can freely attribute value to anything. Any natural kind that is capable of flourishing as the kind of thing that it is always has a possible inflorescent value. On what basis, however, might one attribute dignity to something or say that the thing has inflorescent dignity? It must be something about the entity that makes it appropriate to use the word *dignity* in attributing value to that entity or in describing its flourishing.

What is prior to both the attributed and the inflorescent concepts of dignity is the assumption that the intrinsic value of the entity can be correctly described as intrinsic dignity. It would be very odd to say that a sea urchin's dignity had been violated. It would be very odd to say that a sea urchin was behaving in either a dignified or an undignified manner. The attributed and inflorescent uses of the word *dignity* depend upon a crucial assumption about the value of the entity under consideration – that the value of the entity is a dignity. This implies that intrinsic dignity is the central notion.

Second, no simple property could adequately account for dignity. By a process of eliminating all other options, one is led to conclude that the fundamental ground for dignity is based not upon any property but upon an identity – the value something has by virtue of its being the kind of thing that it is. If dignity were purely an attributed rather than an intrinsic value, then it would be a simple predicate – a property that some members of a particular kind might possess and others might not. Like the word *blue,* it would not depend upon any understanding of the kind of thing of which it was being predicated or of the value of the thing of which it was being predicated.

Attempts to use the word *dignity* as a simple predicate, as a purely attributed value, lead to gross inconsistencies in our deeply held and widely shared moral judgments. No simple property, no simple predicate, can be held as defining dignity in a consistent way across a moral system. To say that dignity depends upon how one appears to others, for instance, leads to the possibility that dignity might depend upon skin color. Surely one would want to reject that idea. To say that dignity depends upon one's freedom and control leads one to ask whether prisoners have any dignity, and if not, why one should care about the rights of prisoners. To say that dignity is purely subjective leads to the absurd notion that unless we have explained what dignity means to each other, we human beings have no understanding that other people have any dignity, and must conclude that, prior to a personal conversation, there are no dignity-based norms governing how we should behave toward each other.

By process of elimination, one is led to the conclusion that all attributions of dignity, as well as all complaints about violations of dignity, depend upon a prior notion of value that is not based on any property or simple predicate. This notion is intrinsic dignity – the notion that the intrinsic value of certain entities depends upon the kind of thing that they are, and not a property. The term *human being* denotes such an entity.

Third, if there are such things as intrinsic values, then what I have called intrinsic dignity must be the value that human beings have by virtue of being the kinds of things that they are. This is true by the definition of the word *intrinsic.* Intrinsic value is the value something has of itself – the value it has by virtue of its being the kind of thing that it is. Whatever is intrinsically valuable is valuable independent of any valuer's purposes, beliefs, desires, interests, or expectations. Truly intrinsic values, according to environmental ethicist Holmes Rolston, "are objectively there – discovered, not generated by the valuer."[13]

By contrast, attributed values are those conveyed by a valuer. Attributed values depend completely upon the purposes, beliefs, desires, interests, or expectations of a valuer or group of valuers. It follows that the more commonly used term *instrumental value* denotes one important class of attributed values. An instrumental value is one that is attributed to some entity because it serves a purpose for a valuer. The instrumental value of the entity consists in its serving as a means by which the valuer achieves his or her end. It is important to note, however, that there can be non-instrumental attributed values as well. For example, the value of humor may serve no clear instrumental purpose.

Accordingly, if there are intrinsic values in the world, the recognition of the intrinsic value of something depends upon one's ability to discern what kind of thing it is. This leads one to the notion of natural kinds, a relatively new concept in analytic philosophy.[14] The fundamental idea behind natural kinds is that to pick something out from the rest of the universe, one must pick it out as a something. This "some-

13. Holmes Rolston III, *Environmental Ethics* (Philadelphia: Temple University Press, 1988), p. 116.

14. Credit for initiation of the discussion of natural kinds is usually given to Saul Kripke in his two essays: "Identity and Necessity," in *Identity and Individuation,* ed. Milton K. Munitz (New York: New York University Press, 1971), pp. 135-64, and "Naming and Necessity," in *Semantics of Natural Language,* ed. Gilbert Harman and Donald Davidson (Dordrecht, the Netherlands: D. Reidel, 1972), pp. 253-355. For a good contemporary approach to the concept of natural kinds, see David Wiggins, *Sameness and Substance* (Cambridge: Harvard University Press, 1980), pp. 77-101, and his *Sameness and Substance Renewed* (Cambridge: Cambridge University Press, 2001).

thingness" implies what David Wiggins calls a "modest essentialism" – that the essence of something is that by which one picks it out from the rest of reality as anything at all – its being a member of a kind. The alternative seems inconceivable – that reality is actually a completely undifferentiated blob that human beings carve up for their own purposes. It seems bizarre to suggest that there really are no actual kinds of things in the world independent of human classification – no such things, *de re,* as planets, mosquitoes, or human beings. Thus, the intrinsic value of a natural entity – the value it has by virtue of being the kind of thing that it is – depends upon one's ability to pick out that entity as a member of a natural kind.

I would then define intrinsic dignity as the intrinsic value of entities that are members of a natural kind that is, as a kind, capable of language, rationality, love, free will, moral agency, creativity, humor, aesthetic sensibility, and a capacity to grasp the finite and the infinite. This definition is decidedly anti-speciesist. If there are other kinds of entities in the universe besides human beings that have, as a kind, these capacities – whether angels or extra-terrestrials – they would also have intrinsic dignity.

Importantly, the logic of natural kinds suggests that one picks out individuals as members of the kind not because they express all the necessary and sufficient predicates to be classified as a member of the species, but by virtue of their inclusion under the extension of the natural kind that, as a kind, has those capacities. In technical language, this is extensional, not intensional, logic. For example, very few bananas in the bin in the supermarket express all the necessary and sufficient conditions for being classified as fruits of the species *Musa sapientum.* We define a banana as a yellow fruit. Yet some specimens in the bin are yellow, some are green, some are spotted, and some are brown. Nonetheless, they are all bananas.

Health care depends profoundly upon this extensional logic. For instance, it is not the expression of rationality that makes us human, but our belonging to a kind that is capable of rationality that makes us human. When a human being is comatose or mentally ill, we first pick out the individual as a human being; then we note the disparity between the characteristics of the afflicted individual and the paradigmatic features and typical development and history of members of the human natural kind. This is how we come to the judgment that the individual is sick. And because that individual is a member of the human natural kind, we recognize an intrinsic value that we call dignity.

It is in recognition of that worth that we have established the healing professions as our moral response to our fellow humans suffering from disease and injury. The plight of the sick rarely serves the purposes, beliefs, desires, interests, or expectations of any of us as individuals. Rather, it is because of the intrinsic value of the sick that we serve them. Thus, intrinsic human dignity is the foundation of health care.

Moral Norms that Follow from Respect for Intrinsic Dignity

Intrinsic dignity is a value that commands respect. To respect something requires both that one recognize its value and that one make choices consistent with the proper appreciation of that value. Respect starts with recognition and acknowledgment. If the value at issue is attributed, one need not make such an acknowledgment. People are free to differ in their attributions. If the value at stake is truly intrinsic, however, then it is an objective value and must be recognized for its proper worth by everyone.

To deny intrinsic value is to make a mistake. To refuse to recognize a value that is intrinsic is incompatible with respect. So, if there is such a thing as intrinsic dignity, then respect requires that it first be acknowledged and recognized for its worth. Further, as an objective value, an intrinsic value has prescriptive and proscriptive potential: it obliges one to make choices that are consistent with the objective value one has correctly acknowledged and recognized. To deny this would be incoherent.

Respect means more than recognition. It means making correct choices. It means choosing in a way that is compatible with the value one is obliged to recognize. So, if there is such a thing as intrinsic dignity, then one is morally obligated to recognize and acknowledge the value of a member of a dignified natural kind as a dignity, and one is morally obligated to make choices that are consistent with a proper appreciation of the dignity of the entity.

Among the moral rules governing the choices we make,[15] assur-

15. For a more complete treatment of the moral implications of recognizing intrinsic dignity, see Daniel P. Sulmasy, "Death, Dignity, and the Theory of Value," *Ethical Per-*

ing that they are consistent with respect for intrinsic dignity, are the following:

(1) a duty of perfect obligation to respect all members of natural kinds that have intrinsic dignity;
(2) a duty to comport oneself in a manner that is consistent with one's own intrinsic dignity;
(3) a duty to build up, to the extent possible, the inflorescent dignity of members of natural kinds that have intrinsic dignity; and
(4) a duty of perfect obligation, in carrying out the previous three duties, never to act in such a way as directly to undermine the intrinsic dignity that gives the other duties their binding force.

Space limitations will not permit a full derivation of these moral rules. Nonetheless, they seem to have validity as partial specifications of what it means to act in a manner that is consistent with recognition of the value proper to the meaning of intrinsic dignity – making choices that respect a member of a dignified natural kind as the kind of thing that it is. While the language of these rules might seem unfamiliar, the concepts are quite familiar.

The second formulation of Kant's categorical imperative might be considered a corollary of number two. Together, one, two, and three elaborate the meaning of Respect for Persons; two sounds as if it comes directly from a Stoic discourse on dignity; three and four are related to Beneficence and Non-Maleficence. Justice arises from the need to balance the requirements of two and three.

It is the intrinsic value of the human that grounds our moral duties toward our fellow human beings and gives these duties their special moral valence. Human beings have a special intrinsic value, and it is this value that governs our choices regarding our fellow human beings. The ground of our duties toward our fellow human beings is not merely that they have interests. As J. David Velleman has argued, from an ethical point of view, there must be something more fundamental to ethics than interests – i.e., a reason to respect a fellow human being's interests in the first place.

---

spectives 9 (2002): 103-18, reprinted in *Euthanasia and Palliative Care in the Low Countries,* ed. P. Schotsmans and T. Meulenberg (Leuven, Belgium: Peeters, 2005), pp. 95-119.

For example, one might ask, "Why should I care about this dying person who has lost a measure of independence that I have the capacity to restore partially through medical treatment?" Velleman's answer is that we seek to protect and promote a fellow human being's interests because we first respect the human being whose interests they are.[16] This fundamental respect is for intrinsic dignity – the "interest-independent" value of a human being. Without this primary respect, there is no basis for any form of interpersonal morality.

Intrinsic Dignity and Christianity

Is intrinsic dignity the fundamental Christian notion of dignity? For some readers, the answer will be an obvious yes. The modest essentialism of natural kinds calls for a theology that can spell out the law-like generalizations and typical history and characteristic development that characterize the human natural kind. In the language of theology, this means a theological anthropology. A properly developed theological anthropology thus becomes the foundation for Christian ethics. Many contemporary Christian thinkers will find such a plan familiar and congenial.

For other readers, however, it will not be obvious that this philosophical notion of intrinsic dignity has anything to do with Christian faith. For such readers, also, it will be necessary to trace the outlines of a theological anthropology; to specify a more specifically Christian understanding of the human in order to convince them that the notion of intrinsic dignity can provide a framework for explicating the Christian notion of human dignity.

Accordingly, one must understand that Christianity would quickly add several assumptions of faith to the brief list of kind-typical characteristics that I provided above (a purely philosophical list that required no faith assumptions). Philosophy can argue that we are, as a kind, capable of language, rationality, love, free will, moral agency, creativity, humor, aesthetic sensibility, and a capacity to grasp the finite and the infinite. Philosophy might also point out that human beings are beings-in-relationship. Yet Christianity would quickly add that the

16. J. David Velleman, "A Right to Self-Termination?" *Ethics* 109 (April 1999): 605-28.

fundamental relationship that human beings have is with God. Human beings are creatures of God. We have been created in the image and likeness of God, and are of inestimable value. Human beings are the apple of God's eye (Deut. 32:10). We are the pinnacle of the created order that we know.

Yet human beings are also finite – physically, morally, and intellectually. Human beings thus occupy a very specific place in the manifold goodness of the web of God's creation. We are "worth more than sparrows" (Matt. 6:26), "more than the birds of the air" (Matt. 10:30-31), and "more than sheep" (Matt. 12:12), yet we are "lower than the angels" (Heb. 2:7). This is our value – our intrinsic dignity – the value we have by virtue of being what we are.

Since this dignity is based upon nothing more than the bare fact that we are members of the human natural kind, it is radically equal among members of the kind. It does not admit of degrees. This is the value that Jesus sees in prostitutes, tax collectors, the poor, widows, orphans, the sick, and the dying. This value inheres in each one equally. Jesus teaches us this by saying that we ought to care as much as he cares for each of the lost sheep (Matt. 18:14) and for each and every child (Matt. 18:15). This dignity is so equal that the reward promised each is also equal. The justice of this radical equality is incomprehensible to the brother of the prodigal son (Luke 15:11) and to the workers who have toiled for many hours in the vineyard (Matt. 20:15). But this idea of equal intrinsic dignity is central to the message of the Gospel.

Intrinsic dignity is inalienable. It can neither be sold nor seized nor abdicated nor erased. Despite human moral failings, we must still recognize the intrinsic value of each, forgiving not merely seven times, but seventy times seven times (Matt. 18:22). Intrinsic dignity is the foundation of all human rights.[17] We respect rights because we recognize intrinsic dignity. We do not bestow dignity to the extent that we bestow rights. Human beings have rights that must be respected because of the value they have by virtue of being the kinds of things that they are.

Intrinsic value is unmerited. We do not create ourselves, and so must recognize that the value we have as the kinds of things that we are

17. Daniel P. Sulmasy, "Dignity, Rights, Health Care, and Human Flourishing," in *Human Rights and Health Care,* ed. G. Diaz Pintos and David N. Weisstub (Dordrecht, the Netherlands: Springer, 2007).

is a gift. As Simone Weil once put it, it is the impersonal in each of us that is of supreme value.[18] That we are, as the kinds of things that we are, is the sole basis for our intrinsic worth. And this is not of our own doing. Simply being human is the foundation of our intrinsic value — more than sparrows, less than the angels. Thus understood, intrinsic dignity is the foundational notion of dignity for Christianity.

"Alien Dignity"

A Christian treatment of dignity, however, must come to terms with the notion of "alien dignity." "Alien dignity" is a phrase apparently coined by Helmut Thielicke in some of his basic theological writings, although some (without supporting textual citation) have attributed the notion to Karl Barth and even to Martin Luther. The notion was directly applied to bioethics by Thielicke himself in 1969, and it has been recently retrieved by Karen Lebacqz.[19] Thielicke writes,

> The basis of human dignity is seen to reside not in any immanent quality of man whatsoever, but in the fact that God created him. Man is the apple of God's eye. He is "dear" because he has been bought at a price: Christ died for him. . . . The Christian tradition has had a special term for referring to this. Instead of speaking of man's own dignity, it has spoken of his "alien dignity" *(dignitas aliena),* a dignity which is imparted to him and which therefore partakes of the majesty of Him who bestows it. . . . Even the most pitiful life still shares in the protection of this alien dignity.[20]

Space constraints preclude a fuller discussion, but I have concluded, after extensive study, that the concept of alien dignity and the concept of intrinsic dignity (as I have developed it here) are really not in

18. Simone Weil, "Human Personality," in *The Simone Weil Reader,* ed. G. A. Panichas (New York: David McKay, 1977), pp. 313-39.

19. Helmut Thielicke, "The Doctor as a Judge of Who Shall Live and Who Shall Die," in *Who Shall Live?* ed. Kenneth Vaux (Philadelphia: Fortress Press, 1970), pp. 146-94; Karen Lebacqz, "Alien Dignity: The Legacy of Helmut Thielicke for Bioethics," in *Religion and Medical Ethics: Looking Forward, Looking Back,* ed. Allen Verhey (Grand Rapids: William B. Eerdmans, 1996), pp. 44-60.

20. Thielicke, "The Doctor as a Judge of Who Shall Live and Who Shall Die," p. 172.

conflict. These terms differ in sense, but not in reference. They denote the same concept but with differing shades of emphasis. Intrinsic dignity, as I have defined it, is not a property ("immanent quality") and does not depend on any properties. Intrinsic value simply depends upon the fact that in order to exist, everything must exist as a something. The value one has intrinsically is the value one has as the kind of thing that one is. Intrinsic dignity is the intrinsic value that a human being has as a special kind of thing – a human being.

If one believes that each human being has been created by God as a human being, and that the human form of being is a form of being-in-relationship-to-God, and that this form of being is the apple of God's eye, then the distinction between intrinsic dignity and alien dignity collapses. Alien dignity looks at human worth from the perspective of God as Creator and Redeemer, and intrinsic dignity looks at human worth from the perspective of the created and redeemed. "Creature" cannot be said without positing a Creator. The value (dignity) of the creature and the value (dignity) imparted to the creature in the act of creation are one and the same value. The terms *intrinsic* and *alien* refer to the same concept but in different senses. As the morning star is the evening star, so intrinsic dignity is alien dignity.

Thielicke and Lebacqz appear to have appealed to the notion of alien dignity, at least in part, in response to the contemporary Western tendency to deny the dignity of individual human beings who do not express one or another characteristically human feature. Presuming that this is not a Christian perspective, they emphasized God's view of the worth of the human as a way of protecting such vulnerable persons from the potentially dire consequences of the claim that they lack dignity.

But the idea of natural kinds and the view that intrinsic dignity is associated with being a member of the human natural kind undermine the claim that various deficiencies can eradicate human dignity just as effectively as does the notion of alien dignity. As I explained above, even if one does not express individually all of the characteristic features with which God endowed the human natural kind, one still has exactly the same intrinsic value as every other member of the kind. Intrinsic dignity does not depend upon the active expression of some necessary and sufficient set of dignity-conferring characteristics. The extensional logic of the concept of intrinsic dignity depends simply upon picking out an individual as a member of the human natural kind. Thus, both the alien and the intrinsic approaches uphold the dignity of the mentally challenged, the comatose, and the deformed.

While much more could be said about the distinction between intrinsic and alien dignity, on the basis of the way I have developed the notion of intrinsic dignity, this distinction ought not divide the Christian community, especially with respect to the care of the dying. Philosophy can offer an indirect argument that proceeds by the elimination of alternative views or by a conditional argument that if there are intrinsic values, then we can understand what dignity means.

Christian faith, by contrast, gives us a positive reason to believe in human dignity. Revelation offers an explanation for our dignity. We are made in the *imago Dei.* We are the apple of God's eye. Christian faith supplies us with a motive for acting in accord with our own dignity and that of others. God loves us enough that the Christ of God died for us. We must therefore live lives worthy of that calling.

Christian faith gives us a model for what it means to have positive regard for the dignity of others; it gives shape to the link between the recognition of intrinsic dignity and the upbuilding of inflorescent dignity (cf. 1 Cor. 14). We have seen God wash our feet as an example. Christian faith gives normative force and shape to duties of beneficence. Christians do not countenance a weak philosophical duty of beneficence but proclaim the agape of the Gospel.

What Does This Mean for the Care of the Dying?

For human beings, the fact of mortality raises questions about one's worth. Dying raises questions about one's value as one is dying; about the value of the life one may have led up to the moment of death; and about whether anything that is valuable about oneself perdures beyond the moment of death. One major spiritual task for the dying is to reject, or to discover, or to re-cover, or to affirm their own grasp of their own intrinsic human dignity. The grounds for attributed dignity will fade inevitably for each of us. As we fail physically, our inflorescent dignity appears to fail as well. At first we flourish, but then we wither like the grass (1 Peter 1:24).

Accordingly, dying persons naturally begin to ask, "Is that all there is? Is there nothing more about me that is of value now except how I feel, how I appear to others, how much I can do without anyone else's help, and how productive I can be?" The only alternative is the belief that one has an intrinsic value. In turn, consideration of the idea that one has an intrinsic value may lead to further questions such as these. What is the source of that value? Can such a belief be validated? Does such value perdure? These are all spiritual questions, whether raised in a religious context or not.

Christianity teaches that one can actually flourish in death, through an open acceptance of one's intrinsic value. This value is one's intrinsic dignity – a worth that is more than that of sparrows, less than that of the angels. Human beings have hearts and minds that reach to the heavens, but they are mortal creatures nonetheless.

Dying Christians must finally and fully accept themselves for who and what they are, in humility and hope. They need to know the value they have by virtue of being the kinds of things that they are – beings in relationship with God and with God's people. They need to know that while they are finite – morally, intellectually, and physically – they are loved radically and exuberantly by the God who created them and offers them redemption in Christ. No human being deserves such love. But God sees in us what we cannot see in ourselves, and became incarnate and died to show us what we could only see imperfectly ourselves, if at all. Death offers us the possibility of seeing this value clearly. An acceptance of our intrinsic value is an integral part of the beatific vision offered to the Christian in death.

The norms governing a Christian approach to death with dignity also place obligations upon the surviving members of the Christian community. Respect for the dying requires attention to their spiritual struggles. Respect, as I argued above, demands not merely recognition of the value at stake, but the making of decisions that are consistent with the meaning of the value. By faith, fellow Christians are called to point out, in word and in deed, the dignity that is already there to be grasped by their dying brothers and sisters. The dying need to be reminded of their dignity at a time of fierce doubt. The dying need to understand that they are not grotesque because of the way disease has altered their appearance; that they are not merely bothersome because they are dependent; that they are not unvalued because they are unproductive; that they are worth the time, attention, and resources of others. In short, they need a demonstration that the community affirms their intrinsic dignity.

Churches can be criticized justly for having neglected the pastoral care of the sick in the twenty-first century. Pastors and congregants increasingly seem to leave the visiting of the sick to professional hospital chaplains. But the intrinsic dignity of the human is, as I argued above, a relational concept. Those relations include, importantly, one's relationship with one's Christian community. Roman Catholics call visiting the sick one of the "corporal works of mercy."[21] Jews consider the practice a mitzvah. The choice to visit the dying is a choice that itself communicates a recognition of the intrinsic dignity of the terminally ill, and can assist them in coming to accept their own intrinsic dignity.

Even families sometimes have responded to the medicalization of dying with avoidance. In our contemporary culture, death is considered something that happens rarely, that is to be avoided at all costs. And when it is about to happen, it should be hidden from view in nursing homes and intensive care units. In developed nations, it has become far too easy to avoid the dying. They are not at home when one returns from work, but are housed in institutions one may elect not to visit. Christians concerned about the dignity of the dying must overcome their own reluctance to visit them. This reluctance may be based on some Christians' inability to accept their own intrinsic dignity, a value they can see reflected in the dying.

All of us, while exalted among the creatures of the earth, are worth less than angels. The dying remind us of this. But the death of a Christian can also communicate the hope that comes from knowing that we are worth far more than sparrows, as well as the humility that comes from knowing that we are finite and fallible creatures. The dying can teach the rest of us about our own dignity. If they have met Christ in their dying, they give witness to the promise of life with God that only comes through dying.

Christians will also uphold the other moral rules that I delineated above, that respect for intrinsic human dignity demands action to build up, to the extent possible, the inflorescent dignity of one's fellow human beings, provided this does not undermine or contradict the intrinsic human dignity that is the ground of moral action. In other

21. *The Catechism of the Catholic Church,* § 2447 (Liguori, Mo.: Liguori Publications, 1994), p. 588.

words, to respect someone's intrinsic human dignity demands that one show that respect in concrete ways.

Physicians, nurses, and others can help dying patients to grasp their own intrinsic dignity by concrete actions that thwart or mitigate the assault that the dying process mounts against their patients' inflorescent dignity. To do so is to preach the Gospel of love by deeds and not just words. To say that one respects the intrinsic dignity of the dying requires that one assist them in their concrete needs. Respect for the dying is shown by bathing them, feeding them, treating their pain, relieving their nausea, and helping them get out of bed. Respect for the dying is shown by being with them, and listening to them attentively, paying careful attention to the lessons they can teach those who survive them.

Respect for the dignity of the dying certainly means that one ought never act with the specific intention of taking patients' lives.[22] This is hardly consistent with respect for intrinsic dignity. It violates rule four from above, that one can never act in such a way as to undermine the intrinsic dignity that gives the other rules their binding force. How can one claim to respect what one intentionally destroys?

Those who claim that "death with dignity" implies the permissibility of euthanasia or assisted suicide can only do so by narrowing the scope of dignity to its attributed meaning. One can justify these actions only if one is convinced that all dignity is lost, or that it has fallen below some threshold. What is truly intrinsic, however, can never be lost and does not admit of degrees – even if one has lost sight of one's own intrinsic worth or others have become blinded to it. Intrinsic dignity is not destroyed by pain or nausea or feelings of dependence or depression. One's intrinsic worth or value is not dependent on any degree of rationality or consciousness. In fact, psychiatrists point out that persons who ask for assisted suicide are often merely testing the waters, looking to see whether others will confirm one of their own deepest fears – that they truly have become worthless.[23] Christianity proclaims that by virtue of having been created by God and redeemed in Christ,

22. Given the focus of this chapter, the argument that leads from respect for intrinsic dignity to a prohibition of euthanasia cannot be described in detail here. A fuller account is given in my essay titled "Death, Dignity, and the Theory of Value," cited in n. 15 above.

23. Herbert Hendin, *Seduced by Death* (New York: W. W. Norton, 1996), p. 156.

no one is ever worthless. The dying have this value by virtue of being human, and nothing more.

Nonetheless, respect for intrinsic human dignity encompasses an acknowledgment that while we human beings are of inestimable value, we are not of infinite value. We are worth more than sparrows but less than the angels. We are made in the image of God, but we are not gods. As the psalmist says, we are made "a little lower than God" (Ps. 8:5).

Thus, while there might be an absolute prohibition on killing, the duty to maintain life is finite. "Extraordinary" means of care are what the Roman tradition has called life-sustaining treatments that go beyond what a finite human being can be obliged to bear.[24] We respect human life, but we do not worship human life. While we cannot make death our aim, we can forego measures that forestall death, realizing that death will likely follow as a consequence. In fact, in some cases, striving to stay alive at all costs can be inconsistent with respect for one's own dignity – if it is rooted in a refusal to accept the finitude that is characteristic of the kinds of things we are as human beings. What Basil of Caesarea wrote concerning his monks' use of medicine in the fourth century is instructive:

> Whatever requires an undue amount of thought or trouble or involves a large expenditure of effort and causes our whole life to revolve, as it were, around solicitude for the flesh must be avoided by Christians. Consequently, we must take great care to employ this medical art, if it should be necessary, not as making it wholly accountable for our state of health or illness, but as redounding to the glory of God and as a parallel to the care given the soul. In the event medicine should fail to help, we should not place all our hope for the relief of our distress in this art, but we should rest assured that He will not allow us to be tried above that which we are able to bear.[25]

Thus, withholding or withdrawing life-sustaining treatments when they are futile, burdensome, costly, or complicated, or when their use

24. For a detailed history of this tradition, see Daniel A. Cronin, "Conserving Human Life," in *Conserving Human Life,* ed. Russell E. Smith (Braintree, Mass.: The Pope John Center, 1989), pp. 1-145.

25. St. Basil the Great, "The Long Rules," Q. 55, in *St. Basil: Ascetical Works,* trans. M. Monica Wagner, SC, in *The Fathers of the Church: A New Translation,* vol. 9 (Washington, D.C.: Catholic University of America Press, 1962), pp. 331-32.

would interfere with our ability to carry out other moral obligations, is perfectly consistent with respect for the intrinsic dignity of the human. Respect for intrinsic dignity implies that we should act in a manner consistent with our true intrinsic value, neither clinging vainly to this life nor denying the intrinsic value of this life.

Respect for intrinsic dignity also requires paying attention to the spiritual needs of patients and giving patients the space to grow spiritually — to attend to their needs for growth in inflorescent dignity. Yes — Christian faith proclaims that we can truly flourish as the mortal kinds of things that we are, even as we are dying. Death has a powerful way of making clear what is really important, what really matters. Death raises questions about meaning, value, and relationship that ultimately have only a transcendent answer.

As Christians, we affirm that this answer has been given to us in Christ and in the Spirit. The dying person brings his or her entire life to the moment of death. If that life has the love of God as the foundation of its value, the source of its hope, and its model of right relationship, Christian theology teaches that this is exactly what will be irrevocably, absolutely, and eternally determined in the dying of that person. One of the most remarkable opportunities I have as a clinician is the privilege of caring for such patients. When I enter their rooms, I sometimes feel the urge to remove my shoes, because I know that the ground on which I am about to tread is holy. I find that I myself am the one transformed, the one to whom enormous grace has been revealed.

In the mystery of death we see the Paschal mystery. Seeing God so purely can inspire us and transform us as caregivers every bit as much as it can transform the patient. For "neither death, nor life, nor angels, nor rulers, nor things present, nor things to come, nor powers, nor height, nor depth, nor anything else in all creation will be able to separate us from the love of God in Christ Jesus our Lord" (Rom. 8:38, NRSV). That love is the cause of our dignity, the lens through which we see dignity in ourselves and in our dying brothers and sisters, the inspiration for our loving service to them, and the destiny to which we are called. The measure in which our society fails to understand these truths is the main stumbling block to improving the care of the dying. The Gospel's vision of death with dignity is one that we must never tire of proclaiming.

CHAPTER 12

Embracing and Resisting Death: A Theology of Justice and Hope for Care at the End of Life

Esther E. Acolatse

From theological and psychological perspectives, death strikes a double chord in human ears. Because it is both a welcome friend and a dreaded foe, it produces ambivalent feelings in us. And because we are often caught betwixt and between, such ambivalence toward death allows it a greater hold and power over humanity than it ought to have. Although death is a mystery and as such ought to strike in us dread and awe, it is possible that the ambivalence might lie more in how humans approach death than in how death presents itself to us. In this chapter, I will think through some of the causes of this ambivalent attitude toward death, causes that must be attended to if their specific manifestations in the dying and the bereaved are to be effectively addressed in pastoral care at the end of life.

Encountering Death

Death is not new to human existence; it is a given. Psychologists tell us that death is present right at the moment of birth.[1] Forms of dying, however, are different. Cultural beliefs about death shape what we con-

1. Freud has eloquently formulated for psychoanalysis the Oedipal complex in his psychosexual theory of development, positing that right from birth the death-and-life instincts are present, witnessed in the birthing process itself. Thanatos and Eros, the death-and-life principles, are always present with us. For an extension of this thought, see M. Mahler, F. Pine, and A. Bergman, *The Psychological Birth of the Human Infant* (New York: Basic Books, 1975).

sider appropriate modes of death and appropriate rituals surrounding dying. Ancient cultures[2] have always "known" what modern culture is now beginning to understand: the distinction between death as a biological occurrence and dying as a sociocultural and religious phenomenon. In these ancient cultures, the experience of dying involves emotional attunement to the event and its concomitants for all involved (i.e., the dying person, the immediate family, and the community at large). The outward shows of emotion follow seemingly laid-down, culturally determined patterns. All of life is lived in preparation for dying and death, for the meaning of dying and death has been assimilated into living. How one views death affects how one lives; how one lives affects how one views dying; and how one dies in turn gives meaning to how the rest of the community continues with their living without the deceased.

It has become increasingly clear in both medical and theological literature that dying, unlike death, is a sociocultural and religious phenomenon, navigated according to cultural norms and attended to by stipulated rites and ceremonies. All people desire a "good death" for their loved ones. What is considered a good death and its attendant effects, however, varies from culture to culture. Among tribes such as the Kikuyu, when the elderly are at the end of their lives and it is clear that death is inevitable, they are carried outside and placed comfortably under a tree and left there until they die. This act may sound bizarre and even cruel to a Westerner, but it is not to the Kikuyu; for the relatives of the dying, this is the kindest act of all.

These cultures may have learned this gracious act by observing animal life. For example, when the dominant male in the pride of lions is nearing the end of his reign, he deliberately picks a fight with a younger male who, by defeating him, becomes the new head of the pack; the defeated male must leave the pride. He goes off to die from his unhealed and festering wounds. In a way this allows the living to carry on the task of living without any undue encumbrances. Given the age-old belief in the care and protection of the ancestors (the good departed), one can appreciate how it may be understood that when all physical

2. In using "ancient cultures" here, I am referring to both those that are gone now and those that are still here but that operate in non-modern ways. I think, for instance, of African (Nubian and Egyptian) cultures and Native American cultures.

care has been exhausted, then the rest of caring needs to be placed in the hands of those who will carry on care to the next life – the ancestors.[3] The final act of caring is no longer seen as anticipated care, but as anticipated reunion with those who have gone before and who keep a watchful eye on the affairs of the living. And herein is hope, when this death and mode of dying are perceived as an end for the dying as well as for the living. Those dying are left to die in peace with as little discomfort and distress as possible.

In most non-Western cultures, the attitude toward death and dying and its attendant grief are exactly as I have just hinted at; death and dying are approached with reverent steps. Death is accepted as a normal part of living, and one is expected to live in a way that makes anticipated death a welcome event rather than an interruption of one's life. Is death necessary and natural? Is death right and just?

At the same time that death is approached as a normal part of life, sometimes certain deaths may be untimely and even unnatural. In such cases, diviners are sought to find the cause and source of what is perceived as untimely death. Mortuary and funeral rites as well as expressions of grief in the wake of untimely death are laced with a haunting mood of defiance that underlies the desperation of the immediate family as well as the community as they try to fathom the inexplicable death.

The kind of ambivalence witnessed in the African understanding of death is certainly not peculiar to Africa. All cultures and religious traditions deal with such ambivalent thoughts and attitudes toward death. The Christian tradition lives with this tension as well. The tensive unity between embracing and resisting death pervades the Scriptures, both Old and New Testaments. On the one hand, we witness an anticipation of death, a preparation for it, and even a welcoming attitude toward it because of what is believed to lie beyond; on the other hand, we witness the dread and terror of those experiencing the approach of death – the bargaining, the desperate pleading, and even the fury at death as it is resisted for oneself or for loved ones. And so, when we ask, "Is death necessary and natural? Is death right and just?" we also ask if such questions can be adequately dealt with from a purely

3. For further discussion and elaboration, see Kwame Bediako, *Christianity in Africa: The Renewal of a Non-Western Religion* (Maryknoll, N.Y.: Orbis Books, 1995).

human and natural-sciences perspective and not from a metaphysical and anthropological perspective.

When we search for the origin and purpose of death, the Christian tradition necessarily leads us to the Fall, to the issue of sin and its repercussions – sickness and death. It is beyond the scope of this chapter to explore the antecedent aspects of the relation of sin and death, and so we leave it for others to explore such troublesome but necessary questions as whether death was always a part of the act of creation (in light of the sovereignty of God), or if it entered the picture only after the Fall.[4]

Whatever the case may be, we usually speak of death as being natural – that is, something that is not alien to creatureliness. When we raise the question of whether or not death is just, we ask, among other things, two intertwined questions: Is it appropriate for humans to die, and is it needful that humans die? Those who point to the distributive justice of God state that it is required by the nature and character of God that human beings face death. It is the outcome of fallenness that human beings are mortal. Again, the issue of whether human beings were made immortal from the beginning and lost their birthright as

4. Though Supralapsarian and Infralapsarian debates usually deal with election and rejection of the reprobate, they have bearings on arguments about creation and sin as one ponders the relationship between sin and death and the issues that stem from it. What complicates thinking about these issues is the differing understandings in theology about the extent of the Fall. For instance, Augustinian and Thomist conceptions differ as to the extent of the results of the Fall on humans. The creation account simply states that Adam was told that on the day he ate of the fruit of the tree of the knowledge of good and evil, he would surely die (Gen. 2:17). We can infer at least two things from that passage, neither of which makes it easy to answer our question. One, that death may have been not only a part of nature but also a part of creation and would take effect in some form with disobedience, or, two, that death came into existence after the disobedient act, an inference that is further supported by Pauline statements in Romans (8:21ff.). At the same time, we need also to accept the account of all creation as being good, and figure out how death factors in to a "good creation." But even with our limited understanding, we know that some aspects of creation serve limited purposes, purposes that procure the greater good for the rest of creation, and death is surely one of those – the death of a grain of wheat for a larger harvest of wheat, for instance (John 12:24). Altogether, while we may not know the mind of God before creation, what has been revealed to us in creation is that the Fall brings with it death. The Christian contention is that death becomes the means of hope and new life for those who believe in the One who took on death for humankind.

immortal beings because of the Fall is debatable. What is clear is that, like the cleaning woman, we all come to dust.

If death is so natural and as such a part of what it means to be human, why is there such resistance to it? Even more pertinent, why do Christians who believe and hope in the resurrection of the body also experience such ambivalent feelings about death? For there is at once both the embrace of and the resistance to death. What is it about death that evokes this dichotomy? It is because death is both friend and foe that it stands as a means of both grace and condemnation by God. It is a means of grace because it is that by which sinful humanity is rescued from perduring in a sinful state. It is a statement of condemnation because it is at the same time the awful reminder of sin's effect. The creature experiences death as both of these possibilities, and hence the tendency to both embrace and resist it, even among Christians who know how the story of death ends.

I want to reflect on this dual approach to death, a dichotomy familiar to us despite the hope of the resurrection. I will argue that this dichotomy is indeed the proper theological and psychosomatic[5] attitude toward death. I will explore this double attitude especially from the perspective of contemporary society and argue that the ambivalence which shrouds death stems only peripherally from what is experienced as the "sacral power of death,"[6] to borrow William F. May's term, and rather largely from what the dying as well as the bereaved experience as an unjust or an untimely death. Whether it is absurd to speak of such things as timely or untimely, the fact remains that some deaths leave us sad and listless but not undone, while others leave us bewildered and angry and quite undone. I will argue that there are practices of the church that can adequately mediate both types of death, especially the latter type, if the community of the faithful will attend to the

5. While the term *psychosomatic,* especially as it relates to disease, has acquired the pejorative connotation of that which is only in the mind or psyche, I use it here in what I hope is its proper rendition to call us back to the important fact that we are embodied souls or besouled bodies, and thus psyche and soma together, undivided, and that it is a composite of these components which constitute human being and which face and deal with death.

6. William F. May, "The Sacral Power of Death in Contemporary Experience," in *On Moral Medicine: Theological Perspectives in Medical Ethics,* 2d ed., ed. Stephen E. Lammers and Allen Verhey (Grand Rapids: William B. Eerdmans, 1998).

core issues that surround death and dying. This, I believe, will facilitate care "now and at the hour of our death" in a manner that engenders hope for both the dying and the community of faith.

Embracing Death

It is my contention that the current reticence about death and dying contributes to the overwhelming power it wields over human beings. Our refusal to name it and turn toward it and to acquaint ourselves with it leaves us fearful and tormented in a death-denying culture. William May suggests that the kind of reticence associated with death could be equated with the kind of awe in which a Jew holds the name of the Tetragrammaton:

> Silence has its origin in the awesomeness of death itself. Just as the Jew, out of respect for the awesomeness of God, would not pronounce the name of Yahweh, so we find it difficult to bring the word *death* to our lips in the presence of its power. . . . [Human beings] evade death because they recognize in the event an immensity that towers above their resources for handling it.[7]

There are kinds of death that we smile at even when we grieve the loss of the departed: the peaceful death that entails no suffering, preferably in one's sleep. Literature on death and dying suggests that all things being equal, people tend to die more peacefully (i.e., they do not struggle when death comes knocking) when they believe that they have set all their affairs in order, have lived good and fruitful lives with little regret, and have experienced what Erik Erikson points to as the final two tasks of psychosocial development: generativity and integrity.[8]

In completing our generativity, we have perpetuated culture and transmitted values to the next generation, and we have lived exocentric rather egocentric, stagnated, and withdrawn lives. At the end we can look back on our life with happiness and contentment, feeling fulfilled with a deep sense that life is meaningful and we have played a part in it. This feeling of contentment with what we have accomplished is what

7. May, "The Sacral Power of Death in Contemporary Experience," p. 197.
8. Erik Erikson, *Childhood and Society* (New York: W. W. Norton, 1963).

Erikson terms integrity. Our deep sense of purposeful strength comes from a well of wisdom that perceives what William James calls "the more."[9]

Paradoxically, this realization leads to a detached concern for the whole of life and an acceptance of death as the completion of life. In this sense, dying becomes one's final act of agency rather than what happens to one involuntarily. It is in light of this kind of dying that one speaks of death and dying as being natural (i.e., what human beings do). Karl Rahner, in his theology of death, offers clues to what one means by death being natural. He writes,

> The end of man, considered only from man's point of view, constitutes a real-ontological contradiction which is insoluble and irreducible to simpler terms. The end of man as a spiritual person is an active immanent consummation, an act of self-completion, a life-synthesizing self-affirmation, an achievement of the person's total self-possession, a creation of himself, the fulfillment of his personal reality.[10]

Death is thus natural, a breaking up of the biological nature and a completion of the task of personhood. But death or preparation for it has been present all along in how one lives. How one lives in a sense is in anticipation of how one hopes to die; how one dies is a reflection of how one has lived. Note that we are making a distinction between what kind of death one dies and the act of dying.

On the other hand, some adults may reach this stage and, rather than having a sense of integrity, despair at their experiences and perceived failures. This fear may cross over into a fear of anticipated death as they struggle in the last years of older adulthood to find a purpose to their lives, wondering if they have lived their best. Alternatively, they may regress into a previous stage, such as adolescence, and feel that they have all the answers. Instead of experiencing "the more" beyond, they may come to the end with a strong dogmatism which implies that only their view has been correct. They have alienated those in their inner circle rather than formed a closer bond with them and in them.

9. William James, *Varieties of Religious Experience* (New York: Penguin Books, 1982).

10. Karl Rahner, *On the Theology of Death,* trans. Charles H. Henkey (New York: Herder & Herder, 1961), p. 48.

Rahner again may have such types in mind when he suggests that the obverse of death as one's final act of completion may also occur. Rather than being an active performance of a personal agent, death becomes for such a one a "destruction, an accident which strikes man from without . . . a dark fate, a thief in the night."[11] To ensure, therefore, that dying is the final act of our existence, the task of all of life, especially that of adulthood, ought to be living in such a way that asks, "How will I die?" and "How will I die comfortably and with dignity?" The hope is that one would die in old age at the end of a fruitful life, anticipating death as a natural end.

A wise friend recalled several conversations with her mother centering on what things her mother would like when she put on her face (i.e., the face of death). It was all said with anticipation and a certain cockiness and attitude. It almost sounded like the best thing that would ever happen to her. Today this friend in turn talks to her son about death by referring to pieces of art that should be placed in the coffin for her burial. And because one such gift graces the refrigerator of their home, opportunities to talk about death come often. In this regard, when death does come, I expect it will be not as the dreaded, fathomless stranger, but the mysterious, fathomable familiar.

It seems that those who in their daily lives as well as in the moments of their dying enter into fierce toe-to-toe fighting with death, who are hell-bent on disarming death, may have lost this awe of death and are the very ones done in by it. They participate in Adam's death rather than in the death of Christ. According to Rahner, death itself can be perceived as a neutral event, to be experienced either as salvation with hope of consummation or as damnation – a participation in the death of Christ or in the death of Adam.[12] Those for whom death is the familiar, fathomable, yet mysterious stranger are the ones who give in to death when death comes and find peace in and through it.

My experience as a chaplain bears witness to this fact. Whether the dying person is a Christian believer or not, much depends on how she thinks about death in its strange familiarity or absence. Of course, the Christian has extra cause and purpose for embracing death when it

11. Rahner, *On the Theology of Death*.
12. Rahner, *On the Theology of Death,* p. 46.

does come because of the hope of the resurrection as well as the certainty of being in uninterrupted fellowship with God and all the saints.[13]

Such hope frames suffering, even the suffering that may lead to death, in a new light. It invites the sick person to bear with fortitude and patience the pain and distress of the suffering moment with an eye to the coming glory. An essay by Stanley Hauerwas and Charles Pinchas underscores the need for the Christian virtue of patience, to temper attitudes in afflictions, especially in bearing the pain of disease. According to the authors, it is not coincidental that the object of the physician's care is named the patient. Although this may sound at first blush like a play on words, the authors rightfully point to the apt description that ought to convey to the suffering/sick/dying the manner in which they bear their afflictions.

The virtue of patience, however, is a Christian attitude birthed in the believer by the Holy Spirit, and as such it is primarily a characteristic of God and not of human beings. By practicing patience in sickness, therefore, the Christian imitates the very nature of God, especially as it is exemplified by Christ in his incarnation, ministry, betrayal, and death.[14] It is through suffering in a Christ-like manner that Christians are perfected. Following Tertullian, Hauerwas and Pinchas make this point:

> Such patience is not only in the mind, according to Tertullian, but in the body, for "just as Christ exhibited it in his body so do we. By the affliction of the flesh, a victim is able to appease the Lord by means of the sacrifice of humiliation. By making a libation to the Lord of sordid raiment, together with scantiness of food, content with simple diet and the pure drink of water in conjoining fasts *to all this;* this *bodily* practice adds a grace to our prayers for good, a strength of our prayers against evil; this opens the ears of Christ *our* God, dissipates severity, elicits clemency." Thus, that which springs from a virtue of

13. One should not take lightly the ramifications of this kind of theology for those who are suffering abuse of one form or another. An awareness that such talk of the glory beyond this life has been used to subjugate and oppress countless people is essential for making such theology a hopeful and fruitful one.

14. Stanley Hauerwas and Charles Pinchas, "Practicing Patience: How Christians Should Be Sick," in *On Moral Medicine,* p. 365.

> the mind is perfected in the flesh, and, finally, by the patience of the flesh, does battle under persecution.[15]

Since this virtue is a fruit of the Holy Spirit, human beings do not have the natural propensity for it, and must subject their flesh to the inclination of the Holy Spirit in birthing patience in and through them. Since it is a supernatural rather than a natural forbearance we speak of here, we can also point out that it is possible that some semblance of patience which comes from the unregenerate heart may be just that. Even with the regenerate, this fruit of the Spirit may not be fully ripe and continues to need the cooperation of the individual with the Spirit for its flowering.

In his treatise on the virtues, Augustine makes a similar point when he says of patience that it streams from God and is a characteristic of God, though we say of God that he is impassible. Furthermore, godly virtue is

> . . . understood to be that by which we tolerate evil things with an even mind, that we may not with a mind uneven desert good things, through which we may arrive at better. Wherefore the impatient, while they will not suffer ills, effect not a deliverance from ills, but only the suffering of heavier ills. Whereas the patient who choose rather by not committing to bear, than by not bearing to commit, evil, both make lighter what through patience they suffer, and also escape worse ills in which through impatience they would be sunk. But those good things which are great and eternal they lose not, while to the evils which be temporal and brief they yield not: because "the sufferings of this present time are not worthy to be compared," as the Apostle says, "with the future glory that shall be revealed in us." And again he says, "This our temporal and light tribulation does in inconceivable manner work for us an eternal weight of glory."[16]

Patience is thus not only a godly virtue and tuned by the Spirit to perfect the believer. It also produces eternal rewards for those who bear with fortitude the afflictions of this temporal world. The impatient,

15. Hauerwas and Pinchas, "Practicing Patience," p. 365.

16. "On Patience," translated by Rev. H. Browne. See http://www.newadvent.org/fathers/1315.htm.

those who live harried lives, who cannot wait for things to take their rightful time and work their way in them — these lose doubly. Not only do they not have their suffering curtailed; they find that they bear heavier loads. At the least they bear the load of a disquieted and restless heart. But a word of caution is in order here, lest we think that what we are called to is purely the obverse of being harried.

In his book *Disciplines of the Spirit,* Howard Thurman explains what this patience ought to look like. He says, "To learn how to wait is to discover one of the precious ingredients in the spiritual unfolding of life, the foundation for the human attribute of patience." Since patience is more than passive endurance — a work of the flesh — Thurman urges that "one has to take a hard and searching look at the environment, particularly the context in which one is functioning . . . so that one's response is informed."[17]

And yet, how often it is the case that usually very sick patients do not have the presence of mind to engage in the kind of deliberate and careful attending to circumstances that is expected. In such cases, it requires the community of faith to pick up the mantle and to be in contemplative prayer for and on behalf of the sick and suffering. Ultimately only the Spirit knows what is truly birthed from above and not born from below. So it is likely that sometimes the patience of the patient may not be patience in this sense of the virtue that stems from life in the Spirit. And I fear that sometimes God may become impatient with the patience of such patients and their relatives, as well as with medical staff.

This is the case when what parades as patience ensues from lack of faith, hope, and love, and borders on fatalism and resignation, not actually to the will of God, but to the desire of the flesh that opposes the will of God. Much as we agree with Hauerwas and Pinchas that patience, a godly virtue, is required not just in illnesses but in all afflictions, we should take care in discerning the nature and quality of this patience and its source. In thus rightly discerning (barring the necessary delimitation of being creatures that are fallible), we are enabled and emboldened in appropriating the Christian practices of care at the end of life. This is the kind of hope fostered by trust in God, which

17. Howard Thurman, *Disciplines of the Spirit* (Richmond, Ind.: Friends United Press, 2003).

paves the way for participating in God's good future in the resurrection of the dead.

All the same, the Christian, even in the midst of this hope of future glory in the resurrection of the dead, needs to understand and see death as an enemy. Herein lies the paradox: while suffering bears eventual glorious fruit in and for the believer, the ultimate fruit being "hope that does not disappoint," death is not to be taken lightly. Death is a result of sin, what Karl Barth calls "the impossible possibility."[18] Sin is that which should not be, but is; and so death is natural but unnatural and thus must be resisted.

At the same time, we must pay attention to a point that Karl Rahner makes. For him, death itself is not unnatural, but neutral. It is human sinfulness that turns what ought to be the natural final act of free agents, which should be experienced as a peaceful culmination of each person's "yes" to God's self-communication in historical existence, into a "no" to truth and love, and so to God, who is the fullness of truth and love. It is as though death were the final embrace of God that terminates earthly historical existence and ushers one into the other side of life with God.

The resistance to death, then, is a continuation of the "no" to the love of God enacted through the history of the person. Yet there ought to be a caveat to this statement, and to what the majority of this chapter seeks to address, which says that at times a properly discerned "no" is uttered first, and only then a triumphant "yes" to that final embrace. Thus there is a good dying and a not-so-good dying, and these are, other things being equal, determined by how one has lived.

And yet what constitutes a "good-enough"[19] death is mediated by cultural norms as well as individual beliefs, characteristics, and temperaments. There is also a recognizable and often unspoken aspect of death which often hinders the dying process from being the peaceable

18. Karl Barth, *Church Dogmatics,* IV/1, trans. G. W. Bromiley et al. (Edinburgh: T&T Clark, 1968), pp. 408-10.

19. I am borrowing the expression from Donald W. Winnicott's theory of object relations, in which he suggests that what constitutes a good holding environment for an infant to develop optimally is a "good-enough" one, not a perfect one. A large part of this "good-enough" environment is dependent on the "good-enough mother" who provides just enough holding for the child's security but not too much. See Winnicott's *Playing and Reality* (New York: Basic Books, 1971).

phenomenon it could be and throws it into a tortuous, agonizing experience: that is, justice. It is a sense that what is happening to one is unjust. In fact, a sense of opposition to the injustice of what is occurring is what is often identified as resistance to death. It is not death qua death that is often the issue, but rather this death – this death within this time and this space.

Resisting Death

If and when we talk about justice or what is fair and unfair as it relates to death and dying at all, we usually forget its multidimensional aspect. We are cognizant of injustice for the dying person and perhaps for the family left behind. But what if we asked the broader question of whence death at all? My contention is that if we asked the larger theological questions apart from the usual "Why this death?" and "Why at this time?" questions that lead us toward theodicy, we would realize that ultimate justice – by which I mean distributive justice – would entail justice for the dying individual, for the community, for God, as well as for death. What mediates the human tendency toward hopelessness and despair in the face of death and gives birth to hope is that what is transpiring is just. By this we mean that this is a timely death rather than an untimely death. What constitutes untimely death in the minds of people will vary from culture to culture and perhaps, on a smaller scale, from person to person. So too will causes of what are considered to be untimely deaths.

Discerning Timely Death

We noted at the onset of this discussion that certain deaths seem to sit easier with us than others. Death in old age or death after prolonged illness, for instance, do not draw out the same agony and crises of faith as the death of a child or an abrupt snuffing out of life before what we consider its time. The Christian tradition says "no" to this kind of death. A good example is the Gospel story of the death of Lazarus recorded in John 11. Here we are taken into the heart of what the Lord of life feels about death, but also about untimely death. As Jesus stands before the tomb of Lazarus, the Evangelist records Jesus' emotions:

> Then again Jesus, angry in himself, comes to the tomb. It was a cave and a stone was lying upon it. Jesus says, "Take away the stone." Martha, the sister of the one who has died, says to him, "Lord, it is stinking now, for it is on the fourth day." (vv. 38-39)

The key word that aids in translating this passage is *embrimoamai.* This is the same word that is used to express Jesus' emotion in 11:33 – hence the word "again" in 11:38. The Greek verb *embrimaomai* connotes anger and indignation and not compassion. In other New Testament passages (e.g., Matt. 9:30, Mark 1:43, Mark 14:5), this verb is consistently interpreted as anger and indignation. Here "groaning in himself" would suggest the expression of intense agitation and anger. In today's parlance, we could even say that he was fit to be tied (i.e., before the full force of the anger explodes).

To die when it is not time to die is not fair. And it is not just. So resistance is in order. But can human beings know when it is time to die or not to die? As human beings oriented toward death, living in preparation for it, can we be attuned to some possibility of when it will occur?[20] More precisely, can the Christian – indeed, the community and fellowship of believers – know if this sickness of a member of the body is unto death? Can they know if this suffering has purpose and meaning and will bear fruit that lasts? Can they be sure that it is a good time to die? How do they distinguish whether this is from the pit of hell, intended "to steal, to kill, and to destroy,"[21] and needs to be resisted, a resistance that should be death-defying, or whether this is from the Father of all life, a clear invitation to cease in this life and begin anew? When do we stand and say "No" loudly to the cruel injustice of sickness and suffering and demand that it ebb its tide? And when do we let the waves come in and engulf us and say in abject trust and not resignation, "Nevertheless, not what I will, but Thy will be done"?

20. Martin Heidegger, *Being and Time,* trans. John Macquarrie and Edward Robinson (London: SCM Press, 1962). See especially pp. 236ff. for a discussion of Heidegger's understanding of the human being as a being oriented toward death. He employs an apt image of a fruit progressing toward its ripeness to illustrate the necessity that "in Dasein [the being for whom being is a question] there is always something still outstanding . . . something in one's potential for being."

21. Jesus sees this as the devil's purpose for humanity and compares this with the abundant life that he has come to give — a life that takes the sting out of all pain, even death (John 10:10).

All of this means that we need to attend to prayer for the sick, the suffering, and the dying with more boldness rather than the tentativeness that often accompanies such prayers. It is possible that our tentativeness comes from fear or maybe disbelief or just the anxiety that comes with encountering this unknown – death. It may also come from the denial with which we skirt and conceal death. Some evidence of this latter aspect can be observed in the rapidity with which we bury our dead and the equal speed with which some widowed spouses remarry. This may be a way of keeping not just death but mourning at bay, and holding them in what I term troubled joy. But hereby we miss the fulsome comfort of God and the support and encouragement of the Christian community. Indeed, the blessedness of mourning and being comforted is denied to both the individual and the whole community. Oftentimes people who would mourn with us are encouraged to hide their grief lest they offend us. By our posture in grief, we silently teach others that mourning is not permitted, and they in turn hide and keep it to themselves, and the cycle continues. Our churches continue to be peopled by many with unresolved grief.[22] The stance I'm advocating here, it is hoped, would mitigate this tendency to hide death and the ensuing grief. When we attend to prayer with such boldness, when our loved ones are ill and suffering pain, when we seek the face of God for their healing and in hope place them in the hands of God, we can know that the outcome is that "acceptable and perfect will of God" (Rom. 12:1). Here hope and justice coincide. We have expectantly hoped in God, not just expressed a wish, and there is a clear distinction here. We have looked at and to God and believed that God will do what is just and good for us, our loved one, and even God in this situation. In other words, all who have a stake in this suffering and dying have banded together in hope and expectation to this perfect end. God, after all, is part of this community, and it is to our shame that we act as though God sits apart from the gathered community and comes only

22. This recalls for me an experience at a drive-in church in Michigan one summer. Part of the reason some of these people were there was that the church had put a moratorium on their days of grieving for whatever losses and ailments they may have had, and their leases had run out. With no more room in the church to express how they genuinely felt, and no more space in their hearts to tell one more lie (i.e., "I am fine"), they found a way to hear from God in the comfort of their steel cocoons in the open space of a parking lot.

in time of need. God is part of this community and has more at stake than we or our loved ones do, especially at the end of life.

What does it mean to attend to praying for the ill with boldness? A story in the Old Testament is a fitting illustration of boldness in prayer. The story of Hezekiah of Judah as recorded in 2 Kings 20:1-11 shows what the Christian community is called to do in the face of illness, death, and dying, as a people who are called to both resist and embrace death. When Hezekiah is ill, God sends the prophet Isaiah, son of Amoz, to inform him that he will die from this sickness and that he has been given time to set his house in order. Hezekiah lets out a loud lament and weeps bitterly to the Lord. Within minutes, we are told, God sends the prophet back to tell the king that his prayers have been heard and that fifteen years will be added to his life.

Now it is the sovereign God who declares that Hezekiah will die at a particular time, and yet this same God, on account of Hezekiah's prayer for mercy for healing so as to avoid dying (what I would term resistance to death and what death stands for), was willing to reverse the decision and grant Hezekiah fifteen more years of life. In accepting this offer, Hezekiah accepts and embraces death, but at its "appropriate" time in the future. One can imagine that when the end of the promised fifteen years approaches, the family and Hezekiah would approach death with a different attitude; they would embrace it with hope. The God of the Bible is a God who would be known, but also One who seeks to reveal his will to those who would walk with him – but, more amazingly, One who is willing to be changed by his creatures. The Incarnation is the ultimate illustration, but throughout Scripture we find a God painted for us in anthropomorphic terms: one who is not unwilling to be affected by his creation, who changes his mind at their request. This is a God who actually invites such a daring approach even though sometimes that approach could cost one's life. But that is the substance of trust which births the hope of salvation that does not disappoint, because either way, one is in God's presence, so "whether we are awake or asleep we may live together with him."[23] Obviously, divine

23. This is from 1 Thessalonians 5:10 (NIV). This whole letter is Paul's discourse about the Christian life as a life lived in anticipation of death and resurrection and Christ's return. It expresses Paul's hope for the Thessalonians to live in the present with an eye to the future hope of promise.

sovereignty and human responsibility are intertwined in this enterprise. One needs to be careful not to lapse into fatalism and resignation on the one hand, or, on the other hand, into the brash boldness that infuses the current prosperity gospel movement and that makes praying for needs a right to demand rather than a privilege of grace.

The Epistle traditionally ascribed to James the Elder to the Jews in the Diaspora begins with an exhortation to them to rejoice in their trials because there is a purpose for the trials and testing they are undergoing – the complete maturity of their faith. To the exhortation to rejoice in trials, James adds a plea that those who lack wisdom in dealing with their trials ask God for it, with the assurance that God gives generously to all who ask. Finally, in the last chapter, James offers a simple procedure for attending to members of the body who are troubled or who become ill:

> Is any one of you in trouble? He should pray. Is anyone happy? Let him sing songs of praise. Is any one of you sick? He should call the elders of the church to pray over him and anoint him with oil in the name of the Lord. And the prayer offered in faith will make the sick person well; the Lord will raise him up. If he has sinned, he will be forgiven. Therefore confess your sins to each other and pray for each other so that you may be healed. The prayer of a righteous man is powerful and effective. (5:13-16, NIV)

Could it be the case that if we take the earlier injunction to ask God for wisdom in large measure together with the injunction to call the elders of the church to pray for healing of the sick, Christians are expected, among other things, to ask God for wisdom in their prayers for the sick, in order to know the difference between an illness that is an affliction from the enemy and thus to be resisted, and one that God has allowed, that one should rejoice in and thus embrace? When we seek such wisdom from the One who grants it in abundance, and have offered prayers – effectual, fervent prayers of the faithful – then the outcome, whatever it may be, is likely to be experienced as fair and just. God and humans have contended, as it were, and justice and mercy have met or kissed.

A contemporary example may help to illustrate the point I am making here. In the early 1980s, a young Christian woman was gravely ill. She had been diagnosed with late-stage septicemia, and most of her vital organs were already infected. In fact, her liver-function test was off the charts; the test result reflected what one should find in a dead body rather than in a living person. Rounds of antibiotics and antiseptics hardly made a dent in the infection attacking her body. The Christian fellowship she was a part of set to praying and fasting on her behalf. Then came a point when she herself was sure that she would be dead before the week was out. On Wednesday of that eventful week, a Christian brother called on her, lifted her out of bed (for by this time she weighed no more than eighty pounds), and supported her so that she could stand up, if only for a few seconds. He placed her back in bed and said to her, "I just came to tell you not to go." Then he prayed with her and left. Since only this young woman knew of her expectation to slip away by Friday, she understood the implicit message and its source as coming from God. It could be that God was answering the prayers of the saints who were crying before him day and night for the life of their sister and friend, or, more importantly, that God himself had set himself up against the intrusion of death and joined the believing community to say "No" to death. That woman is still alive today.

But perhaps I am calling us into a premodern world of the miraculous, of expectations that the church is still meant to be the primary place of healing for the sick, not barring cure that comes from modern medicine or traditional herbs or whatever other means. In all of this, I need to reiterate that God is the ultimate healer and decision-maker about whom God would heal for continuation of life here on earth, and whom God would heal for life in the resurrection.

Yet if the church is to function in this scriptural manner in its care for the sick and the dying, it needs to start from the theological schools, with the formation of clergy for pastoral ministry. This means that, among other things, clergy need to have a clear sense of their own theologies of death and dying and the implications of such theologies for their pastoral ministry. The trickle-down effect is that the Christian community (and it is the community at large, especially in the Reformed tradition, which together care for one another) is then equipped to speak openly first about suffering, and then about death and dying, and the hope of the resurrection. Our affirmations of faith during worship would then take on new meaning and poignancy, and become a springboard for us to form a caring community in which vulnerability regarding issues of death and dying is commonplace, and the practice of caring acts of comfort and support becomes second nature. Our sacramental practices, such as baptism and the Eucharist, in which we invite ourselves to death of self and proclaim that our living comes out of our dying, would be continual reminders that we are living toward dying. Unfortunately, this is not now the case. Our baptisms are no longer a reflection of dying in Christ and being resurrected with him; especially when the one baptized is an infant, thoughts of death even as a symbol are far from our minds.

A recent survey on attitudes toward death, which included clergy attitudes toward death and their uneasiness in talking about death to their parishioners, and visiting and ministering to the dying, indicates that the majority of pastors are discomforted about their own mortality. It seems that many clergy do not have a sustainable theology of death that allows them to adequately teach their congregants about living faithfully in suffering, death, and dying.[24] The fear of death, the aversion to physical suffering in any form, the assumption that when we are sick, we must become well at all costs – all sustain and nourish the current over-medicalization of death in our culture. It might appear strange, at first blush, that a chapter which insists on resisting death would deplore the tendency to over-medicalize death. I am not advocating a cure for all disease or the staving off of all death; rather, I am saying "No" to injustice begetting death, especially the death of the very young and those in the prime of life. And we cannot talk about Christian practices of care at the end of life without attending to some of these causes of injustice begetting death.

Various causes and sources of untimely death today range from accidents caused by drunk and underage drivers to suffering and death from medical malpractice and discrimination against certain races. There is ample information in the medical literature indicating the disparities and inequities in health care between whites and nonwhites, from the failure of pharmacies in predominantly nonwhite neighbor-

24. ETC Institutes' "Compassion Sabbath Survey, 1999," which looked at 350 faith leaders in Kansas City, reports, for instance, that only 37 percent of ministers see themselves as ministering very effectively to those who are seriously ill or dying, and only 44 percent consider themselves very prepared to minister to the seriously ill and dying. This survey was brought to my attention by Richard Payne in a presentation at Duke Divinity School titled "From Pulpit to Bedside: Engaging Clergy in End-of-Life Care."

hoods to stock opioid analgesics for alleviating pain[25] to the denial of fully informed consent to minority patients, who through lack of knowledge and the imbalance of power between health-care provider and patient may give consent without fully understanding all the issues at stake, or without even being aware that they are being used for clinical trials. Here research findings trump caring for the patient, and in the United States, African-American bodies have consistently been used for experimentation for drugs and new procedures that benefit mainly rich, middle-class white persons. The Tuskegee syphilis experiment is still fresh in the minds of black people, but such incidents are by no means relegated to the past, as one would think. Violations of informed consent persist in the medical community today. Farfel and Holtzman (1984) offer this report: "Of 52,000 Maryland women screened annually for sickle cell anemia between 1978 and 1980, 25 percent were screened without their consent, thus denying these women the benefit of prescreening education or follow-up counseling, or the opportunity to decline screening."[26]

If patients are unaware of the policy of informed consent and are thus denied input in their health care during early stages of their disease, what are the chances that they will be given full facts, complete disclosure, or even be able to understand what is explained to them when they are at the final stages of life, and the diseases from which they might die leave them unable to function mentally? When medical professionals require them to make life-and-death decisions at the end of their lives, especially when such opportunity has been denied them during routine check-ups, such supposed care appears cynical to those who in many ways have been and continue to be victims — objects of medical care rather than meaningful subjects of care. There is a question of justice and medical ethics here, which is why such people need advocates, both in the health-care system and in the community. And for the purposes of this chapter, the primary community is assumed to be the church.[27]

25. R. S. Morrison et al., "'We Don't Carry That' — Failure of Pharmacies in Predominantly Nonwhite Neighborhoods to Stock Opioid Analgesics," *New England Journal of Medicine* 342, no. 14 (April 6, 2000): 1023-26.

26. Annette Dula, "Bioethics: The Need for a Dialogue with African-Americans," in *"It Just Ain't Fair": The Ethics of Health Care for African-Americans,* ed. Annette Dula and Sara Goering (Westport, Conn.: Praeger, 1994), p. 18.

27. I am assuming that there is no need to argue for why this ought to be the case.

Justice Issues in Health Care and Care at the End of Life

Negotiating care and advocating health-care issues, especially care at the end of life, require the church to look far beyond the caregiving issues at stake at the end of life to the causes of ailments leading to death, especially preventable deaths, in which cases the church is sometimes called in to attend to and provide pastoral care for the dying and the bereaved. But long before the critical illnesses and disease that usher in death appear, certain factors — such as poverty, which fosters malnutrition, lack of adequate health care, and so on — could have been alleviated in some form. The history of Christianity from its inception shows that the church was the place where the gathered people of God found refuge from the ravages of the cares of the world. The book of Acts and the ordination of the diaconate speak to and support the role of the church in this holistic care not only of its members, but of the whole of creation. If the church is serious about its ecclesial and public role in holistic care for faithful living and hopeful dying, it does not need to look far to realize that inequities in distribution of basic human amenities are central to some of the most intractable health problems in our society today. In many ways, poverty has become a bane to adequate health care for the ill and dying, not to mention to the preventive care for the healthy. Many people are caught up in the cycle of poverty and disease that culminates in untold and sometimes preventable deaths, especially among minorities. So to speak to such people about hope at the end of their lives or to practice rituals that purport to translate them into celestial, blissful death does not represent to them the love of a just God working on their behalf, or the hope they can have for tomorrow, even the tomorrow that comes through death.

What continues to make the health care of the dying a little shaky and even shady is the inherent hypocrisy that foregrounds care. The dying — who are transitioning from the "doing" mode to the final "being" mode, crippled with disease, and are thus more acted upon than actively acting — find themselves interrupted frequently with the sudden insistence from medical practitioners that they revert to the "doing" mode again, that they again take responsibility for life-and-death decisions, even though many such opportunities were blatantly denied them when they were functioning somewhat optimally. Usually human development progresses from dependence in infancy through independence in young adulthood to mutual interdependence in mature adulthood. Often in old age, as death approaches, it reverses to dependence again. The aged and dying find themselves no longer in charge of their lives. Under normal circumstances, most people are overwhelmed by medical settings, especially when they are in the presence of high-tech equipment and "med-speak" from physicians and other health-care providers. This sense of being overwhelmed is accentuated for the very old and the dying. And these circumstances are especially challenging for minorities because of their sociocultural background, educational level, and/or language barriers. In medical settings, such people regularly experience themselves as being acted upon, and are therefore in a "being" mode rather than a "doing" mode where they are actively involved in and perhaps in charge of their own care. For such individuals, the current medical expectations of decision-making and the strenuous efforts made to sustain life and abate death do not replicate daily life and experience. In fact, research indicates the circumstances that many black Americans face:

> The legacy of slavery, abuses in medical experimentation, economic injustices, racial-profiling practices, and the disproportionate numbers of incarcerations, to name a few, reflect societal and ethical misconduct that has led to a general loss of credibility of many institutions, including the health-care system. Death often has been associated with these societal patterns. For example, compared with whites and other minorities, African-Americans have higher mortality rates from conditions such as cancer, cardiovascular disease, acquired immunodeficiency syndrome, other disease states, illnesses and homicides which have been correlated with social and environmental disparities.[28]

In daily life, many of these individuals living on the edge of poverty and on the boundaries of illness and death continually surrender themselves to the inevitability of death. Living and dying are always intertwined, for there is always death in one form or another in close proximity to one's life. For many such, death becomes intentionally the

28. LaVera Crawley et al., "Palliative and End-of-life Care in the African-American Community," *JAMA* 284, no. 19 (November 15, 2000): 2518.

welcome friend that escorts them from the pain and sorrow of this world. Occasionally, by circumstances beyond their control, such individuals may find themselves in a medical facility at the end of their lives, and the medical system (in its "doing" mode, driven by success, control, productivity, and measurable gain) works against the desire of the dying to just be that. The medical establishment, which conceives of death as the ultimate defeat of the human being as well as of medicine, resists death at all costs. In its bid to sustain life at the end and probably to score a point for modern technological advances in medicine, it all too often interferes with dying and robs people of dying in peace.[29] Oddly, this may be the final injustice committed against the dying, especially to the population that is usually discriminated against in health-care delivery. Such incessant desire for a cure and maintenance of life at all costs speaks to a culture of death-denying people and an inordinate fear of death.

Attending to Spiritual Death: The Cure for Denial and Fear

The main thrust of this chapter has been to foster a balanced view and attitude toward death; it is a call to hold a resistance to death and an embrace of death in tensive unity. Many times we are discerning what the proper stance ought to be as we live faithfully with God together with our communities of faith. In our discernment about death, we may ask if at this time hope, Christian hope, and justice require letting go? Should we allow the ebb and flow of life and death to go on, especially when one comes to the end of life as we know it? Is this the good, the beautiful stance and thing to do? It is only within this framework that we can legit-

29. I am aware that Richard Payne's APPEAL program cites data which shows that African-Americans (even African-American physicians) are much more likely than whites to choose and maintain extraordinary, life-extending care, even if the quality of life is apparently gone (e.g., flat brain scan, rampant cancer, late-stage dementia). This apparently stems from the history of health-care inequities and allows families to feel that they have done everything possible even when the doctors "give up." Furthermore, Payne's research indicates that African-Americans would rather have their loved ones die in the hospital than be cared for at home. Combined, these issues drastically reduce the numbers of African-Americans receiving hospice and palliative care at the end of life and increase the numbers dying in the painful and noisy environment of a hospital.

imately ask and attend to what care at the end of life – or, put another way, physical care at the end of physical existence – looks like.

In current Western culture, one gets the impression that justice for the dying person all too often resembles demanding a pound of flesh from death. It entails fighting to the battle's end with every medical weapon available in the arsenal, and if eventually death "wins," we walk upright and stoically away, and usher death clearly and primly away from us to the grave until the next battle. We must also be cognizant of the fact that what we may be resisting, what we may be calling untimely death, may be our inability to let go, which is symptomatic of our clinging to this world and the desires of the world. There does not seem to be a healthy respect for death, or an acceptance of its right to be among us and to take our loved ones or us even when it is time. But what if the obverse were to take place? What if we were to tiptoe around death and dying with reverence when we sensed its approach, and were to wait for it to come and take our loved one? And what if we then raised a loud lament and sang dirges and mourned, even if in a preset, ritualistic manner? Maybe how we live is what prevents us from coming to the final task of our autonomous existence in an authentic manner consistent with our nature. One African poet sums it up this way: "The man, who died, died because he loved life."[30] When life is over, dying is the necessary and natural thing to do.

It sounds quaint, but the Scriptures are right when they point to dying daily as the way to find life.[31] Jesus tells the disciples that they would lose their lives if they cling to them but find their lives if they lose them. It is the self-transformational experience that comes to many through conversion experiences, and to the Christian through the working of the Holy Spirit in sanctifying the believer. Suffering daily humiliations, mortifying and denying the flesh its unwonted pleasures, is like little deaths of the flesh, a dying consciously, not unconsciously, while still alive. Karl Rahner refers to this as the axiological presence of death[32] (i.e., where wise words or wisdom leans). It is

30. Kobena Eyi Acquah, *The Man Who Died: Poems, 1974-1979* (Accra: Asempa Publishers, 1984).

31. By this I mean more than the Christian Scriptures, because other world religions have the same philosophical principles about abundant living, although it is called by different names.

32. Rahner, *On the Theology of Death,* p. 51.

a daily self-negation, which paradoxically births self-affirmation, a submission in which one finds one's true authority. Ultimately it is a willingness to surrender to God's will on a daily basis, and then, finally, in death. The daily dying in which one finds oneself again – a new and better self, I must add – becomes preparation for this final death, in which one will, by God's promise, find oneself again, and definitely a better self. For what is sown rises a glorified body.

Implications for Pastoral Ministry at the End of Life

While the majority of the discussion here has been on navigating physical death, it is clear that in the final analysis, psychological and spiritual death are the linchpins on which death actually hangs. One's spiritual aptitude for navigating daily dying to self and one's willingness to surrender to God anticipate the form that suffering, dying, and death will take. Our discussion also suggests that sociocultural factors play a large role in what constitutes health and wholeness, also determinants of how death is apprehended.

In light of the foregoing discussion, what would our Christian practices of care at the end of life look like? First and foremost, Christian practices of care have to take seriously the current disparities in health care and advocate for the just and fair treatment of all peoples, ensuring adequate and timely preventive care and treatment for the disadvantaged. When it comes to care on a one-on-one basis, we must meet individuals where they are in their understanding of what is happening to them and at what level they fall on the continuum of psychological and spiritual death. On the question of justice, we must take care not to pass judgment on what we might assume to be apathy or passivity on the part of those who need care. We must pay attention to the tension between what may present itself as acquiescence in the view of caregivers, and what in reality may be a learned resistance for the care receiver who has spent a lifetime negotiating the health-care bureaucracy and other bureaucracies.

While social and economic care is needed, at the point where it is clear that the individual will not transition from care to cure, supporting the patient and the family by providing spiritual care becomes more needful. In fact, at the point where good health is no longer attainable, many who are dying, when left to their own devices, are not as interested in slowing the progression of their illness as they are in ensuring that their loved ones are taken care of. The individual is more preoccupied with the issue of the last stage of human psychosocial development – generativity[33] – and with recapturing dreams, and with dying well despite serious disease.

There are times, however, when the nature of the disease demands that someone make decisions regarding the intentional ending of life. In such instances, we must take care to factor in the views of all members of the family. This is difficult because different family members may be at different levels of comfort and/or preparedness in their attitude toward death. Some may be facing their mortality daily as they die to self; others may not ever have given death a thought; and there will be some in between. Showing consideration to all and waiting for all to come to the place of a comfortable decision (assuming that time permits this) is the just thing to do, and is essential for working through later grief and mourning.

Above all, caregivers must avoid using the Christian doctrine of the hope of the resurrection as a mantra for the relief of pain and grief. Death is still a mystery that our faith, however staunch, cannot completely resolve on this side of eternity. At the same time, we know that Christ has conquered death for us, and so we will not be undone by this mystery called death. This is our hope; this is our justice.

33. Erikson, *Childhood and Society,* p. 266.

CONCLUSION

Attending to God in Suffering: Re-Imagining End-of-Life Care

John Swinton and Richard Payne

As we have moved through this book, we have covered a lot of ground and found ourselves taken to many strange, wonderful, and sometimes difficult places. As we have reflected on the theological and medical complexities of end-of-life care, our horizons have been broadened and deepened and our imaginations presented with new possibilities and options. We sometimes equate imagination with fantasy, assuming that it is a mode of fiction that bends or transcends the rules of the known world. But to think of imagination in such a way is to misunderstand the ways in which we encounter the world. Stanley Hauerwas describes imagination as "a pattern of possibilities fostered within a community by the stories and correlative commitments that make it what it is."[1] Through our imagination we make sense of the world and make decisions about how we should respond to our experiences. Imagination allows us to anticipate and understand what is going on around us based on previous experience and expectation. Importantly, the boundaries of our imagination enable or prevent our seeing certain things, asking particular questions, and responding in particular ways.

As Hauerwas suggests, our imagination is not an independent, free-floating entity, somehow filled with innate ideas and concepts that appear out of nowhere. Our imagination is deeply tied to our cul-

1. Stanley Hauerwas, "The Church and the Mentally Handicapped: A Continuing Challenge to the Imagination," in *Critical Reflections on Stanley Hauerwas' Theology of Disability: Disabling Society, Enabling Theology,* ed. John Swinton (London: Routledge, 2005), p. 56.

tural contexts and the assumptions and values of the communities that we inhabit. To a great extent, one can only imagine what one has been taught to imagine. This might seem a strange observation, but it is important for current purposes. One thing that has become clear as this book has developed is that we are clearly taught to imagine the experience of dying and death in quite particular ways by the various communities that we are involved with. Some of these dominant images that fund our imaginations are powerful and ideological and profoundly shape the ways in which we understand end-of-life care. But, as we have seen, there are other ways in which our imaginations can be funded in relation to death and dying – ways that enable us to imagine quite different responses to this basic human experience. Perhaps one way of summing up this book is that it is intended to offer alternative and complementary images that will re-fund the imagination of Christian caregivers in ways that are liberating, transformative, and healing.

Funding the Pastoral Imagination

In his book *Texts under Negotiation: The Bible and Postmodern Imagination,*[2] Old Testament scholar Walter Brueggemann argues that Scripture (and, by implication, the type of theological reflection presented in this book) is intended to re-fund our imaginations – to enable us to enter into new worlds that reveal fresh truths and allow us to break through the hegemony of modernity and see something of the nature and practice of the Kingdom of God *in the present.* He asserts,

> The task is to *fund* – to provide the pieces, materials, and resources out of which a new world can be imagined. Our responsibility, then, is not a grand scheme or a coherent system, but the voicing of a lot of little pieces out of which people can put life together in fresh configurations.[3]

Like Hauerwas, Brueggemann views imagination as "the human capacity to picture, portray, receive, and *practice the world* in ways other than it

2. Walter Brueggemann, *Texts under Negotiation: The Bible and Postmodern Imagination* (Minneapolis: Augsburg Fortress Press, 1993), p. 18.

3. Brueggemann, *Texts under Negotiation,* p. 20.

appears to be at first glance when seen through a dominant, habitual, unexamined lens." He writes, "Our knowing is essentially imaginative, that is, an act of organizing social reality around dominant authoritative images."[4] One of the questions this book asks is whether our therapeutic imagination in relation to end-of-life care has been so influenced by the rationalist and scientistic presumptions of modernity that we have lost the ability to recognize the radical, countercultural imagination that the Christian tradition provides us with. If we have indeed lost this dimension of our imaginations, our practices have become theologically impoverished. The chapters presented in this book offer new ways of re-funding our imaginations, which will change the meaning of death and offer people the opportunity to die well and to die faithfully.

Re-imagining End-of-Life Care in Community

In closing this book, we would like to offer one final image that we hope will contribute to the process of re-funding that the offerings here have initiated.[5] We would like to re-imagine Christian end-of-life care practices in terms of the image of a migrating flock of geese. The geese fly overhead in a V formation. Their shape, form, and direction are not incidental. At the head of the flock is the windbreaker. She takes the wind full on and breaks it in order that the passage of the others can be made smoother and their efforts and stresses can be eased. But she can only do this for so long. When she tires, she moves back, and another goose takes her place. Now she can rest and be strengthened and encouraged by the other geese as they move toward their destination. The journey is hard work. Sometimes one of them becomes exhausted or ill and falls to the ground. When this happens, other members of the flock join the fallen one until he dies or until his strength returns. If he regains his strength, he flies back with the others to join the V.

This image seems to us to sum up something essential about the

4. Brueggemann, *Texts under Negotiation,* p. 13, p. 18.

5. This image was put forward originally by the pastoral theologian Michael Wilson in his book *A Coat of Many Colors* (London: Epworth Press, 1983).

task of the Christian caregiver and the Christian community in the context of end-of-life care. The key to the effective functioning of the flock is its formation. Geese in formation can fly much faster and farther than they do individually. If they hold this formation and share the trials of their journey fairly, they will reach their destination and discover fresh pastures. Of course, not all of them will arrive safely at their destination. But their journey remains important and respected by the others who seem quite happy to break off their own journey in order to offer companionship, compassion, and hope to those who become weak and who may eventually die.

In the case of the geese, this journey is initiated, guided, and energized by instinct; in the case of the church, the journey is initiated, guided, and energized by God.[6] As we are formed by engaging in the types of spiritual practices that have been outlined in this book, so we are formed into the type of people who can travel together toward their divinely ordained destination — a people who can embody a different imaginative vision of what it means to deliver end-of-life care that takes most seriously the reality of God and God's destination for all human beings. Such an imaginative vision is not an alternative to what currently occurs. We would emphasize that nothing in this book is intended to suggest that medical approaches to end-of-life care are wrong or necessarily misplaced. Nevertheless, what the vision of this book does do is to offer other ways of seeing things, to imbue in established practices new meanings and ways of seeing the world. In doing this, we hope that we will at least have succeeded in the task of reminding Christians who work within the field of end-of-life care that our primary task is to enable people to love God in all things and at all times, and to present modes of theological and practical assurance that God is with us in all things and at all times. As the apostle Paul puts it, "For I am persuaded that neither death, nor life, nor angels, nor principalities, nor powers, nor things present, nor things to come, nor height, nor depth, nor any other creature shall be able to separate us from the love of God, which is in Christ Jesus our Lord" (Rom. 8:38-39, KJV).

6. It is interesting to reflect on the fact that within the Celtic Christian tradition in Ireland and Scotland, the Holy Spirit is represented as a wild goose. The wild goose embodies the untamable and unpredictable nature of the Spirit and is a reminder that the Spirit is disturber as well as comforter.

Ensuring that people who are journeying toward the end of their lives can discover and encounter this assurance is our hope, our prayer, our vision, and our goal. This book is a small but, we hope, important contribution to the achievement of such a goal. We offer it to you with peace, joy, and much love.

Contributors

Esther E. Acolatse is Assistant Professor of Pastoral Theology at Duke Divinity School. She holds a B.A. from the University of Ghana, an M.T.S. from Harvard Divinity School, and a Ph.D. in practical theology from Princeton Theological Seminary. She has taught theology at Loyola College in Baltimore.

Tonya D. Armstrong currently serves as Lecturing Fellow in Pastoral Theology with the Institute on Care at the End of Life at Duke Divinity School. She is a graduate of Yale University, where she completed a double major in psychology and music. From the University of North Carolina at Chapel Hill, she earned master's and doctoral degrees in clinical psychology with a focus on child, adolescent, and family issues. After completing her pre-doctoral internship in pediatric psychology at Duke University Medical Center (DUMC), Dr. Armstrong pursued a postdoctoral fellowship at the Center for Developmental Epidemiology, also at DUMC. She continues her engagement in clinical work and seeks interdisciplinary collaborations for the faithful integration of theology and mental health care, particularly in the development of caring practices for dying and bereaved youth and their families.

Abigail Rian Evans (M.Div., Ph.D., L.H.D.) currently is Charlotte W. Newcombe Professor of Practical Theology at Princeton Theological Seminary. She founded and directed National Capital Presbytery Health Ministries in the 1980s in Washington, D.C., was Director of New Programs at the Kennedy Institute of Ethics at Georgetown University, and was a member of the Clinton Health Care Task Force, the American Association for the Advancement of Science Human Embryonic Stem Cell Working Group, and the IRB of the Neurology Institute at the National Institutes of Health. Her graduate degrees are from the University of Basel, Princeton Theological Seminary, and Georgetown University. She has been a missionary in Brazil, a pastor in churches around the country, an evangelist in Appalachia, a campus minister at Columbia University, and a synod executive. She has written numerous articles and books on bioethics and health ministries, including *Healing Liturgies for the Seasons of Life* (2004) and *Negotiated Death: Is God Still at the Bedside?* (forthcoming from Eerdmans Publishing). Her current research, teaching, and speaking include the subjects of aging and ministry with older adults, death and dying, health and spirituality, health-care decision-making, and addiction.

Stanley Hauerwas is Gilbert T. Rowe Professor of Theological Ethics at Duke Divinity School. Professor Hauerwas has sought to recover the significance of the virtues for understanding the nature of the Christian life. This search has led him to emphasize the importance of the church as well as narrative for understanding Christian existence. His work cuts across disciplinary lines, as he is in conversation with systematic theology, philosophical theology and ethics, political theory, as well as the philosophy of social science and medical ethics. In 2001 he was named "America's Best Theologian" by *Time* magazine. Dr. Hauerwas, who holds a joint appointment at Duke Law School, delivered the prestigious Gifford Lectures at the University of St. Andrews, Scotland, in 2001.

M. Therese Lysaught is an Associate Professor in the Department of Theology at Marquette University, where she teaches theological ethics. Her writing focuses (variously) on liturgy, medicine, anointing of the sick, biotechnology, and Haiti. Her first book, *Gathered for the Journey: Moral Theology in Catholic Perspective* (Eerdmans, 2007) was co-edited with David McCarthy. Her ongoing work in theology and medicine moves in two directions. Specifically, her work on the practice of anointing the sick seeks to rethink medicine and bioethics with particular attention to economics. More generally, her overall project moves toward envisioning what bioethics and medicine might look like as practices rooted in a vision of reconciliation and peacemaking rather than in an ontology of violence. Since 2005, she has had the privilege of serving as the Chair of the Board of the Ekklesia Project.

Amy Plantinga Pauw is Henry P. Mobley Professor of Doctrinal Theology at Louisville Seminary. She majored in philosophy and French at Calvin College. She also studied at Calvin Seminary before completing her M.Div. at Fuller Seminary in 1984. In her doctoral studies at Yale, she became particularly interested in the writings of Jonathan Edwards. Dr. Pauw has a growing interest in theologies of the global south and in the theological interpretation of Scripture. She is a consulting editor for the new theological commentary series by Westminster John Knox and serves on various other editorial boards.

Richard Payne is Professor of Medicine and Divinity and Esther Colliflower Director of the Duke Institute on Care at the End of Life. Dr. Payne is an internationally known expert in the areas of pain relief, care for those near death, oncology, and neurology. He has served on numerous panels and advisory committees, many at the national level. He has given expert testimony to the Congressional Black Caucus National Brain Trust and the President's Cancer Panel in the area of health-care access disparities in cancer care, palliative medicine, and end-of-life care. He also has received a Distinguished Service Award from the American Pain Society, of which he is president; the Humanitarian Award from the Urban Resources Institute; and the Janssen Excellence in Pain Award.

Christina M. Puchalski is Founder and Director of the George Washington Institute for Spirituality and Health and Associate Professor in the Departments of Medicine and Health Care Sciences at the George Washington University. She has pioneered the development of numerous educational programs for undergraduate, graduate, and postgraduate medical education in spirituality and medicine. Her spirituality curriculum at the George Washington University was one of the first in the country and received the John Templeton Award for Spirituality and Medicine. Since 1996, she has been directing a national award program for medical-school curricula in spirituality and health. Her research interests and expertise include the role of spirituality in health and end-of-life care, the role of clergy in health and end-of-life care, and the evaluation of education programs in spirituality and medicine.

Karen D. Scheib is Associate Professor of Pastoral Care and Pastoral Theology at Candler School of Theology, Emory University. Professor Scheib works in the area of practical and pastoral theology. She is the author of *Challenging Invisibility: Practices of Care with Older Women* (2004). Her current writing explores the intersection of ecclesiology and practices of care. Her other research interests include faith and health, the theological and cultural dimensions of crises and trauma, and narrative theory and therapy.

Daniel P. Sulmasy holds the Sisters of Charity Chair in Ethics at St. Vincent's Hospital, Manhattan, and serves as Professor of Medicine and Director of the Bioethics Institute of New York Medical College. He received his A.B. and M.D. degrees from Cornell University and completed his residency, chief residency, and postdoctoral fellowship in General Internal Medicine at the Johns Hopkins Hospital. He received his Ph.D. in philosophy from Georgetown University in 1995. In 2005 he was appointed by Governor Pataki to the New York State Task Force on Life and the Law. He serves as editor in chief of the journal *Theoretical Medicine and Bioethics.* He is also the co-editor of *Methods in Medical Ethics* (2001), and the author of three books: *The Healer's Calling* (1997), *The Rebirth of the Clinic* (2006), and *A Balm for Gilead: Meditations on Spirituality and the Healing Arts* (2006). His numerous articles have appeared in medical, philosophical, and theological journals, and he has lectured widely both in the United States and abroad.

John Swinton holds the Chair in Practical Theology and Pastoral Care at the University of Aberdeen, Scotland, United Kingdom. He is also an honorary professor at Aberdeen's Centre for Advanced Studies in Nursing. Professor Swinton is an ordained minister of the Presbyterian Church of Scotland who worked for sixteen years as a registered nurse specializing in psychiatry and intellectual disabilities. He also worked for a number of years as a hospital chaplain and a community mental-health chaplain. Professor Swinton's areas of research include the relationship between spirituality and health and the theology of disability.

He is the founding director of Aberdeen University's Centre for Spirituality, Health, and Disability.

Allen Verhey is Professor of Christian Ethics at Duke Divinity School. Dr. Verhey's work has focused on the application of Christian ethics, especially in the area of medical and health practice. He has published widely: he is the author, editor, or co-editor of twelve books. *Reading the Bible in the Strange World of Medicine* is his latest publication. Before coming to Duke Divinity School, Verhey was director of the Institute of Religion at the Texas Medical Center for two years. Prior to that, he served as the Evert J. and Hattie E. Blekkink Professor of Religion at Hope College for ten years.

Index

AARP North Carolina patient survey, 210-11, 214
Advocacy, prophetic, 54-55
African-Americans: and health-care, 265, 267-68
After Virtue (MacIntyre), 92
Against Heresies (Irenaeus), 38
Airing, C., 218
Althaus, Paul, 118-19, 120
American Medical Association (AMA), 194
Anointing with oil, 26, 27, 168; primary effects of, 63-64
Aquinas, Thomas, 70-71, 220, 227
Aristotle, 227
Association of American Medical Colleges (AAMC), 193-94
Augustine, 255
Autonomy, patient, 89-90, 98

Balint, Michael, 176
Barclay, Aileen, 10
Barth, Karl, 91, 93, 174
Basil of Caesarea, 244
Becker, Ernst, 35
Benedict XVI, Pope, 70
Benson, Herbert, 61
Bernardin, Joseph, Cardinal: example of faithful dying, 77-85; and love for accuser, 74-77; and prayer, 59-60, 71-74, 76-77
Beyond Silence and Denial (Bregman), 37-38, 44
Bluebond-Langner, Myra, 142-43, 144
Bonhoeffer, Dietrich, 133-35
Bregman, Lucy, 37-40, 44
Brody, Howard, 214, 221-22
Brueggemann, Walter, 273-74
Byock, Ira, 225

Callahan, Daniel, 35
Calvin, John, 23, 91, 93
Caritas, 70-71, 73; kenotic, 74-81
Cassell, Eric, 173, 176
Chaplain, 166; role of, 177-85
Charity, 70-71
Child mortality, 141-42
Christianity: and dignity, 236-38, 241
Christianity and death, 7, 17; ambivalence about, 248-50; and belief, 21-24; and communal practice, 17-20, 29, 30-31, 44-46, 48-50, 179-80; and ecumenism, 26; and judgment, 25-26, 41-42, 248-50; and medieval practices, 26; and mercy, 27-28; and patience, 254-57; protest against, 24, 257-58; in relation to contemporary

culture, 24; theology of, 41-43, 252-65. *See also* Death; Sacraments
Christian funerals, 21-22, 23, 28-29; shift in focus from dead to bereaved, 38-39
Church, the: and end-of-life care, 17-20, 29, 30-32, 44-49, 55-56, 179-80, 274-75. *See also* Sacraments
Clinical Pastoral Education (CPE), 166
Coles, Robert, 88-91
Compassion, 147-48, 188-89; and caring presence, 159-60, 177-78, 196-97; and the church, 151, 161-62; clinical practice of, 195-201; and "compassion fatigue," 105; crisis of, 149-51; cultivation of, 150; ethical model for, 193-95; and freedom, community, and creativity, 153-55; of God, 151-52, 153-55; and healing, 190-93; and health-care providers, 192-93; Jesus as model of, 151-57; and looking heavenward, 102-6; and practicing faithfully, 139-40; relationality of, 155-56; as spiritual practice, 157-58; tangible practices of, 159-62; training in, 201-3; as way of life, 152-54
Compassion (Nouwen, McNeill, and Morrison), 152
Compassionate Ministry (Stone), 152-54
Complicated Losses, Difficult Deaths (Karaban), 39-40
Cook, Stephen, 75-76, 83
Crawley, LaVera, 267
Cross, the: as new reality, 120; theology of, 116-20

Dalai Lama, 188
Damien of Molokai, Blessed, 62
David, 134
Davies, Oliver, 150, 151, 154, 156
Death: ambivalence toward, 246, 248-50; "bad death," 20-21; befriending of, 79-80; and Christian community, 17-18, 19-20, 29, 30-31, 44-46, 179-80, 242; Christian language of, 41-42, 49, 51, 52; contemporary response to, 18-19; and the Cross, 80; cultural narratives of, 34-36; across cultures, 247-48; definition of, 34-35; and dignity, 240-45; and divine judgment, 25-26, 41-42, 248-50; and divine mercy, 27-29; embracing of, 251-58; encountering of, 246-50; and ethical decisions, 52-54; and forgiveness, 25-26; and funeral homes, 18, 19; and imagination, 272-76; and injustice, 264-65; Jesus on, 7, 17, 258-59; and lament, 21-22; and liturgy, 49-50; as loss, 38-40; many faces of, 20-21; and modern medicine, 19, 34-35, 65-66, 84, 165-66; relationship to life, 4-8; resisting of, 24, 257-58; and resurrection, 44, 49-50, 51; and sin, 257; spiritual, 268-70; timely and untimely, 258-64; and thanksgiving and hope, 21-23. *See also* Christianity and death; End-of-life care; Prayer
Death and Dying, On (Kübler-Ross), 37
death as natural, 37-38, 41; Christian response to, 41-42
Death awareness movement, 37-38; and Christianity, 38-39
Dignity, 226; "alien," 238-40; and care for the dying, 240-45; and Christianity, 236-38, 241; different notions of, 229-31; intrinsic, 229-34, 236-38; and moral norms, 234-36; theological history of, 227-29
"Dignity of Man, On the" (Mirandola), 228
Disciplines of the Spirit (Thurman), 256
Doctor, the Patient, and Illness, The (Balint), 176
Donne, John, 18; and modern medicine, 19
Dualism: of soul and body, 64-65, 170

Dudley, Martin, 181
Dying children, 139; and child development, 142-43; and community support, 147; and compassion for, 141-47; emotional experience of, 143-44; and the family, 140-41, 144-47, 161; and family spirituality, 145, 146
Dying well, 225; and faithfulness, 77-85; and hope and thanksgiving, 21-24; and lament, 21-22

Ecclesial care, at the end of life, 30-32, 44-49, 55-56, 179-80. *See also* the Church
Empathy, 216-19
End-of-life care: beginning of, 4-5; and care for the body, 27; and the church, 30-32, 44-49, 55-56, 179-80, 274-75; collaborative model of, 168-71; and dignity, 240-45; and errors of communication, 160-61; and forming communal contexts for ethical decision-making, 52-54; and "glorious medicine," 122-23, 125; and hope and loss of hope in patients, 222-23, 206-8; and incurable illnesses, 208-11; and justice, 266-68; and lament, 135-38; narrative practices of, 47-49; and narratives of restitution, 114-16; and pastoral care, 177-85; and relational care, 50-55; and relationship to rest of life, 4-5, 7-8; and over-reliance upon medicine, 110-14; and spiritual care, 167-69; and spiritual formation, 8; theology of, 108-10; and theology of the cross, 121-27. *See also* Death; Pastoral care and death
Erikson, Erik, 198, 251-52
Erwin, Deborah, 124-25
Ethics, AMA code of, 194
Ethics, medical, 89-90, 94, 174, 193-95, 226, 243-45; and fallibility, 97-98; and injustice, 264-68; and prayer, 87-88, 106
Eucharist, 49-50; and action, 70; as center of liturgy, 68
Euthanasia, 243-45

Faith communities, 179-80. *See also* the Church
Ford, David, 8-9
Four Things That Matter Most (Byock), 225
Francis, Saint, 62
Frank, Arthur, 114-15
Frankl, Viktor, 222
Freud, Sigmund, 215
Funerals, 18, 19; Christian, 21-22, 23, 28-29, 49

Gift of Peace, The (Bernardin), 59-60, 71-85
God: compassion of, 151-52, 153-55, 157; silence of, 149, 157. *See also* Jesus Christ
God, glory of: and disappointment, 135; and suffering, 129-30
God Is Love (Benedict XVI), 70
Guroian, Vigen, 29

Hall, Douglas John, 119, 120
Hauerwas, Stanley, 71, 254, 272-73
Havel, Václav, 221
Health-care providers, 159, 168-71; clinical practice of, 195-201; and compassion, 192-93; and empathy and sympathy, 216-19; and honesty, 214-16, 219; and incurable illnesses, 208-11; and spiritual concerns of patient, 211-12; and upholding dignity of patient, 243-44. *See also* Physician
Hell, 36
Hezekiah, 261
Hobbes, Thomas, 228
Holmes, Oliver Wendell, 218
Hope: Aquinas on, 220-21; cases of,

206-8; fostering of, 221-24; and honesty with patient, 214-16; loss of, 206-8; and miracles, 221, 224-25; and placebos, 205-6; and supportive interventions, 224; and terminal illnesses, 219-25
"Hope" (Brody), 214, 221-22
Hospice, 209-10
Hunsinger, Deborah van Deusen, 223

Illness: incurable, 208-11, 219-25; and inwardness, 78-79
Illness as Metaphor (Sontag), 129
Imago Dei, 154, 240
Irenaeus, 38, 149

Jesus Christ: as crucified healer, 125-27; on death, 7, 17, 23, 258-59; and lament, 21; as model of compassion, 151-57; as redeemer and healer, 95-96; as teacher of prayer, 133-35
Job, 148
John of the Cross, Saint, 193
Johnson, Elizabeth, 45-46
Joseph's House, 199-200

Kant, Immanuel, 228-29, 235
Kavenaugh, Eve, 27
Kingdom of God, 11
Kleinman, Arthur, 137
Kolb, Robert, 118, 119
Kübler-Ross, Elisabeth, 37

Lament, 98; and community, 100; definition of, 130; vs. dirge, 99-100; and health-care providers, 137-38; and hope, 132-33; as language of praise, 133-35; prayer as, 98-100, 130-31; and the Psalms, 127-36
Lawrence, Brother, 8, 11-15; on suffering, 14-15. *See also* Practice of the presence of God
Lazarus, death of, 6-7, 23, 258-59
Lebacqz, Karen, 238-40

Life, abundant, 8; Jesus on, 5-6, 11; and suffering, 6
Life-sustaining treatments: withholding or continuing, 243-45
Liturgy: and end-of-life care, 180-81. *See also* Sacraments
Long, Tom, 39
Luther, Martin: theology of the cross, 116-20; theology of glory, 117-19
Lysaught, Therese, 14-15, 86-87

MacIntyre, Alasdair, 92-93
McNeill, Donald, 152, 155
McVay, M. R., 204
Manual for Ministry to the Sick, A (Dudley), 181
Marcel, Gabriel, 196
May, William, 251
Medicine, modern: and battle metaphors, 124-25; and Christian faithfulness, 96; and dying, 19, 34-35, 65-66, 86; "glorious," 121-27; and glory to God, 108-9; and narratives of restitution, 114-16; over-reliance upon, 110-14; as a spiritual practice, 203-4
Merton, Thomas, 10; on assurance, 15-16; on prayer, 136
Meyer, B. C., 214
Mirandola, Pico della, 228
Morrison, Douglas, 152, 155
Mourning, 260, 269
Myers, Gary, 115, 123

Narratives, 33-34; Christian, 32, 41-43, 47-49, 55-56; of dying, 34-36; of resistance, 55; of restitution, 114-16, 122-23
National Hospice Work Group (NHWG), 210-11
Nouwen, Henri, 79-80, 152, 155, 156-57, 161
Nussbaum, Martha, 156

Osler, William, 193

Osmond, Humphrey, 175

Palliative care. *See* End-of-life care
Parish nursing, 168; and the pastor, 172-73
Pastoral care and death, 65, 166, 177-85, 270-71; and chaplains, 166; education about, 263-64; and imagination, 273-74; and medical ethics, 89-91; and narrative practices, 47-49; and parish nursing, 172-73; and physicians, 169-71; and proclaiming truth, 185-86; and psychology, 88-89; and shift in focus from dying person to grievers, 39-40; and spiritual assessment, 183-85
Pastoral Care Emergencies (Switzer), 40
Patient, the: and autonomy, 89-90, 98; desires at end of life, 210-11; dissatisfaction of, 195; as healer, 173-77; and physician, 173, 176
Paul, 109, 275; on the body of Christ, 150, 178; on death, 6, 25, 30-31, 40-41; on God's compassion, 157-58; on ownership of life, 43; on prayer, 129, 182; on the resurrected state, 47-48
Pellegrino, Edmund, 168-69
Physician: and comfort with spiritual topics, 223-25; of cross, 126-28; of glory, 126-28; and pastors, 169-71; and patient, 173, 176. *See also* Health-care providers
Pinchas, Charles, 254-55
Plantinga Pauw, Amy, 36
Practical theology, 31-33; of dying, 31, 33-38; and pastoral care, 38-41
Practice of the presence of God, 11; and formal spiritual practices, 13; and mundane life, 12-13; and suffering, 14-15
Prayer, 59-60, 86; with boldness, 260-63; as confession, 96-98; for death, 101-2; example of, 59-60, 71-77; and forgiveness, 74-77; guiding care for dying, 87-88, 91-93; as invocation, 93-96; Jesus as teacher of, 133-35; as lament, 98-100, 130-31; looking heavenward, 102-6; and the Lord's Prayer, 101; medical effectiveness of, 61-62, 86-87; and medical ethics, 87-88, 106; of medical practitioners, 102, 105-6; and pastoral care, 182-83; as petition, 101-2; and the Psalms, 133-36; and the saints' health, 62-63; as thanksgiving, 98-100; and virtue, 92-93
Price, Charles P., 180
Private World of Dying Children, The (Bluebond-Langner), 142-43
Psalms, book of, 27, 107, 244; in clinical practice, 136-38; and lament, 127-36; as language of Jesus, 133-35; as language of praise, 133-35; and praying, 133-36
Purgatory, 36
Pushing Daisies, 36-37

Rahner, Karl, 252-53, 257, 269
Ramsey, Paul, 19
Rayson, Daniel, 110, 136

Relational practices of care, 50; accompanying, 51-52; and ethical decision-making, 52-54; and prophetic practice, 54-55; remembering, 50-51

Remen, Rachel Naomi, 198
Rerum Novarum, 229
Rhodes, R., 215
Rolston, Holmes, 232
Ronald McDonald House, 146

Sacraments, the, 82-85; and action, 70-71; and the church, 67-69; effects of, 61-66; and end-of-life care, 180-81; and faithful dying, 60-61, 80-81; and health, 61-63; and the individual, 64, 67, 69; instrumental views

of, 63-66; and the saints, 62-63; theology of, 63-66, 67; transformational power of, 68-69
Saunders, Dame Cicely, 216
Schmemann, Alexander, 69
Shea, William M., 18
Siegler, Miriam, 175
Sontag, Susan, 129
Soubirous, Bernadette, Saint, 62
Spiritual assessment, 183-85, 212; two models of, 213
Spiritual formation, 10-11; and loving God, 8-9; and the practice of the presence of God, 11-15
Stairs, Jean, 44, 48
Stone, Brian, 152-54
Suffering, 6, 150-51; and Brother Lawrence, 14-15; and Christianity, 82, 107-10; and compassion, 102-6; contemporary attitudes toward, 147-49; and dying children, 148-49; faithfully, 108-10; and "glorious medicine," 123; and invoking God, 94-95; and Jesus Christ, 126-27, 129; and illness, 189-90; and lament, 98-100, 127-31; and technology, 148; and theodicy, 149; and a theology of the cross, 116-20, 126-27
Sullivan, M. D., 223
Summa Theologica (Aquinas), 220
Switzer, David, 40

Texts under Negotiation (Brueggemann), 273-74
Theology of Compassion, A (Davies), 150, 151, 154, 156
Theology of the Cross, 116-20, 127-28; and end-of-life care, 121-27; practical, 125-27; and the Psalms, 133-36
Theology of Glory, 117-20, 136; and medical language, 124. *See also* Medicine, modern: "glorious"
Thérèse of Lisieux, Saint, 62
Thielicke, Helmut, 238-40
Thurman, Howard, 256

Uniform Definition of Death Act (UDDA), 34

Vatican Council, Second, 67
Velleman, J. David, 235-36

Waddell, Paul, 68
Weil, Louis, 180
Wells, Samuel, 71
Westminster Catechism, 109
"Whatever Happened to the Christian Funeral?" (Long), 39
Wolterstorff, Nicholas, 24, 28-29, 149, 160
Worship, 68-69; relationship to action, 70